ANTHROPOLOGICAL PAPERS

MUSEUM OF ANTHROPOLOGY, UNIVERSITY OF MICHIGAN

NO. 58

# THE YOMUT TURKMEN:
# A STUDY OF SOCIAL ORGANIZATION
# AMONG A CENTRAL ASIAN
# TURKIC-SPEAKING POPULATION

BY

WILLIAM IRONS

ANN ARBOR

THE UNIVERSITY OF MICHIGAN, 1975

© 1975 William George Irons

ISBN 978-1-949098-03-7 (paper)
ISBN 978-1-951519-13-1 (ebook)

# PREFACE

THIS monograph is based on field research conducted among the Yomut Turkmen in 1965-67 and 1970. Most of the material presented here was contained in a doctoral dissertation submitted at the University of Michigan in 1969. Many members of the faculty of the University of Michigan guided and encouraged me in various stages of the work leading to the writing of this monograph. The most important of these were William Schorger, my dissertation advisor, Richard Beardsley, Napoleon Chagnon, Mervyn Meggitt, Eric Wolf, and Henry Wright.

Also I am grateful to the institutions which supported my research financially. The Foreign Area Fellowship Program supported eighteen months of field research in Iran (July 1965-August 1966 and October 1966-April 1967) and seven months of data analysis and writing in the United States (November 1967-May 1968). The University of Michigan Center for Near Eastern and North African Studies supported six months of research in Iran (May 1967-October 1967) and five months of analysis and writing in the United States (June 1968-October 1968). The Johns Hopkins University financed three months of research in Iran (June 1970-August 1970).

During my residence in Iran (June 1965-August 1966; October 1966-November 1967; June 1970-September 1970), I was shown hospitality and given assistance by innumerable individuals and it is impossible to thank them all. By far my greatest debt of gratitude is to the Turkmen of Aji Quī. Although I doubt that any of them will ever read these words, I would like to say that they lived up to their tradition of hospitality to outsiders in a manner that won my admiration. Among the many others to whom I am grateful are the following: Hūshang Pūrkarīm of the Ministry of Culture and Fine Arts, Office of Anthropological Research, Mahmūd Khaliqī, Director of the same office, Ihsān Narāghī, then Director of the Tehran University Institute of Social Studies and Research, Nādir Afshāri Nādirī, then Director of the Section for Tribal Studies of the above Institute, David Stronach, Director of the British Institute of Persian Studies, Brian Spooner, then Deputy Director of the British Institute, William Sumner, Director of the American Institute of Iranian Studies in 1970, Eugene and Marjorie Garthwaite, residents of Tehran, November 1966-April 1967, 'Aṭā'ullāh Muʻtadil, then a member of the Iranian Office of Community Development, Tāghān Muḥammad Shamsī, then Dihyār in Kalāleh, and Barkley Moore, Peace Corps Volunteer in Gunbadi Kāvūs from 1964 to 1970. Also I wish to thank two individuals who assisted while doing four months of archival research in Tehran: Dr. Īraj Afshār, Tehran University Reference Librarian, and Hajjī Husayn 'Āqā Malik, owner of the Malik Library.

Since completing the research on which this monograph is based, I have undertaken additional research among the Turkmen of northern Persia. This research is designed to elaborate and test some of the hypotheses discussed in this study. I have been able to undertake this current research because of generous grants from the National Science Foundation (NSF Grant GS-37888 for 1973-74), and the Ford and Rockefeller Foundations Program in Support of Social Science and Legal Research on Population Policy (1974-75).

A brief comment is necessary concerning the spelling of Persian and Turkmen words used in this study. Whenever possible I have used spellings that appear in *The American College Dictionary*, or *Webster's Geographical Dictionary*. For Persian words which have no standard English orthography, I have used the system of transliteration employed by Ann S. K. Lambton in *Landlord and Peasant in Persia* (see pp. x-xii of that study). For Turkmen words, I have used a system of transcription which is explained in Appendix III. However, I have made a few exceptions in cases of words which, although not found in any English dictionary, appear extensively in various relevant sources. Thus, I have spelled "Basseri" as it appears in Fredrik Barth's *Nomads of South Persia*, and I have used the spellings of Turkmen names which appear in V. and T. Minorsky's translation of V. V. Barthold's "A History of the Turkmen People." In using V. and T. Minorsky's spellings I have replaced "ï" with "i̵."

The diacritics necessary for Lambton's system of transliteration and for my system of transcription make it impractical to follow the usual practice of italicizing foreign words. In order to be consistent, I have not italicized any of the foreign words that appear in the text.

William Irons
Pennsylvania State University

# TABLE OF CONTENTS

|  | Page |
|---|---|
| PREFACE | iii |
| LIST OF TABLES | vii |
| LIST OF FIGURES | vii |
| LIST OF PLATES | viii |

I. INTRODUCTION ................................. 1

    The kinship system and its environment ............... 2
    The ethnographic setting ........................ 4
    The recent history of the Turkmen ................. 8
    Data and research methods ...................... 13

II. ECOLOGY ..................................... 21

    Traditional ecology and economy .................. 21
    Recent changes .............................. 27
    The current ecology of Ajī Quī ................... 30

III. POLITICAL STRUCTURE .......................... 39

    Descent groups .............................. 40
    Residence groups ............................ 46
    The relationship between descent groups and residence groups ..... 49
    Peace, war and feud .......................... 61
    Sacred lineages .............................. 65
    Relations with the Kajar government ............... 66
        The office of thaqlau ....................... 67
        Nomadism and politics ...................... 69
    Nomadism and feud .......................... 71
    Nomadism and relations with the state .............. 72
    The recent political history of Ajī Quī .............. 75

IV. DOMESTIC GROUPS ............................. 83

    The normal developmental cycle .................. 84

|  |  | |
|---|---|---|
|  | Exceptional patterns of household development | 88 |
|  | Household types in a particular oba | 90 |
|  | Inheritance | 92 |
| V. | KINSHIP NORMS AND CATEGORIES | 95 |
|  | Parent-child | 95 |
|  | Grandparent–grandchild | 99 |
|  | Siblings | 99 |
|  | Husband–wife | 102 |
|  | Affines | 104 |
|  | Uterine relatives | 112 |
|  | The contrast between agnatic and non-agnatic kinship | 113 |
|  | The extension of kinship | 115 |
|  | The place of deceased ancestors in the kinship system | 118 |
|  | Slavery and kinship | 121 |
|  | The prominence of the father–son relationship | 122 |
|  | Kinship norms and domestic groups | 125 |
| VI. | MARRIAGE | 127 |
|  | Choice of marriage partner | 127 |
|  | Endogamy and agnation | 132 |
|  | Marriage negotiations | 134 |
|  | The development of a marriage | 136 |
|  | Widows, widowers, remarriage and polygyny | 141 |
|  | Divorce | 142 |
|  | The demographic context | 143 |
|  | Population regulation through social conventions: an hypothesis | 150 |
| VII. | DOMESTIC ORGANIZATION AND ECONOMICS | 155 |
|  | Differential productivity and the distribution of wealth | 155 |
|  |    Livestock as a form of capital | 156 |
|  |    Shepherding contracts | 157 |
|  |    Agriculture | 158 |
|  |    Carpet weaving | 159 |
|  |    Other secondary sources of income | 159 |
|  |    Wealth profile in a particular community | 160 |
|  |    The relationship between family size and wealth | 161 |
|  | Leveling institutions | 163 |
|  |    Bridewealth | 163 |
|  |    Other leveling institutions | 167 |
|  |    The overall effect of economic leveling institutions | 168 |
|  |    Household size and economic viability | 169 |
| VIII. | OVERVIEW | 171 |
| APPENDICES |  |  |
| I. | THE WEALTH PROFILE OF AJĪ QUĪ | 175 |
| II. | INCOME OF A PASTORAL FAMILY OF MEDIAN WEALTH | 179 |
| III. | NOTES ON THE TRANSLITERATION OF TURKMEN WORDS | 181 |
| BIBLIOGRAPHY |  | 187 |

## LIST OF TABLES

| | | Page |
|---|---|---|
| 1. | Composition of Ajī Quī Households | 91 |
| 2. | Consanguineal Relationships of Wives to Husbands in Ajī Quī for First Marriages | 129 |
| 3. | Consanguineal Relationships of Wives to Husbands in Ajī Quī for Second Marriages | 130 |
| 4. | First Marriage and non-Yomut Descent in Ajī Quī | 130 |
| 5. | Second Marriage and Non-Yomut Descent in Ajī Quī | 131 |
| 6. | Marriage and Sacred Descent: The Case of the Qara Makhtum | 132 |
| 7. | Customary Bridal Payments | 135 |
| 8. | Age and Sex Composition of the Population of Ajī Quī, August 1967 | 144 |
| 9. | Dissolution of First Marriage and Remarriage | 149 |
| 10. | Breakdown of the Yomut Population of Ajī Quī by Age, Sex, and Marital Status | 152 |
| 11. | Wealth Profile of Ajī Quī | 160 |
| 12. | Holdings of Capital in Ajī Quī | 175 |
| 13. | Capital, Labor Resources, and Other Sources of Income in Ajī Quī | 177 |
| 14. | Estimated Income for an Ajī Quī Family of Approximately Median Wealth | 179 |

## LIST OF FIGURES

| | | Page |
|---|---|---|
| 1. | Principal Turkmen descent groups | 6 |
| 2. | Ecological zones and predominant modes of economic production before 1950 | 23 |
| 3. | Approximate pattern of Yomut migration before 1930 | 24 |
| 4. | Predominant modes of economic production among the Yomut of the Gurgan Plain in 1967 | 31 |
| 5. | Migratory pattern of Ajī Quī residents | 33 |
| 6. | Descendants of Oghurjīk according to a written genealogy | 41 |
| 7. | Genealogy of the Yomut | 42 |
| 8. | Genealogy of the Daṯh | 43 |
| 9. | Genealogy of the Aq-Atabay | 45 |
| 10. | Locations of tribes in the Gurgan Plain before 1930 | 50 |
| 11. | Distribution of Yomut tribes in 1967 | 52 |
| 12. | Agnatic relationships of household heads in Ajī Quī, 1967 | 54 |
| 13. | Lineage A of the Chenthulī | 55 |
| 14. | Distribution of dominant descent groups among Daṯh obas | 57 |

15. Segmentary political system of the Gurgan Yomut . . . . . . . . . . . . . . . . 59
16. Location of Sherep and Choni̅ tribes . . . . . . . . . . . . . . . . . . . . . . . . 64
17. Agnatic kinship terms . . . . . . . . . . . . . . . . . . . . . . . . . . . . . . . . . . 100
18. Uterine kinship terms . . . . . . . . . . . . . . . . . . . . . . . . . . . . . . . . . . 101
19. Affinal kinship terms: relatives of spouse . . . . . . . . . . . . . . . . . . . . 108
20. Affinal kinship terms: affines of consanguineal kin . . . . . . . . . . . . . . 109
21. Ages at first marriage for 133 individuals in Aji̅ Qui̅ . . . . . . . . . . . . 146
22. Labor resources and wealth for the households of Aji̅ Qui̅ . . . . . . . . . . . . 162

## LIST OF CHARTS

1. Turkmen vowels . . . . . . . . . . . . . . . . . . . . . . . . . . . . . . . . . . . . . . 182
2. Turkmen diphthongs . . . . . . . . . . . . . . . . . . . . . . . . . . . . . . . . . . 182
3. Turkmen consonants . . . . . . . . . . . . . . . . . . . . . . . . . . . . . . . . . . 184

## LIST OF PLATES
(following page 193)

1. A Yomut woman assembling her family tent after a migration
2. A Yomut woman milking a sheep
3. A Yomut man hunting in the Gōkcha Hills
4. Preparing a hide after the slaughter of a goat
5. A nomad camp in the Gōkcha Hills
6. Setting up camp after a short migration

# I

# INTRODUCTION

IT could reasonably be argued that anthropology has contributed more to the understanding of kinship than it has to any other facet of human social relations. The topic has attracted the interest of a large number of anthropologists for several generations and a voluminous literature now exists on the topic. Yet, despite considerable progress, there are serious lacunae in the existing literature. If we are to understand fully the role of kinship in organizing human social relationships we should presumably strive to document as wide a range of variations as possible in the form of kinship organization. An important part of this documentation should consist of recording as fully as possible kinship structures in the different geographical regions of the world. Yet many areas of the world are represented only scantily in the literature.

One group of societies for which documentation is insufficient is that of the Central Asian Turkic peoples. There are a few good studies (Aberle, 1953; Hudson, 1938; König, 1962; Krader, 1963b; Lattimore, 1962; Pūrkarīm, 1966a, 1966b, 1967, 1968a, 1968b, 1968c, 1970; Vreeland, 1957), but these are only sufficient to indicate that these societies present some interesting variations in the area of kinship. Many more such studies will be needed before anthropologists can have a full picture of social organization and kinship among these populations.

The primary objective of this monograph, therefore, is to provide a description of the kinship system and social organization of one of these societies, that of the Yomut Turkmen of northern Persia. In particular, an attempt has been made to describe those aspects of social organization which are most likely to be of interest for comparative purposes: the lineage system, the developmental cycle of domestic groups, norms and modes of interpersonal kinship relations, kinship categories, choice of marriage partner, and the economic transactions accompanying marriage.

A second objective is to describe the ecological and social context in which the kinship system operates, as well as the context in which it has operated in the recent past. Many aspects of the kinship system of the Yomut appear to have a definite relationship to certain features of their physical and social environment. Several relationships of this sort are explored briefly in this monograph: (1) the relationship between the lineage system and the external political relations of Yomut descent and residence groups, (2) the relationship between the organization of domestic groups and the economy of the Yomut, and (3) the relationship between certain practices surrounding marriage and population growth.

## THE KINSHIP SYSTEM AND ITS ENVIRONMENT

The Yomut, and other cognate Turkmen groups like the Göklen, Teke, Salor, and Sarik, are organized into a segmentary system of territorial groups which functions in a manner similar to that described for stateless segmentary societies in other areas of the world (Evans-Pritchard, 1940; Fortes and Evans-Pritchard, 1940; Middleton and Tait, 1958). This feature of the indigenous political structure of the Yomut and other Turkmen groups stands in strong contrast to the political organization of other tribal groups in Persia which tend to be sharply stratified in their political structure and have traditionally been more closely integrated into the state organization (Irons, 1972). The hypothesis that such a political organization is especially suited to predatory relations with neighboring groups seems to be borne out in the case of the Yomut (Sahlins, 1961). There are, however, some peculiarities of the Yomut segmentary system which appear to be adjustments to an emphasis on the exploitation of nomadic mobility for military purposes. The Yomut have a political system which makes it especially easy for families or entire lineages to establish their residence in a new locality as a response to hostile political relations in their original location. A number of features of the political rules of the society make this possible. The implications of these rules are discussed briefly at the end of Chapter III.

It should also be noted that this commitment to mobility for political and military purposes is reflected in many other respects of the total way of life of the Yomut. The most obvious manifestation of this is the fact that their nomadic residence pattern itself is not completely a response to economic conditions (as is often assumed to be universally the case among Middle Eastern, Central Asian, and North African nomads). Rather, their nomadism is in large part a direct response to political conditions (Irons, 1974).

Household organization is a second aspect of the kinship system which appears to be an adjustment to environmental circumstances. In the predominantly pastoral community where most of my data was gathered, there is a salient connection between household size and economic prosperity. Larger households are decidedly wealthier and it seems clear that, in this case, size comes closer to being the independent variable. Another way of stating this is to say that the long-term economic well-being of a domestic group depends more on the number of adult laborers in the group than on the capital (livestock and arable land) owned by the household at any point in time. This circumstance is largely a result of a situation of free access to pasture and water and extensive opportunities for employment as shepherds, where it is relatively easy to convert labor into the capital needed for economic survival. Until recently good arable land was also available in excess of demand, and unused land could be claimed by anyone willing to expend the labor necessary to cultivate it. Thus in the recent past the relative importance of labor and capital favored labor sharply.

Certain features of the developmental cycle of domestic groups appear to be adaptations to this circumstance since they have the effect of increasing household size, or, more precisely, of minimizing the frequency with which the adult labor pool of a household falls below the viable level. These features include the late date at which sons usually establish separate domestic units economically independent of their father's household, ultimogeniture, and the adoption of sons by men without male issue. This argument is developed in Chapter VII.

It should be pointed out that this characteristic of the economy of the pastoral Yomut—the ease of converting labor into capital—was shared by the agricultural Yomut until recently. Before recent changes, arable land existed in surplus of demand among the agricultural Yomut, and large tracts of cultivatable land were left unexploited. Under these circumstances the amount of land a family cultivated depended on its labor supply rather than on any claims of ownership of land. Thus, the situation described in Chapter VII as existing among the pastoral Yomut in 1966 and 1967 existed in an even more exaggerated form among the agricultural Yomut until recently. This situation, however, no longer existed among the agricultural Yomut at the time of my first research in 1966 and 1967. As a result of agricultural development beginning in the 1950s, all arable land and all water available for irrigation had been claimed. The purchase price of land, especially irrigated land, was high and inflating rapidly. Under these conditions ownership of capital will probably have a greater effect on a domestic group's prosperity than will its labor resources.

A third area in which certain features of the kinship system appear to be adaptations to environmental conditions is that of practices surrounding marriage, especially bridewealth and delayed co-residence of spouses. Bridewealth among the Yomut, unlike the situation among many groups, is ordinarily not lower for poorer families than for wealthier ones. The level at which bridewealth is ordinarily set places an economic burden on many families and leads to delays in marriage for the poorer strata of Yomut society. The situation is further exaggerated by the fact that payment of bridewealth is ordinarily followed by a period of several years during which the bride remains in her father's household and is forbidden any contact with her husband. The statistical result of this situation is that a fairly high proportion of fecund women—in the one community for which detailed census data are available—are either unmarried or not co-resident with a spouse. This fact suggests that these aspects of Yomut kinship behavior may be significant in regulating population size, or at least may have been so in the recent past. This possibility is discussed at the end of Chapter VI. Firm conclusion concerning this particular possibility, however, cannot be drawn until research currently in progress is completed.

All of the theoretical issues outlined above are the subject of more extensive discussion in other publications (Irons, 1972, 1974, n.d.). Also, research designed to further explore the second and third propositions above is currently in progress, and it is hoped that after the completion of this research it will be possible to subject these propositions to a more thorough empirical testing. Since more data relevant to these hypotheses will be available in the future, they have not been discussed as thoroughly as they might have been in this monograph. *The Yomut Turkmen* is, in a sense, a preliminary report on research not yet complete, and as such it emphasizes the basic descriptive material which is the necessary starting point for any anthropological research.

It should also be emphasized at the beginning that the kinship system and the general ecological and social context described in this monograph was that of a conservative community at the time of research. Considerable attention has also been given to the recent history of the Turkmen. What is presented here is not representative of the Yomut as a whole today. This choice of focus on the conservative rather than on the typical is not arbitrary. When I began my research among the Yomut, they were caught up in a process of social change which will transform them soon into modern citizens of an economically prosperous and politically powerful nation. What was then observable among the more conservative element of the Yomut population will soon no longer be observable anywhere. At the same time, the traditional kinship system of the Yomut appeared to be in many ways an adaptation to the environmental conditions of the recent past, conditions which partially survived in conservative areas, and were still clear in the minds of many potential informants. Thus, the study presented here, and the research currently in progress, will soon not be possible. Considering this situation it seemed more important to concentrate on describing the more traditional form of Yomut social organization and the environment to which it was an adjustment than to concentrate on the process of social change which, in one form or another, will be observable for some time to come.

## THE ETHNOGRAPHIC SETTING

The Yomut are one of several large descent groups that share the ethnic designation, Turkmen, and together occupy a contiguous region in the southwestern portion of Soviet Central Asia and adjacent areas of Iran and Afghanistan (see Fig. 1). All of these groups speak the same language, share basically the same cultural tradition, and maintain a theory of common origin either by descent from the same mythical ancestor, Oghuz Khan,[1] or by absorption through co-residence with descendants of Oghuz Khan.[2] The Central Asian Turkmen are all Moslems of the Sunnite sect and Hanafite rite, and they identify themselves closely with Islam, even though they do not follow its precepts as closely as some of their religious teachers might prefer. The Turkmen language, which the Turkmen themselves refer to variously as Türkī, Türkmenche, and Türkmen Dil, is classified by philologists as belonging to the Oghuz or southwestern group of Turkic languages and has close affinities to Azerbaijani and modern Turkish (Menges, 1967: 72-74). Like the latter languages Turkmen is heavily laden with Arabic and Persian borrowings. The linguistic relationship of Turkmen to Uzbek, Kazakh, and Kirghiz is considered more distant than to Azerbaijani or Turkish (Menges, *ibid.*). The cultural affinities of the Turkmen, however, are stronger with the other Turkic peoples of Central Asia, especially the Kazakh and Kirghiz, than they are with their closest linguistic relatives, the Azerbaijanis and Turks. The latter point is more relevant to the present study, since the kinship system of the Yomut shows stronger similarities to those of the Kazakh and Kirghiz and even to that of various Mongolic groups than to those of the Azerbaijani or Turks.[3]

The recorded history of the Turkmen covers approximately a millenium.[4] The specific details of the early portion of this history are, for the most part, irrelevant to the present study. One pertinent fact does emerge from Turkmen history: for at least a thousand years, the Turkmen have been in contact with urban civilization and have had important economic and political relations with sedentary and urban people. It is important to keep this fact in mind while appraising their recent history.

---

[1] Oghuz Khan and Oguz Khan are the usual spellings of this name. The Yomut pronunciation, however, is Oghuth Han.

[2] There are also small, scattered groups designated Turkmen in Anatolia, the Caucasus, and the Fertile Crescent. These groups, although historically related to the Central Asian Turkmen, have lived in isolation from them for a number of centuries and, probably as a result, are culturally and linguistically distinct from them. Many of these "diaspora" Turkmen groups are Shiite in religion, but the Central Asian Turkmen are all Sunnite, and all those with whom I am acquainted maintain that one cannot be a Turkmen if one is not Sunnite. The location of these groups can be seen in S. I. Bruk and V. S. Apenchenko, 1964:28-32, 70-71. Throughout this study the word Turkmen is restricted in meaning to the Central Asian Turkmen.

[3] For descriptions of the kinship systems referred to see: Aberle, 1953; Hanessian, 1963; Hudson, 1938; Krader, 1963b; Stirling, 1965; and Vreeland, 1957.

[4] For an introduction to Turkmen history, see Barthold, 1962:73-187.

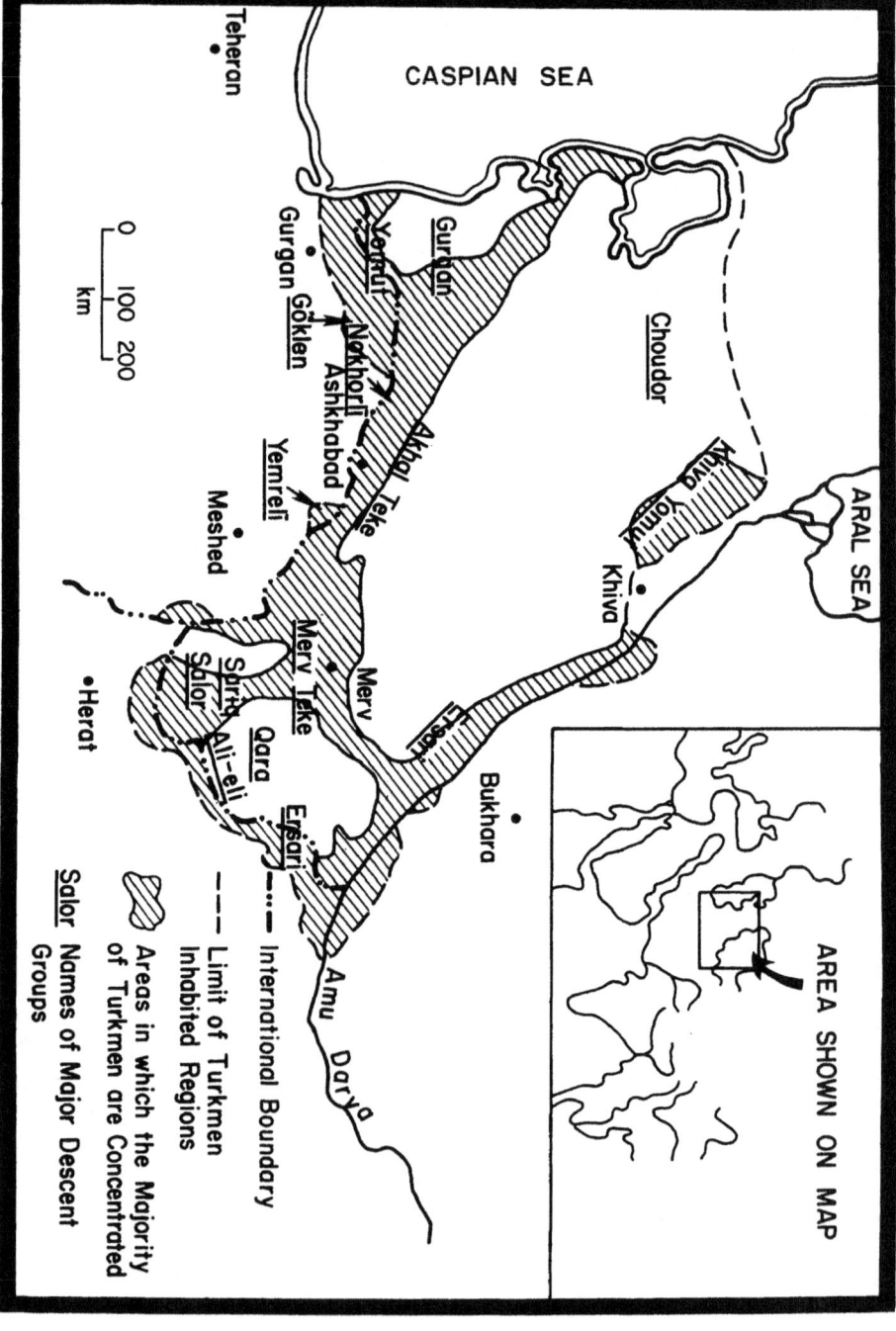

Fig. 1. Principal Turkmen descent groups.

During the past century, the Turkmen have experienced many pressures for social change. The Russian conquest of the majority of the Turkmen during the last part of the nineteenth century and later conquests by the Persian and Afghan governments provided the initial impetus for change. During more recent decades increasingly effective government control and the penetration of government into wider and wider spheres of Turkmen life have increased these pressures. Anthropologists are familiar with similar processes in other parts of the world. The experience of the Turkmen in this regard, however, is different from that of most of the "primitive" peoples of the Americas, sub-Saharan Africa, and Oceania in that they had, throughout their recorded history, been in contact with "civilization." Many peoples studied by anthropologists have only recently become familiar with the state as an institution and have only recently been integrated into an economy articulated by urban markets. The Turkmen, in contrast, have been familiar with such civilized institutions as the state and the urban market for at least a thousand years. What they have experienced recently has been merely a drastic increase in the ability of the state to exercise control over them.

Historical evidence indicates that prior to the recent appearance of these forces of change the Turkmen had achieved a stable relationship with both their physical and social environments and, as a consequence, the broad outlines of their culture and social structure probably had not changed for some time.[5] This stable adjustment can be summarized as follows. The Turkmen were oriented to production for trade in urban markets. By trade they acquired many goods which they could not produce themselves or at least could not produce as well. These goods include grain, cloth, metal tools, guns, and gun powder. The Turkmen, especially the tribes south of the Kara Kum desert, were, for the most part, free of effective political control by any neighboring sedentary state, although they often recognized sedentary rulers as their suzerains. They often viewed the recognition of a suzerain as an alliance between two autonomous political groups rather than as an acceptance of authority, and their interpretation of their political status was by no means unrealistic. Despite their ability to resist government control it would be unrealistic to think of them as influenced only superficially by the state as an institution. The centralized administrative and military apparatus of settled society has been a factor with which they have had to reckon. Those who could completely resist the power of the state by military means did so, and in effect maintained full de facto political sovereignty while regulating their political affairs in terms of a segmentary political system. Those who for one reason or another could not do this granted the government's agents some limited degree of control over their affairs. The extent of autonomy left to

---

[5] Probably the conversion of the Turkmen to Islam in the tenth century and their integration into the Mongol Empire in the thirteen century had similarly far-reaching effects on their culture and social structure (see Barthold, *ibid.*).

the Turkmen, or, conversely, the degree of government control consented to by them, reflected more than anything else a balance of power.[6]

The Turkmen have also been a force with which sedentary states have had to cope. States based on sedentary society have often adopted a largely defensive policy against the Turkmen (for example, see Barthold, 1962:146, 167). At other times, sedentary political leaders have sought military support from various Turkmen groups. For example, the Turkmen of Iran were instrumental in the establishment of the Kajar dynasty of Iran in the late eighteenth century, and opponents of the Iranian constitution sought Turkmen support in the revolution of 1909.

This long history of economic and political relations with settled and urban people is quite naturally reflected in many ways in Turkmen culture and social structure. Much of Turkmen culture is a modification and simplification of more sophisticated Islamic urban traditions. Other aspects of their culture represent continuation of pre-Islamic Turkic traditions.

One area in which urban influences are especially evident can be found in what might be described as the intellectual tradition of the Turkmen. The Turkmen began to adopt Islam in the tenth century, and their adherence at present to that religion is by no means superficial. Most adult Turkmen males are assiduous in carrying out such obligatory Islamic rituals as the prayers required five times a day and the annual month of fasting. Wealthy Turkmen usually make the pilgrimage to Mecca and after their return are much respected for having acquired the status of ḥajjī. Turkmen also observe the requirement that they give a prescribed portion of their property annually for charitable or religious purposes (see Coon, 1958:109-111, and Lane, 1908:92-93). Those Turkmen who study religion become literate in Arabic, and once they have done this it is relatively easy for them to read and write their own language using the Arabic alphabet. Among the literate minority of religious teachers, a small body of literature in the Turkmen language has developed, most of which is religious poetry (see Köprülü Zāde, 1931: 898-899). A small quantity of history has also been written.[7]

The influence of urban civilization in the sphere of kinship is less extensive than in the domain of religion but is nevertheless visible. The influence of Islamic tradition is most evident in the permission of marriage with close agnatic kin, a practice which the Turkmen share with their Middle Eastern co-religionists and also with the sedentary Uzbeks of Central Asia. Islamic law also affects inheritance and the treatment of widows.

## THE RECENT HISTORY OF THE TURKMEN

The recent history of the Islamic world is primarily the history of the

---

[6] A similar situation has been described in southwestern Iran (Garthwaite, 1969).

[7] The most widely known history written in Turkmen is that of Abul-Ghāzī, 1958.

penetration of western influence, and the Turkmen are no exception. Like the other nomadic peoples of the Islamic world, they have been more conservative than sedentary and urban people, adjusting more slowly to western influences.

During the past century, all of the Turkmen have been brought, by force of arms, under the effective control of one of three governments— Russia, Iran, or Afghanistan. As a result of government influence the majority of Turkmen have, in recent decades, become sedentary. These changes, however, have occurred piecemeal, affecting some areas sooner and more drastically than others. The particular community which forms the focus of this study is a conservative group that had remained nomadic up to the time of my first research in 1965-67 (and, in fact, remained fully nomadic until 1970). Much of their culture and social structure had remained as it was before the loss of political independence, and much of it, therefore, made sense only when viewed in the context of previous political conditions. For this reason, a brief review of the recent history of the Turkmen, especially those of northern Iran, is useful as an introduction to the more specific discussion of kinship.

A century ago the larger subdivisions of the Turkmen were distributed as follows.[8] The bulk of the Turkmen population was concentrated, as it is now, along the more fertile fringes of the Kara Kum desert. Their population was estimated then at about 900,000 individuals (Vambery, 1865:355). Their present population is about a million and a half (Krader, 1968:408). The most powerful and numerous tribe was the Teke which occupied the Akhal Mountains south of the Kara Kum and the Merv oasis to the west of the Akhal Mountains. Second in military strength and reputation were the Yomut who occupied the Gurgan Plain and Balkhan Mountains south of the Kara Kum and west of the Teke. Another group of Yomut lived north of the Kara Kum near the city of Khiva. The Salor and Sariq, whom the Teke had recently driven from the Merv oasis, were small in number, but had a reputation for sending out formidable raiding parties. The Choudor, west of the Yomut of Khiva in the very arid Ust Urt, were not numerous, but like many tribes inhabiting especially arid regions they were effective raiders and much feared by their neighbors. The Qara tribe in the very arid regions southeast of Merv similarly were a small tribe inhabiting an especially arid region and enjoying a reputation as formidable brigands.

The other large tribes were not as noted for military prowess. The Ersari, inhabiting the banks of the Amu Darya, were relatively peaceful subjects of the Khans of Bukhara. The Göklen, occupying a well-watered region southeast of the Gurgan Yomut, were primarily agricultural and were considered to be the most civilized of Turkmen tribes, as well as the most religious and the most addicted to opium.

[8] On the nineteenth century distribution of the larger Turkmen descent groups, see Vambery, 1865:347-355; and Jarring, 1939:35-51.

These were the larger and politically more important tribes, and much was written about them. There were also politically less significant tribes which received less attention. Among these were the Ewlad, scattered groups who claimed descent from the first four Caliphs and whose sacred descent gave them the status of non-combatants in intertribal warfare. There were also small groups, such as the Nokhorli of the Akhal Mountains and the Ali-eli of Andkhui who were thought of as originally non-Turkmen and only recently Turkmenized. Because of their putative non-Turkmen origin these latter groups were considered socially inferior by the larger and more powerful tribes.

The Turkmen were, before their conquest, notorious for slave raiding. Most of the raiding was done by four tribes—the Teke, Yomut, Salor, and Sariq—and most of the raids were directed against northeastern Persia and northern Afghanistan. In their raids they exploited two factors to considerable advantage: surprise and the great endurance of their horses (see Marvin, 1881:177-200, for a good discussion of Turkmen slaving). Raiding parties moved into the area they hoped to raid by traveling at night and hiding in a secluded spot during the day. After carefully reconnoitering a village or caravan selected as their target, they would arrange an ambush. Once captives were taken they would retreat quickly to their own territory. Their horses were a breed outstanding for endurance, and they kept their better horses fresh for the retreat by riding inferior mounts to the scene of the raid and during the ambush. This usually made it easy for them to outrun any pursuers who might be mustered after the raid.

Captives taken in these raids could be held for ransom, sold among their own tribe, or sent by caravan across the Kara Kum to the slave markets of Khiva, Bukhara, or Merv. The evidence that survives indicates that slaving was often very profitable (Marvin, *ibid*.; Coon, 1958:223). It is interesting to note that, while Islam forbids one Moslem from enslaving another, the Turkmen justified their practice by appealing to the fact that their victims were not orthodox Moslems like themselves, but rather Shiites. Slave raiding, they reasoned, brought many errant souls into the orthodox Sunnite fold.

The Czarist empire brought the majority of the Turkmen under its control in the last quarter of the nineteenth century and put an end to most of the slave trade. In 1873 Czarist forces took Khiva and subdued the northern branch of the Yomut (d'Encausse, 1967*a*:147-149). A rapid succession of conquests followed. The conquest of Qizil Arvat in 1877 brought the southern branch of the Yomut, excepting those south of the Atrak River, under Russian suzerainty. After a setback at the hands of the Teke in 1879, the Russians pushed on, taking Ashkhabad in 1881 and Merv in 1884.

Historians usually cite the conquest of Merv in 1884 as the final blow to Turkmen independence. This conquest closed the last Central Asian slave market and gave the Russians control of most of the Turkmen-inhabited regions. However, not all of the Turkmen were actually brought under Russian rule. In the Gurgan Plain, the region from which the data for this study were drawn, the Russian conquest stopped at the Atrak River, leaving a large portion of the Yomut tribe, and most of the Göklen tribe, under the nominal suzerainty of Persia. Control of these Turkmen by the Kajar government of Persia was weak at best and varied considerably from one area to another. These conditions continued in the Gurgan Plain until 1925.

Fortunately there are a few good written descriptions of the Gurgan Plain during the latter part of the nineteenth and the first part of the twentieth centuries.[9] Also, the early part of the twentieth century falls within the memory of my older informants. This makes it possible to combine written and oral sources in studying the conditions that prevailed at that time. The picture that emerges from written records and informants' oral accounts is a consistent one.

During this period, the Göklen tribe was under the control of the Kurdish chiefs of the city of Bujnurd who appointed a governor of the Göklen and supplied him with a militia of 200 mounted men. The governor and most of his officers were drawn from the Kurdish population of the Bujnurd region, but the mounted militia were Göklen. The primary functions of the governor and his militia were to collect a light tax and to prevent raids by the Göklen against Bujnurd. The power of the governor was not sufficient to regulate the internal affairs of the Göklen or to protect them from the Yomut. Internal feuds and relations with the Yomut were matters handled by the Göklen without the intervention of the governor or his militia. Relations with the Yomut were characterized by continual raids and counter-raids. As a result, there was a strip of uninhabited territory, a no-man's-land, between these two tribes.

Control over the Yomut was much looser. The Yomut, then, as today, divided themselves into two groups along economic lines. One group, the charwa, were pastoral; the other group, the chomïr, were agricultural. The charwa were, for the most part, free of any form of government control, although some of them migrated seasonally into Russian territory where the Czarist authorities maintained a measure of control. Those chomïr that occupied territory distant from the administrative center of the Gurgan Plain were also free of government control. The chomïr nearer the administrative center, the city of Asterabad (modern Gurgan), paid taxes, though lighter ones than the Göklen, and they had tribal leaders supplied with a mounted militia at government expense. More details concerning the political conditions of the Yomut of the Gurgan Plain before 1925 are presented below in the discussion of political structures.

[9] See Bustāmī, 1878; Qūrkhānchī Saulat Nizām, 1903-04, 1909-1910; Rabino, 1928:67-104; Yate, 1900:212-281. Concerning more recent conditions see Pūrkarim, 1966a,b, 1967, 1968a,b,c, 1970.

In 1925 the situation of the Iranian Yomut changed sharply as a result of events occurring throughout the nation of Iran. During the 1920s the Iranian government underwent a vast transformation under the leadership of Reza Shah, a transformation toward a government committed to reform, economic development, and the exclusion of foreign influence from Iranian affairs. An important part of this transformation was the subjugation and disarming of the various tribes which up to that point had enjoyed considerable autonomy—and often de facto independence. This was an extensive task which kept the army occupied with military operations against one tribe or another for most of the decade. It was as a part of this general effort to bring all the tribes of Iran under effective control, that the Iranian army began a campaign to subdue and disarm the Yomut and Göklen in the autumn of 1925.

The Yomut at first put up a stiff resistance, but after finding their opponents too strong for them, most of them fled with their families and livestock across the border into Russian territory. Thus, immediately after being brought under control, the territory formerly occupied by the Yomut was largely uninhabited. The Iranian army, however, continued to hold the territory and allowed the Yomut to return only if they surrendered their arms and promised to accept Iranian authority.

Administration on the Russian side of the border was largely ineffective then. During the revolution, Russian authority had completely collapsed in the Turkmen regions of Russia and by 1925 the new revolutionary government was only beginning to reestablish administration of the region. Many of the Yomut who had fled Iran in the autumn of 1925 preferred the less effective administration on the Russian side of the border and remained there until the mid-1930s, though others returned sooner. In the mid-1930s, the revolutionary government began a much more strenuous attempt to intervene in the affairs of the Yomut. Attempts were made to collectivize property and to curtail religious activities. Most of those who had fled Iran in 1925 and had not yet returned, returned at this time. They were joined by many Yomut who had always lived on the Russian side of the border.

Soon after these events, the Iranian administration also began to intervene more extensively in the affairs of the Yomut. It was during this period that the Iranian government began a general policy of forced sedentarization of nomads. During the Russian occupation of northern Iran (1941-1946), there was a partial reversion to the condition of ineffective government control characteristic of the period before 1925. This was especially true of the more arid regions in which the Russian occupying force had little administrative interest. An Iranian administration was reestablished with Russian approval shortly after the invasion of 1941, but its authority was very limited, particularly in the less populous portion of Yomut territory.

After the Second World War, effective Iranian administration was reestablished in the Gurgan Plain, and in the more populous and better watered southern portion of the Plain a period of rapid economic development began. The southern portion of the Gurgan Plain was ideal for mechanized agriculture. It was quite level, and had both a high rainfall and numerous streams from which water could be taken for irrigation. In addition, it had a low population density and large tracts of arable uncultivated land. These attributes led to the rapid development of commercial mechanized agriculture. As a result, all of the Turkmen south of the Gurgan River have become sedentary cotton farmers.

In the more arid regions north of the Gurgan River change has been less drastic. This is especially true of the Gōkcha Hills region where this study was conducted. The Turkmen of this region reverted completely to nomadism in 1941, and were still nomadic at the time of my study. A fuller description of how this region was affected by these changes is given in Chapter II (pp. 27-30).

## DATA AND RESEARCH METHODS

The data presented in this monograph are based on sixteen months of field research conducted between December 1965 and November 1967. Most of this research was carried out in a single nomadic community approximately thirty miles north of the city of Gunbadi Kāvūs. In addition, considerable time was spent gathering data in a recently settled community about fifteen miles northeast of Gunbadi Kāvūs. I also traveled extensively, making shorter visits to 39 of the approximately 250 Yomut communities in the Gurgan Plain, and seven Turkmen communities belonging to the Göklen descent group. Throughout this study the ethnographic present refers to the time period 1965-67. All of the descriptive material in Chapters IV-VII refers to conditions in the nomadic community mentioned above, at this time, unless specifically stated otherwise.

A few remarks about the manner in which my research was conducted will probably assist the reader in evaluating the data presented. Like many anthropologists I began my field research with no knowledge of the language of the group I was to study. The task of learning Turkmen began the same day as my field research. The linguistic problems of field research were, however, eased by several things. First, I had had good training in linguistic field methods while a graduate student at the University of Michigan. As a result of this training I was better equipped to tackle the job of learning a language without the benefit of textbooks, grammars, or professional language teachers. Second, Turkmen is closely related to standard Turkish, a language for which excellent elementary grammars and textbooks are available for native English speakers. Turkmen is not as similar to standard Turkish as most written sources claim. The phonology is quite distinct, roughly half of the vocabulary is different (consisting either of noncognates or false cognates), and although the grammar is similar in its general form almost every grammatical structure is different in its details. Nevertheless, I found a textbook designed for teaching Turkish very useful as a guide to what to look for as I put together my own crude grammar and sketchy vocabulary lists. I also made some use of G. K. Dulling, *An Introduction to the Turkmen Language*. It was not much assistance, however, being both superficial and inaccurate as a guide to the speech of the Turkmen of northern Iran. A third factor easing the initial linguistic problems of field work was the fact that when I began my study I knew Persian, the national language of Iran, and was able to communicate with many Turkmen through Persian.

At first progress in learning Turkmen was slow because it is a difficult language, and one totally unrelated to any other language I know. After about six months of field research, I had learned enough Turkmen to be able to conduct my interviewing in Turkmen and after ten months I was able to understand most conversations between native speakers.

While living in the community which was the focus of my attention, I established what amounted to a semi-independent household, consisting of myself and one servant, occupying a canvas tent. During the later months of my research, we expanded our equipment by adding a small Turkmen tent. For all but a few weeks of my time in that community I camped next to the headman's tent and the women of his household baked the bread which formed the staple of our diet. While visiting other Turkmen communities I was a guest of local families. The Turkmen, like other Moslem people, have a tradition of hospitality which greatly facilitates travel. Strangers who appear at their doors are invariably invited in and offered tea and bread. If it appears that a visitor needs lodging for the night, his host asks simply "Are you staying?" and if the answer is affirmative, the guest is fed and supplied with a place to sleep without further ceremony. This ease of access to Turkmen homes proved beneficial to my work. When I occupied my own tent, the situation was reversed and I was obliged to offer bread and tea to all who chose to visit my tent, other than immediate neighbors who were in and out several times a day. When my servant prepared meals I usually invited the headman, his father, and some of his brothers to join us. While with the Turkmen I adhered as best I could to Turkmen rules of etiquette and personal conduct. My objective in doing these things was to minimize my outlandishness in their eyes, and to maximize opportunities for personal contact. My intention was not to become a Turkmen, which would have been impossible, but to smooth the way for communication across cultural boundaries.

My initial attempts at doing this were an utter failure. The gap between myself and the subjects of my research was too great to bridge in a few days. The extent to which the Turkmen of the Gurgan Plain have had experience with outsiders varies greatly from one area to another. In the urban centers of the Gurgan Plain, one can find highly sophisticated Turkmen: government officials, entrepreneurs, and capitalistic farmers who practice mechanized agriculture. Many of these people have obtained a modern education, in Iranian schools or abroad. In economically less promising portions of the Gurgan Plain, one finds more conservative people, people who live in tents and raise sheep for a living, and whose only contact with urban life has been an occasional visit to a nearby city to shop in a store owned by another Turkmen, often a relative, or to sell sheep or carpets to a Turkmen middleman. Like many anthropologists, I was most interested in the people least influenced by modernization, and so I chose to study a conservative, nomadic community. This, however, vastly increased the barriers to communication. Lack of a common tongue was by no means the only difficulty. The local people viewed me, first and foremost, as an infidel whose presence could only be a source of misfortune. Although they did not have the courage to ask me to go away, imagining that I must have great influence with the government and, therefore, was potentially dangerous, they, nevertheless, made their discomfort with my presence clear. I unwittingly aggravated the situation by asking what they considered indecent questions, such as inquiries about their sisters, and by committing acts they considered sacreligious, such as tossing bread crumbs into the fire. Much of the information I sought they would not give readily to any stranger. Portions of their genealogies were carefully guarded secrets, because this information, in the wrong hands, could make them targets of blood vengeance.[10] Questions about their sisters and daughters were indecent. Asking the ages of young men involved the touchy matter of conscription. The man I had hired as a servant and interpreter, a Turkmen from another region, realized that my isolation from the local community increased my dependence on him, and so he set about to improve on what he saw as a good situation. He did this by warning the local people that I was suspected of having a dangerous covert political mission and it was his job to watch me on behalf of the Iranian gendarmerie. He added that they should, therefore, never deal with me directly, but only through him.

As a result of these difficulties, my research made little progress during the first few months of my stay with the Turkmen. Eventually, as I learned more of the local language and culture, I began to realize the sources of my difficulties and to correct them. A proper understanding of, and respect for, the local code of personal behavior, and a new, more honest servant opened the way for a better rapport with the people I wanted to study. Eventually I built up a relationship of trust with a number of Turkmen and was able to gain

---

[10] In general the sixth and seventh ascending generations are difficult to gain information about. Obtaining information about lower generations is not difficult. Usually genealogies above the seventh generation are admittedly incomplete and imprecise (see pp. 45-46, 115-116). Genealogies of the sort that exist for generations above the seventh generation—genealogies which I have referred to in this book as putative genealogies—are not difficult to gather.

their assistance as informants. Most of my information came from a limited number of informants, and much of my interviewing had to be done at irregular intervals when I was able to be alone with them. Much of the information I sought was not information local people felt comfortable sharing with outsiders.

However, working within these limitations, it was possible to obtain the data I wanted. The community I studied was small and the adults of the community knew each other's business well. Thus, while I could gather certain types of information *from* only a limited number of people, I was able to gather information *about* a much wider circle of people. Comparing the information given by different informants provided a check on the accuracy of my data. I was also able to check much of what I was told by direct observation.

Three men who were my primary informants were exceptionally intelligent, knew Persian well, and were literate. Two were religious teachers who had received a traditional religious education and were residents of the community I studied. One of these was 61 years old when I first met him and had fought in intertribal wars in the days before the Iranian government took effective control of the Gurgan Plain. The other was 30 when I first made his acquaintance. The third of my principal informants was my second servant, a man of 30 years when I first met him, who was born and raised in the community I studied but had later migrated permanently to another community. He had a limited religious education, but had perfected his literacy, as well as his knowledge of Persian, while a conscript in the Iranian Army.

I first became acquainted with these men soon after my research began, so that I received their assistance over a long period of time. All three became sympathetic to my work and came to understand what sort of data I wanted. All three were honest in supplying information, and readily admitted ignorance when they did not have the data I sought. They were all willing, as well, to seek out information which I wanted if they did not already have it, or to find informants who could supply special kinds of information. Each of these men was recognized as a leader in local affairs and often people who would not have trusted me on my own merits, trusted me because one of these three men vouched for the innocence of my intentions.

A wider circle of people supplied more limited assistance, some of them acting frequently as informants. I was only able to interview adult women if they were considerably older than I, and my contact with women was much less extensive than with men. On the other hand, for most of my time with the Turkmen, I was the only non-Turkmen in the community and, life being what it is in a tent, most of their household affairs were readily observable. I had ample chance to observe Turkmen interacting with one another and to interact with them myself.

In addition to direct observation of Yomut life and the experience of living with and dealing with Yomut on a daily basis, the data collected consisted primarily of the following: genealogies, census material (including household composition, ages, ages at marriage, and property holdings), brief life histories, accounts of social norms and of values and beliefs, descriptions of particular events such as disputes or negotiations of bridal payments which illustrate Yomut social life, accounts of recent local history, sketch maps of the distribution of camps, wells, and agricultural land over the grazing territory of a particular community at different seasons (made with compass and pedometer), and sketch maps showing the locations of residence groups, data on the descent group composition of residence groups, and history of these residence groups.

A few comments should be made about portions of this data. In contrast to situations encountered elsewhere by anthropologists, Yomut informants know their own ages and those of their relatives and acquaintances. Age reckoning is done in terms of a cycle of twelve animal years.[11] Each year is associated with a particular animal and the weather and other events of that year are in some ways characteristic of the animal. Each new animal year begins ten days before the spring equinox. The animal years in which people are born are remembered, although the precise day of birth is usually forgotten. By comparing the animal year of a person's birth with the current animal year it is possible to determine his age as being one of several possible ages, each twelve years apart. Thus, when my research began in the year of the snake, anyone born in the year of the pig would be either six, 18, 30, 42, 54, 66, or 78. Given this much assistance it is not difficult to determine precisely which age to select. The Turkmen use this memory device to remember specific events of significance as well so that intelligent informants can provide accurate dates for past events. (In converting their ages to ours, however, one has to remember that their New Year's Day falls on March eleventh and that a child is considered to be one at birth, and two after it has seen one New Year's Day.)

Concerning ages, it should be noted that all ages change on the same day, so that a person's age by Turkmen reckoning may differ during a part of the year from his age by ordinary western reckoning. The ages I was given

---

[11] The use of animal years is obviously a result of Far Eastern influence. The Turkmen names for these years are, beginning with the first year of the cycle and proceeding in order: thichin (mouse), thighir (cow), barth (leopard), tawshin (rabbit), baliq (fish), yilan (snake), yilki (mare), qoyin (sheep), bijin (an unidentified animal which is described as being small, red, and living in the sea), taok (chicken), it (dog), dongith (pig). The complete cycle of 12 years is called a müje, and a period of three müje, 36 years, is called a hengam. A hengam is approximately the period over which the Islamic lunar months make a complete cycle in terms of the solar year; thus, if a particular date in the Islamic calendar falls in a particular solar year on the spring equinox, it will fall close to the spring equinox one hengam later.

were by and large not those I would have guessed. Most individuals under 20 appeared younger to me than their actual ages, while those over 40 usually appeared older than their actual ages. Presumably the Yomut population matures later and, after reaching maturity, ages faster than the population of middle-class America.

My census of the community from which most of my data comes had to be taken at first indirectly from a few informants. After this it was possible to visit the tents of various families on one occasion or another and during the course of each visit to note the number of individuals and their sex and apparent ages in order to check the accuracy of the initial indirect count. It was also possible at milking time to make a rough count of the livestock holdings. Because of the time consumed in such work, however, I used it to check the accuracy of informants' accounts rather than doing a complete new census of my own. The only inaccuracies that direct observation revealed in census data gathered indirectly were occasional omissions of girls under five, a category of individuals that is not considered very important in Yomut society. These inaccuracies were not numerous, however, and could be remedied in most cases by further inquiries, and comparing different informants' accounts.

Unfortunately, because of the way my census was taken, precise ages could not always be obtained and I was often forced to record an informant's impression of someone's age. Cross checking with other informants, however, revealed that such estimates were usually within two or three years of the correct age.

My own counts of livestock holdings, again because of the way they were taken, could not be precise and those given by informants were usually in round figures. However, the size of a herd is continually changing, increasing at lambing season and decreasing during the remainder of the year, so that precise counts at one point in time would not be especially meaningful. Again my own counts indicate that my informants were supplying accurate data.

Maps of Yomut country were made by visiting a number of communities and in each community asking the headman to draw a sketch map of the territory of his own tribe including rivers and other landmarks as well as residence groups. By obtaining several maps for the same area it was possible to check for omissions. These sketch maps were then combined with maps obtained from the U.S. Army Map Service (Series N502, 1951 edition) to prepare maps showing the location of all the Yomut communities in Iran and indicating such data as the predominant mode of economic production (agriculture or pastoralism) in each community and the distribution of Yomut descent groups among these communities.[12]

---

[12] Most of the Yomut residence groups were not shown on the U.S. Army maps and over half of those shown were given a name that bore no similarity to any name recorded in my survey. For this reason, only a few communities could be accurately located; the rest were located approximately in terms of such landmarks as rivers or the sites of those communities that could be located. Figures 2-9 are simplifications of the maps prepared from the U.S. Army maps and my survey data.

INTRODUCTION 19

These visits were also used to gather information on local histories and the genealogies of larger descent groups.[13] Most of this work was done by going to the headman of a community and requesting that he gather the elders (yasholĭs) of the community together so that we could make our inquiries from them as a group. This is by no means an unusual procedure in Yomut social relations.

Details concerning the location and history of the community in which most of my time was spent are given below. It should be observed, however, that although the location and historic events are accurate, the community has been given a fictitious name, Ajĭ Quĭ (Brackish Well). The names of individuals have also been changed by substituting names of individuals from other communities. Occasionally, names of smaller descent groups have also been changed by substituting names of similar size groups from other regions; footnotes indicate which descent group names are fictitious, and all those not so indicated are the actual names of the groups referred to.

---

[13] These genealogies were not sensitive matters and therefore not difficult to gather; see note 10 above.

## II

## ECOLOGY

THIS chapter proceeds from a description of the traditional ecology of the Yomut to a discussion of the shift toward sedentarization, the introduction of mechanized agriculture and other major changes which have affected the majority of the Yomut. Finally the current ecology of the pastoral community from which most of my data are drawn is described. The most significant point that emerges from this description is that the traditional economy of the Yomut, and the economy of conservative pastoral communities at the time of observation, could easily be combined with a semi-sedentary residence pattern. The more nomadic residence pattern they actually practice—traditionally in all areas and at the time of my research in conservative areas—offered no *economic* advantage over a semi-sedentary residence pattern.

### TRADITIONAL ECOLOGY AND ECONOMY

The Gurgan Plain, the habitat of the Iranian Yomut, is the southwesternmost portion of the Central Asian lowlands which extend eastward from the Caspian Sea to the Pamirs and the Altai Mountains and northward from the Iranian Plateau to the forests of Asiatic Russia. The western portion of this plain, adjacent to the Caspian Sea, lies below sea level and rises gradually to the east until it reaches the Gōkcha Hills and Kopet Dagh which form its eastern border. The southern part of the plain is bounded by the Elburz Mountains which rise sharply to peaks of 2,500 to 3,000 meters. This dramatic rise in elevation is responsible for the unusual climatic conditions of the Gurgan Plain. Air moving to the south over the lowlands rises when it encounters the Elburz Mountains and releases most of its moisture on the northern slopes of the mountains and the southern edge of the plain. These slopes have an annual average rainfall of over sixty centimeters, and, where uncultivated, are heavily forested (Bobek, 1968:284-285). Rainfall decreases sharply to the north, causing the terrain to change from forest to steppe, and then to steppe-desert over a short distance (see Fig. 2).[1] Thus, for example, if one starts moving to the north from the 500 meter contour in the mountains south of the city of Gurgan, within 20 kilometers, one will reach the edge of the forest at an elevation just below sea level. If one continues northward, in another 20 kilometers one will reach the edge of the region in which rainfall agriculture is possible. Farther to the north lies a steppe-desert which, without irrigation, can only be used for raising livestock.

These three ecological zones—forest, steppe, and steppe-desert— correspond to three ethnographically distinct regions. The forest area stretching from the northern slopes of the Elburz to the southern portion of the Gurgan Plain is inhabited by Persian-speaking and Turkic-speaking, sedentary peasants. These peasants all adhere to the Shiite sect of Islam, and all are referred to by the Turkmen as Welayet.[2] Immediately north of the forest region is a steppe zone which is inhabited by Turkmen who are primarily agriculturalists. The Turkmen term for this group of people is chomir, in contrast to the pastoral Turkmen, who are called charwa. This third group, the charwa, occupies the desert region north of the Gurgan River.

Before the sedentarization program of the 1930s, the chomir were unusual in that they were nomadic even though agriculture was the mainstay of their economy. They lived only in the Central Asian type of tents, called yurts, which consist of hemispherical wooden frames covered with felt, and they made short migrations, camping near their fields when engaged in planting or harvesting. Like the sedentary villagers of the forest area, they also had small flocks of sheep and goats.[3]

The seasonal movements of the chomir corresponded to the colder and warmer parts of the year (see Fig. 3). During the winter they camped near their agricultural land which was concentrated in the southern extreme of their territory, adjacent to the forest zone. During this season, they did their plowing and planting. The primary crops were wheat and barley. Occasionally, near a river or spring where it was possible to cultivate rice without constructing extensive irrigation works, they would plant small plots of rice. Not all of the cultivable land was put to plow and so grazing land was also available in this area for their livestock. Because of the surplus of arable land,

---

[1] Steppe here will consistently refer to a treeless region characterized by a continuous, thick grass cover. Steppe-desert will refer to a more arid region with thinner grass cover interspersed with patches of barren earth. The classification is that used in the following sources: Bobek, 1968; Krader, 1963:10-14; Kovda, 1961:175-218.

[2] Welayet is used throughout as an ethnic designation following the Turkmen usage. It is, therefore, capitalized.

[3] The breed of sheep exploited by the chomir and the Welayet is different from that of the charwa. The charwa sheep are of the fat-tailed variety. The Welayet and chomir sheep are smaller and thin-tailed.

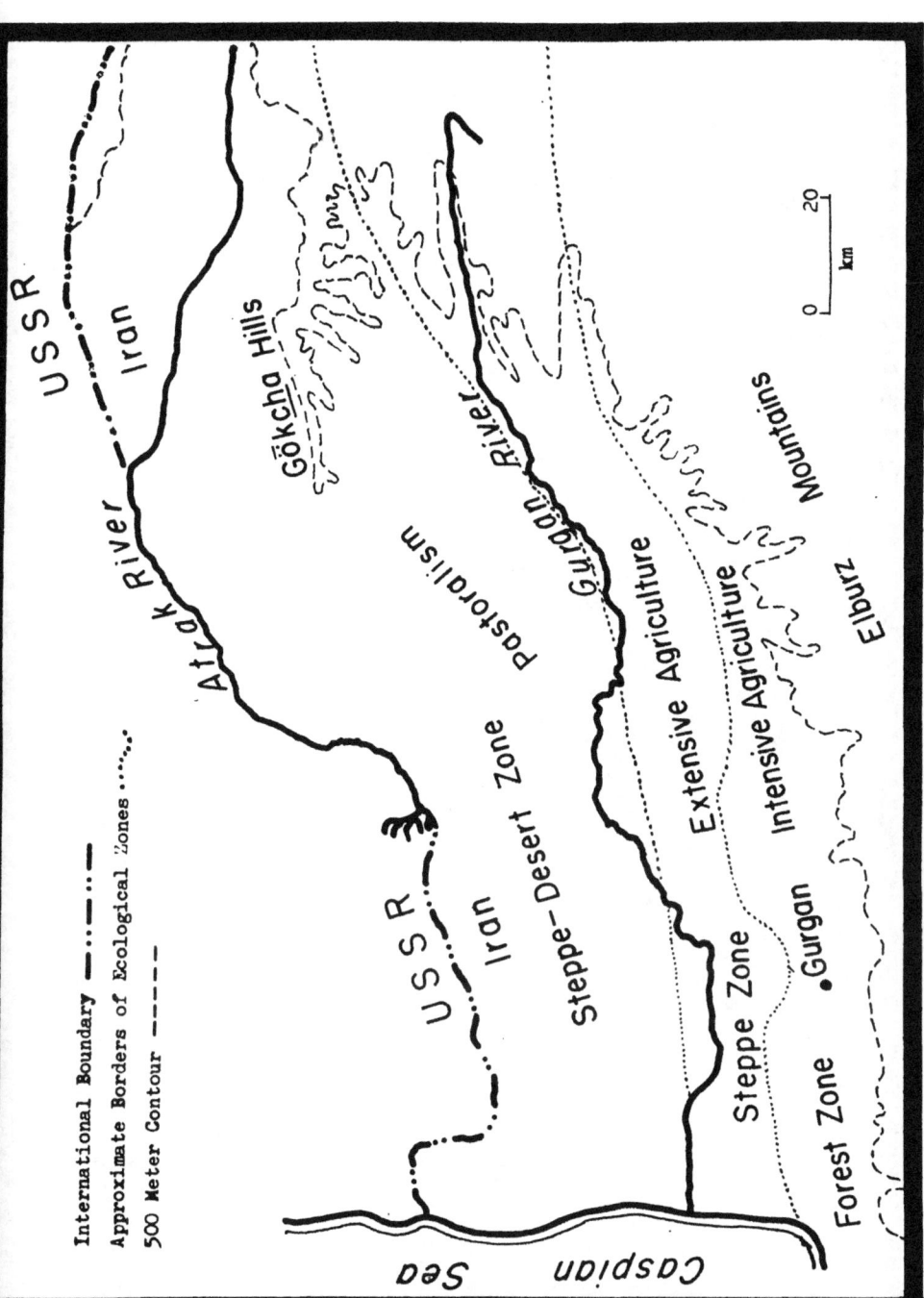

Fig. 2. Ecological zones and predominant modes of economic production before 1950.

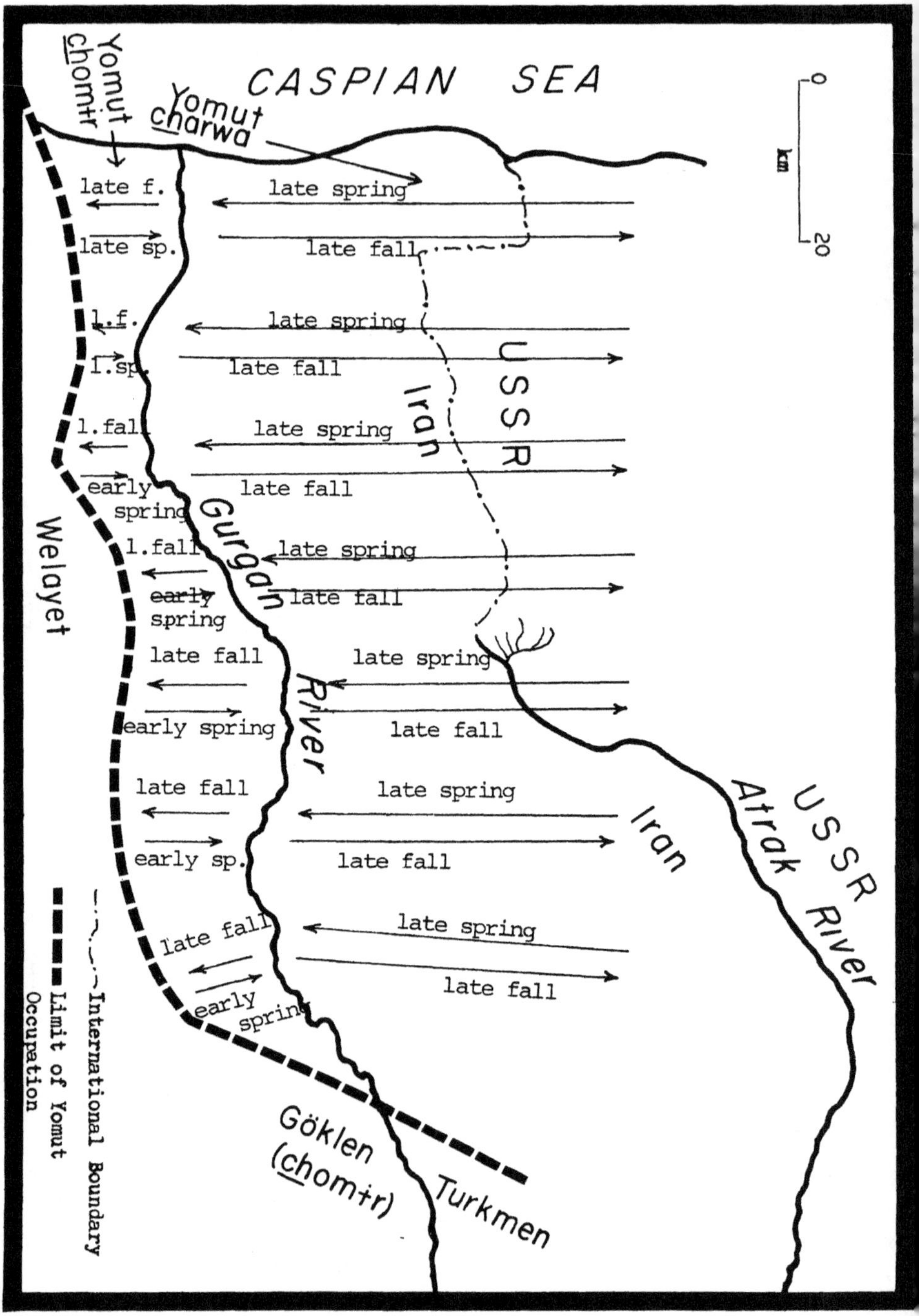

Fig. 3. Approximate pattern of Yomut migration before 1930.

it was possible for any family needing additional land to plow up unused land and claim it as its own.

During the spring most of the chomır migrated north to the banks of the Gurgan River to escape, to some extent, the flies and mosquitoes of the forest zone. These pests were not only a source of discomfort but also a hazard to both their own and their livestock's health. The chomır remained on the Gurgan River through the summer, leaving a few families behind to guard the fields. At least part of each family moved south to harvest their crops at the end of the spring, returning again to their camps on the Gurgan River. In late fall, the chomır moved back to the edge of the forest.

The migrations of those charwa immediately north of the chomır followed a similar north-south movement corresponding to the wet and dry seasons (see Fig. 3). During the dry season (winter and spring) they camped on the banks of the Gurgan River, and in the wet season they moved north into the steppe-desert. Charwa farther north followed a slightly different pattern, which is basically the same as that explained as part of the current ecology of Aji Qui described later in this chapter. In the winter and spring there were scattered rain water pools in the steppe-desert region from which the charwa could obtain water for their household needs and for their animals. Although the charwa were, and still are, primarily pastoral, they cultivated small plots of land in this area between the Gurgan and the Atrak. Scattered depressions which collected rain water could be cultivated and during the wetter years, despite the general aridity of the region, a crop of barley, and occasionally a small amount of wheat, could be harvested.[4] These fields, like those of the chomır, were planted in the winter and harvested in late spring.

Winter was the lambing season. During this season the pastoral Turkmen camped near their livestock, keeping the lambs and kids inside their yurts at night to protect them from the cold. Because the young animals were weak and unable to move far to daily pasture, camps were set up near good pasture. Whenever the pasture near a camp site became exhausted, short-range migrations were necessary. During the spring the milking season began. Camps had to remain close to the livestock in spring as well, because sheep and goats required daily milking.[5] This was the season during which many of the pastoral Turkmen crossed the Atrak into Russian territory to find good grazing land and to escape the flies and mosquitos of the forest areas.

In the dry season (summer and fall) the pattern of residence for these Turkmen changed. There was no need to keep livestock and camp site close together. Further, it was less convenient to do so. Pasture was poor at this

---

[4] Concerning the means of cultivation employed see Kovda, 1961; see also the techniques of rainfall agriculture employed by the Marri Baluch (Pehrson, 1966:8-9).

[5] All milk and milk products are consumed by the producer, except for the very wealthiest families.

time of year and herds had to be moved frequently. Thus, keeping livestock and camp together would have required frequent migration. Most of the labor involved in relocating would have fallen on the women who were busy weaving carpets. Also, frequent migration would have been an inconvenience for the most important segment of the population, the older men. Thus, as a matter of efficiency, each household was split into two groups that lived separately. The household's yurt or yurts were placed near a permanent source of water and the older men, women, and children resided there, remaining at a single location throughout the dry season. The younger men lived separately in small lean-to-like tents, moving daily with the livestock.

The economy of chomïr and charwa alike combined subsistence production and production for market exchange. The chomïr offered wheat and barley for exchange while the charwa offered livestock, wool, felts, and carpets. A few chomïr communities specialized in manufacturing the wooden frames for the yurts of other chomïr and those of the charwa. Both groups acquired rice, sugar, tea, salt, cloth, metal tools, rifles, and gunpowder by purchase. The charwa, in addition, were dependent on trade for the staple of their diet, wheat. Both chomïr and charwa relied on mills in the Welayet country to grind their wheat into flour. Market exchange took place through a number of channels. On occasion Turkmen traveled to urban markets for purchases, and, at other times, they did their trading through itinerant merchants. A few Turkmen were merchants traveling among their own tribe selling products bought in other areas in exchange for local products, or for cash. Welayet merchants also traveled among the Turkmen under the protection of Turkmen traveling companions, who were paid a portion of the merchant's profits for their trouble.

The charwa were wealthier than the chomïr and were generally considered to have the preferred occupation. Informants frequently cited poor health conditions as the reason for viewing the chomïr's lot in life as an undesirable one. Before the mid-1950s, malaria was an especially serious problem in both the forest zone and in the steppe region of the chomïr. The charwa, in contrast, were generally able to avoid exposure to malaria, and had a much healthier environment overall. The Yomut were, and for the most part still are, unaware of the relationship between mosquitos and the most troublesome disease of the chomïr territory, malaria. They maintained that the air of the Atrak region was healthier, causing people to have "more blood," while that of the Gurgan region was unhealthy, causing people to be "deficient in blood." The different conditions were visible in the complexions of chomïr and charwa, they claim.

Because of these differences, those among the chomïr who became wealthy would buy livestock and take up a pastoral mode of life north of the Gurgan River. Those among the charwa who became poverty-stricken had several avenues open to them. One was to work as a hired shepherd for wages.

(To some extent, it was also possible to rely on economic assistance from kinsmen.) Another alternative was to migrate south of the Gurgan and take up the agricultural life of the chomïr. The economy of the chomïr was clearly seen as a less preferable niche, to which the Turkmen resorted only when unable to maintain the pastoral life of the charwa. All of the Yomut tribes included both chomïr and charwa, and usually they occupied adjacent territories. This made it possible for people to move from one occupation to another within the territory of their own tribe.

## RECENT CHANGES

The dominant ecological trend among the Yomut in recent decades has been an increase in agriculture at the expense of pastoral pursuits, and, especially in the decade preceding my field research, the introduction of agricultural machinery and a greater emphasis on cash, as opposed to subsistence, crops. These trends have affected some areas sooner and more drastically than others, and the particular community which forms the focus of this study represents the conservative extreme, a group that has remained predominantly pastoral. Nevertheless this community and others like it have felt these changes in various ways.

During the 1930s the ecology of the Yomut was disrupted by the closing of the Russian border to migration, and by the Iranian government's policy of forced sedentarization. The first truly effective attempts to prevent Yomut pastoralists from crossing the Russian border during their seasonal migrations were made in 1928. Prior to this date, according to older informants, movement across the border had been forbidden for some time in theory, but actual enforcement was ineffective. Russian border patrols attempted to prevent crossings only when they caught nomads at the actual moment of moving across the border. In these instances, gun battles ensued and the nomads retreated into Iranian territory and waited for a better chance to cross. It should be noted that Russian Central Asia was in a general state of political turmoil during the decade of the twenties and the Bolshevik government's control of much of Turkmen territory was weak (d'Encausse, 1967b, 1967c). From 1928 to 1930, some of the nomads were able to cross using official permits from the Russian authorities; but after 1930 the border was effectively sealed off to nomadic movement. Some of the Yomut pastoralists who had been in the habit of crossing the border seasonally remained permanently in the Soviet Union and others remained in Iran. Since that date, occasional movements across the border occur for political reasons: Turkmen on either side of the boundary who are in trouble with the authorities seek permanent refuge on the opposite side, but such movement has little in common with the migrations of pastoralists seeking pasture.

The pastoralists who remained in Iran had to readjust their seasonal movements; some who were unable to find adequate grazing territory turned to agriculture. Those who remained pastoral shifted their migratory movements to the east since in the eastern portion of the Gurgan Plain the border swings to the north leaving more territory suitable for grazing on the Iranian side (see Fig. 3). The necessity to alter migratory paths fell on the Yomut at a time when they were economically weak. The years 1925 and 1926 had been bad for livestock and had been years of political disruption. The combined effect was a serious loss of livestock from which they had not fully recovered in 1928, when their pattern of migration was disrupted. These difficulties were soon followed by the initiation of a government policy of forced sedentarization entailing still further disruption of their economy.

In comparison with the much publicized difficulties of the Zagros tribes, the Yomut did not suffer great economic difficulties from forced settlement. Among the agricultural Turkmen, migration was not necessary for economic purposes and, therefore, building permanent houses and remaining throughout the year in one location, although distasteful, did not in itself cause an economic decline. Among the pastoral Turkmen, a semi-sedentary existence was possible without economic problems. This residence pattern entailed permanent settlements in which the bulk of the population lived during the dry season while the young men of each family migrated separately with the livestock. During the wet season they were permitted to live in tents and make the short-range migrations necessary for their economy.

During the period of forced settlement, economic activities were closely regulated by the government. Most of the territory of the Yomut had become the private property of the King during this period, a factor which facilitated close administration of the local economy (see Lambton, 1953:243-244, 256-257). The Yomut became tenants of the King and paid a rent for cultivated land and a grazing fee for pasture to the bureau established to administer the royal estates, the Estates Administration (idārehyi amlāk). These rents and fees were not high. Agents of the Estates Administration made the important decisions concerning local economic activities. What crops were planted and in what amounts, and where and when livestock should be taken to pasture were decisions handed down from above. Sometimes these decisions were unwise in terms of the local environment. For example, during the first few years of forced settlement, Turkmen northeast of the city of Gunbadi Kāvūs were forced to cultivate cotton, though the area was too dry for cotton. After a few years of such errors, the government officials responsible for these areas learned from their mistakes and the economic administration of the Yomut became more reasonable.

The Soviet occupation of northern Iran from 1941 to 1946 put an end to forced sedentarization and close administration of the economic affairs of the Yomut. In general, government administration of the Yomut was considerably weakened. It was also during this period that the royal estates fell under new laws allowing previous owners to reclaim their land under certain conditions (Lambton, 1953), and much of the crown land was returned to its original Yomut owners. (In a few cases even rather dubious claims of original ownership were respected.)

The period since the Second World War has been one of impressive economic development in the Gurgan Plain (see Okazaki, 1968, for a full discussion). The fertile southern portion of the plain provided unusual opportunities for agricultural development. This region, having a high rainfall, permits profitable dry cultivation of wheat and barley. It also provides, as mentioned earlier, ample opportunities for irrigation, which the Welayet exploited but the chomir ignored. The fact that this area is extremely level provides an ideal situation for the use of agricultural machinery. An extremely low population density in relation to the productive capacity of the land made conditions ideal for the introduction of machinery. The Yomut, who were strongly committed to an extensive rather than intensive exploitation of their environment, maintained a population level well below what their territory could support if cultivated more intensively. Shortly after the Second World War, various local merchants, both Turkmen and non-Turkmen, who had accumulated fortunes during the war by taking advantage of the rapid rise in the price of grain, leased large tracts of crown land and began to cultivate them with machinery imported by the government (Okazaki, 1968). Such operations proved profitable and a number of men of wealth and influence from Teheran began similar large-scale operations in the Gurgan Plain. Turkmen entrepreneurs of this sort employed other Turkmen as wage laborers in these operations, while non-Turkmen capitalists imported labor from the poor regions of southeastern Iran, the Zabul region of Sistan, and Baluchistan. The result was an increase in population density south of the Gurgan.

The process of agricultural development was accelerated in 1955 when the government began selling crown land to ordinary Turkmen tribesmen in two hectare plots of irrigated land or 10 hectare plots of dry land.[6] These Turkmen had been tenants on crown land up to this point, in most cases occupying the same region they and their immediate ancestors had occupied before 1925. The annual payments for the purchase of such land were lower than the annual rent which had been paid up to that time.[7]

About three years prior to this distribution of crown land to Turkmen

---

[6] This distribution of crown land was a prelude to a general program of land reform throughout Iran (see McLachlan, 1968:691-692).

[7] Rents for dry land in the area northeast of Gunbadi Kāvūs, for example, were 30 tumans annually per hectare. Payments for purchase of the same land consist of 25 annual payments, the first being 15 tumans and the remainder being 10 tumans each.

agricultural tenants, the tenants began to rent agricultural machinery from large farm owners. Cultivation by machine was much easier than by draft animals and enabled the farmer to increase the amount of land under cultivation. This in turn decreased the area of pasture available for livestock. Thus, in the 15 years prior to the field research on which this study is based, agriculture expanded and livestock production decreased drastically throughout that part of the Yomut territory in which agriculture is possible. Climatic conditions prevented the spread of a predominantly agricultural ecology throughout the northern portion of Yomut territory, a region which is still used for livestock production (see Fig. 4). In this region dependable agriculture is possible only where land is irrigated with water from the Atrak. A few communities in the area in which the Atrak disperses into salt marshes on Russian territory are predominantly agricultural. There the banks of the river are low and irrigation is relatively easy. Similarly, a few communities near Marāveh Tappeh rely on the Atrak for irrigation. The rest of this territory is devoted primarily to grazing.

In the western part of the Plain, the region that is too dry for rainfall agriculture consists of a thin strip of land which is now occupied only seasonally by shepherds from sedentary Turkmen communities. The grazing area in the eastern portion of the Plain is large, and here completely pastoral communities can still be found. Ajī Quī is one of these communities and the data presented in Chapters III—VI are based primarily on what I observed and was told of life in that community. It can be taken as representative of the approximately 10,000 pastoral Yomut in the northeastern portion of traditional Yomut territory. It is also largely representative of earlier social conditions among all of the Gurgan Yomut, including those north of the Atrak River in what is now Soviet territory.

## THE CURRENT ECOLOGY OF AJĪ QUĪ

The communities in the more arid and thinly populated northeastern portions of the Gurgan Plain had remained pastoral up to the time of my first study and provided a sharp contrast to those in the more fertile southern portions of the Plain.[8] Something of the contrast between this region and the southern portion can be gained by looking at the population density of each region. The predominantly agricultural southern portion of Yomut territory had a population of more than 122,000 people in 1966 with a density of more than 68 persons per square mile; the northern portion had a population

---

[8] The mountainous region immediately south of the Gurgan Plain is similar to the arid region in the sense that it forms an economically conservative area immediately adjacent to a region that has experienced rapid and extensive economic development. Here the ruggedness of the countryside and lack of virgin arable land inhibit the development of large mechanized farms (see Okazaki, 1968:5, 51).

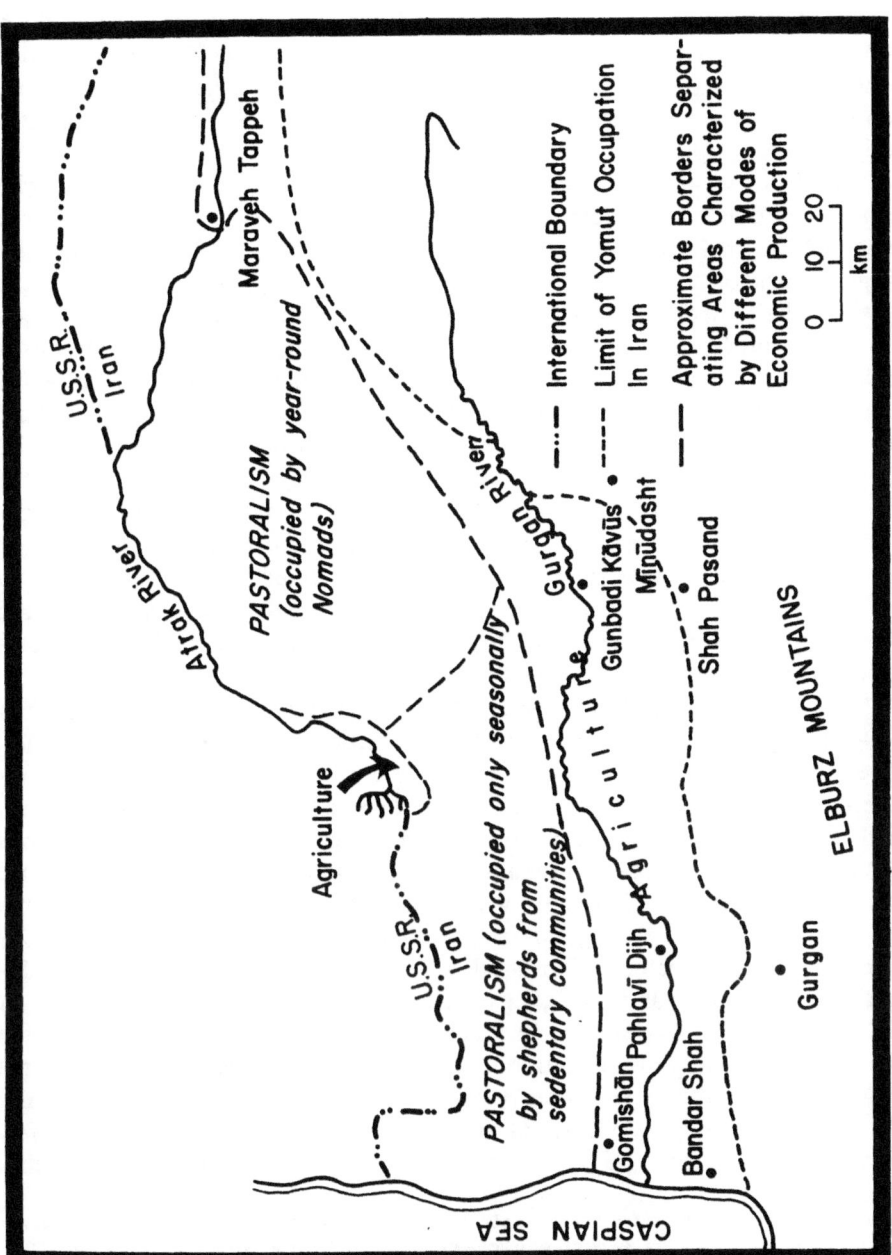

Fig. 4. Predominant modes of economic production among the Yomut of the Gurgan Plain in 1967.

of about 16,000 people and a density of about six persons per square mile.[9] The southern portion of Yomut country can be compared in its productivity to the southern Caspian littoral, of which it can be considered an extension. The northern portion is more typical of the arid regions of Iran that support a largely pastoral population.

Ajī Quī is one of several predominantly pastoral communities in the northeastern portion of Yomut country. The Yomut of Ajī Quī derive the main part of their income from their flocks of sheep and goats and their annual pattern of short-range migration is determined in large measure by the needs of their flocks. Other productive activities consist of raising horses, cows, and camels, and the cultivation of marginal agricultural land. Many of the families in this area also derive a portion of their income from plots of agricultural land on the north bank of the Gurgan River. These are 10 hectare plots of productive land used for dry cultivation of wheat and barley obtained as a result of the distribution of crown lands mentioned above. Though at the time of division of land these pastoralists were not tenants in the communities on the Gurgan, land was made available to them to encourage them to settle. Most of those who have such land rent it for a fixed amount of money to local residents who then cultivate it. Thus, they manage it as absentee land holders while devoting their own productive efforts to pastoral pursuits and the cultivation of marginal land in their own territory.

The productive activities and patterns of migration of the Turkmen of Ajī Quī in 1965-67 differed little from the traditional pattern described earlier. Between 1936 and 1941 they were forced to take up a semi-sedentary existence, but in 1941 they reverted to their traditional residence pattern. Figure 5 shows their seasonal movements. During the dry season their camps are scattered over an area of roughly 20 square miles around a group of wells. Two of these wells yield potable water throughout the dry season and serve their household needs during this season. Some of the other wells yield water suitable only for livestock. During this period some beasts of burden and a few goats are kept near their camps. The goats remain nearby as a source of milk. The few animals retained in this area during the dry season must be fed on cut fodder, which is cut and stored during the latter part of spring. In the dry season, most of the livestock is sent with the younger men of each family to graze the stubble of cultivated fields north of the Gurgan River. A few animals also are sent to the Atrak where both grazing and water can be found.

---

[9] These population estimates included only the rural populations of the regions involved. The estimates are based on several sources: (1) published data from the 1956 and 1966 Iranian censuses: Government of Iran, 1961:21-24; and Benham, 1968:468-485; (2) U.S. Army Map Service Maps: Gasan Kuli, 1:250,000, Sheet No. NJ40-9 of Series N502, and Shahrud, 1:250,000, Sheet No. NJ40-13 of Series K502; and (3) my own survey data. The estimate for the soutern portion of Yomut country does not allow for the extensive immigration of agricultural laborers and their families from poorer regions of Iran, and therefore is an underestimate.

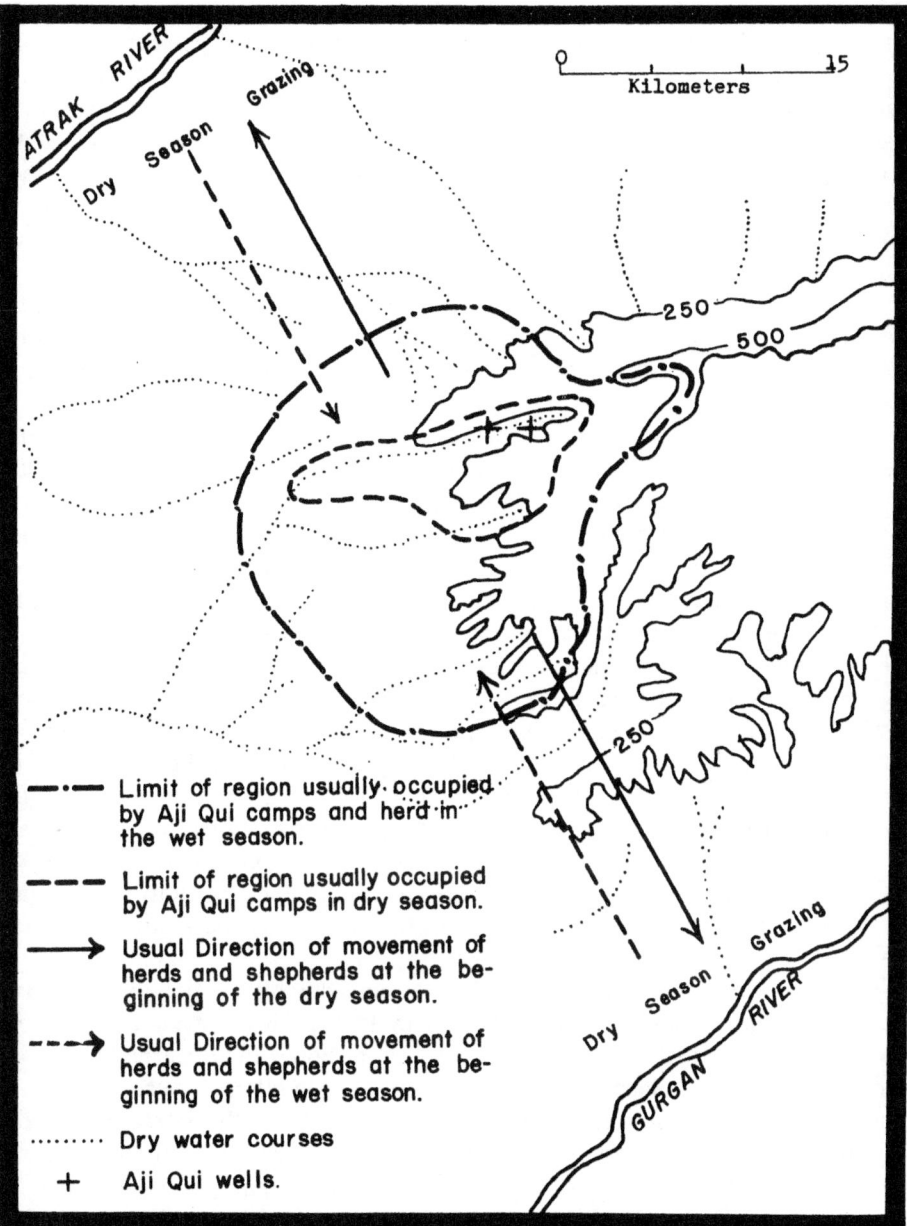

Fig 5. Migratory pattern of Ajī Quī residents.

The livestock and shepherds sleep in the daytime when temperatures are high (in August, the hottest month, daytime maximum temperatures recorded inside a yurt ranged from 100°F to 110°F). Shepherds use small lean-to-like tents during this season, since no shade is available on the treeless steppe. At night the animals graze and every other night they must be watered at the river. The usual pattern is to water the animals one night and then move them slowly to the north allowing them to graze as they travel. The next night the animals are brought back, grazing along the way, to the river where they can again be watered.

In the Gurgan Plain the wet season begins in the winter, and during this season much of the Gōkcha Hills and surrounding area are covered with a short, but relatively thick, crop of grass. In the Gōkcha Hills, for example, slopes exposed to the north are green and those exposed to the south are barren. During the winter temperatures are mild, rarely dipping below freezing, and the snow which occasionally falls seldom lasts more than a day. There is a fair amount of rain and rain water, in addition to occasional melted snow, collects in scattered depressions to form pools from which the nomads take water for their household needs. In good years when the grass is lush and contains much moisture the livestock rarely need water during the winter, but in drier years they, too, must use the scattered temporary pools. Because of the intensive care of lambs and kids in the winter and because of milking in the spring, camp and herd must be kept close together during these seasons. During the wet season, winter and spring, the nomads camp where water and suitable pastures can be found. Usually ample pasture can be found not too far from their dry season camp site so that most of their migrations are quite short. The pastoralists of Ajī Quī, during most years, spread out over an area of about 120 square miles surrounding their dry season location (see Fig. 5). If pasture becomes exhausted in one location, they migrate to another location, usually making a short move that can easily be completed in one day.

This pattern of movement differs considerably from that of many pastoral groups in and around the Iranian Plateau who make long seasonal moves ranging across vastly different ecological zones. The Kurds of northern Khurasan and the Sangsarī from the Elburz Mountains southwest of the Gurgan Plain are pastoralists who make migrations of the latter type. These groups come to the Gurgan Plain in the winter when their summer quarters are covered with snow, and then return to mountain pastures in the late spring. They travel a distance of about 150 miles twice each year between their summer and winter pastures. The pastoral Turkmen, in contrast, make only a series of short moves during a year, most of them less than 10 miles. Each of these groups claim that their breed of sheep is adapted to their characteristic pattern of migration. The Kurds and Sangsarī maintain that their sheep would not prosper if they were kept in the Gurgan Plain in the hot, dry summer rather than returning to cooler, fresher mountain pasture. The Turkmen in turn claim that their sheep would not do well if they were forced to make the long migration through rugged mountainous terrain like the sheep of the Kurds and Sangsarī.

During the winter, the residents of Ajī Quī also plow their scattered plots of marginal agricultural land and sow wheat and barley in the hope of a late spring harvest. As mentioned earlier, most of these plots are individually owned, although occasionally when there are several heirs to a small plot they hold it jointly rather than dividing it into smaller individually owned plots.

In addition, since 1959 the Yomut of Ajī Quī have jointly cultivated a large valley bottom, covering about 100 hectares, with the assistance of a wealthy merchant who is a distant agnate of most of the residents of Ajī Quī. The merchant owns agricultural machinery which he uses to cultivate this land. The high labor input necessary to cultivate such a large piece of land with draft animals, combined with the high risk of crop failure, precluded earlier efforts at such large scale cultivation. However, since most of the grazing territory of Ajī Quī is hilly and cannot be reached by agricultural machinery, large-scale cultivation of this sort is possible only at a few favored locations where a level valley bottom makes cultivable land accessible to machinery. The tractor belonging to the wealthy merchant mentioned above plows the area he cultivates jointly with the local people and also for a fee plows a few other favored plots. The remainder of the plowing in Ajī Quī is done by draft animals, horses, and camels.

Harvesting of the jointly cultivated valley bottom discussed above is done with a combine owned by the merchant kinsman of the local Turkmen. But because combines claim a higher fee, the local people do not engage it for the few individually owned plots that can be reached by agricultural machinery. All harvesting is done by traditional means except for the one large valley plot.

At harvest time, in those years in which a crop can be harvested, each family gives a harvest feast (oroq thadagha). A yearling goat, as a rule, is killed for this purpose. Most of the men of Ajī Quī attend such feasts and on that day they donate their labor toward the harvest of land belonging to the family giving the feast. This speeds up, but usually does not complete, the laborious process of harvesting the crop with sickles. Afterward, threshing is done by traditional means: draft animals are driven over the stalks of wheat or barley. For winnowing, the simple technique of tossing grain and chaff into the wind is used. Finally the grain, other than that set aside for immediate use, is stored by burying it in deep pits. All of the plowing, planting, and harvesting is done by men.

Shearing takes place in the late spring, usually by fleecing a few animals each day when they are brought in for milking. It is the task of the men, as is all labor concerned with the direct care of the livestock. Milking, however, is done by women. Families with few men occasionally give a shearing feast (qirqim thadagha) and are then assisted in their labor by all attending the feast. Those with many men find such assistance unnecessary in the spring. However, the fall shearing is always accompanied by a shearing feast since it is done when the animals are far away from their camp site and the older men must generally spend a day traveling to the spot where the livestock are grazing in the care of the younger men. The shearing feast gets the labor over with quickly so that the older men can return as soon as possible to their camps where they pass most of their time during the dry season sitting in their tents drinking tea and talking.

Harvest time occurs as the dry season begins. The green pastures of spring gradually change to a barren brown, and the rain water pools of the wet season disappear. When this happens, the Turkmen of Ajī Quī move to camp sites near their wells and send their livestock with the young men to the banks of the Gurgan or Atrak (see Fig. 5).

During the dry season most of the women are busy turning the spring wool into carpets.[10] Washing the wool, carding, spinning, dyeing, and weaving are all the work of women. Often several closely related families pool their wool and female labor to produce one or several large carpets. The weaving is more easily done by several women who take turns weaving between their domestic chores. The weaving is all done with a simple flat loom. The fall wool is of poorer quality and is usually not suitable for manufacturing carpets. Most of this wool is used for making felt, also the work of women.

The end of spring is ideal for selling yearlings, since they are fattest at this time. Nevertheless, many families sell livestock sporadically at other seasons to meet immediate needs. Because of the large number of animals sold in the late spring, early spring is the season when herds are at their largest. Fall, when herds are smaller, is the time for reckoning thakat (see Coon, 1958:109-111, and Lane, 1908:92-93).

The most remarkable aspect of the ecology of the Yomut charwa is the fact that their migration pattern is so circumscribed and could be so easily combined with seasonal use of permanent settlements, as it was between 1936 and 1941 under government coercion; yet they prefer to avoid permanent houses and live only in yurts. All charwa readily admit that in the grueling heat of summer a good mud house (tam) is much cooler and therefore more comfortable than a yurt. The reasons for their eschewing of houses are partly a matter of tradition and the implications are discussed in the next chapter.

[10] All stages in the production of carpets by Yomut pastoralists, from fleecing the sheep to the final step of cutting the warp threads that hold the carpet to the loom, are carried out by either a single domestic unit or several such units pooling their resources in wool and labor. Artificial dyes are the only raw materials used which the nomads do not produce themselves. This method of production contrasts sharply with that described for other regions of Iran (see English, 1966:125-127).

Similar ecologies combining short-range nomadism with a predominantly pastoral economy have been described for such other groups in Central Asia as the Teke Turkmen charwa (König, 1962:46-53) and the Khalkha Mongols (Vreeland, 1957:34-47). The general pattern of movement and economic production also bears a definite similarity to that of the darshin nomads among the Marri Baluch (Pehrson, 1966:5-16).

## III

## POLITICAL STRUCTURE

THE indigenous political institutions of the Yomut consist of a hierarchy of descent groups and a hierarchy of residence groups. Each of these categories has different, though at times overlapping, functions. It is important to note that these two types of groups do not have the same composition. Each residence group has a numerically dominant descent group which can, and usually does, control any group action by the residence unit. Nevertheless, most residence groups contain a large number of households[1] that do not belong to the dominant descent group, and yet are counted as full members of the residence unit. For this and other reasons elaborated below, the geographic arrangement of the Yomut reflects their genealogical subdivisions only in a very imprecise way. Therefore it is necessary, to some extent, to discuss residence and descent separately.

It is also necessary, in order to present even a brief discussion of politics among the Yomut, to discuss the role of nomadism in their political structure. In a very real sense nomadism is a part of the political system of the Yomut, and neither their politics nor their ecology can be understood without an appreciation of this fact. The Yomut exploit their nomadic mobility for both economic and political purposes. This would not be possible if rights of residence were tied, as they are in many societies that emphasize patriliny, to one's descent group. Fully effective exploitation of nomadic mobility, a salient feature of traditional Yomut life, is possible only if each household and each lineage is free to move over a wide area and, if necessary, to take up permanent residence among people with whom they share no close ties of kinship (see Lewis, 1961:2-3, 89).

Furthermore, any discussion of the political affairs of the Yomut must take into account the effects of both indigenous political institutions and the

---

[1] In Turkmen reckoning, no distinction is made in discussing descent groups between the agnatic core of a household and its total membership. Throughout this study the same usage is followed. Thus, households are referred to consistently as the smallest units in the descent system.

Persian government. The role of the government in the political affairs of the Yomut has changed extensively in recent decades and, therefore, a few brief comments on the recent political history of the Gurgan Plain are also necessary. A detailed discussion of local administration in the Plain, either as it existed at the time of my research or in recent history, is, however, beyond the scope of this study. Rather, we are here concerned only with the effect of the Persian administration on the Yomut, especially on the pastoral Yomut who form the focus of this book.

## DESCENT GROUPS

The Turkmen as a whole can be described as a descent group which includes a million and a half people. Starting with this rather large group, numerous levels of segmentation can be identified, dividing the Turkmen into progressively smaller and more closely related groups until ultimately the level of small groups consisting of 10 to 40 households is reached. All of these descent groups can be referred to in Turkmen as "taypa," regardless of the level of segmentation. The larger subdivisions are often termed "halq." Such groups as the Yomut, Teke, and Göklen (see Fig. 1) are frequently designated halq. The very smallest groups—consisting of 10 to 40 households—are usually called "tire." For purposes of this study, taypa is translated either as descent group or lineage.

There are written genealogies recounting the descent of all Turkmen from a single mythological character, Oghuz Khan. Two large modern descent groups, the Göklen and Choudor, are descendants of two of Oghuz Khan's 24 grandsons, Qayɨ and Javuldur (see Barthold, 1962:109-110, and Rabino, 1928:101). The remainder of the modern large descent groups are all the descendants of Oghurjɨq, a man who was in turn a descendant of Salor, another of Oghuz Khan's grandsons. Figure 6 summarizes a written genealogy tracing the derivation of several large modern descent groups from Oghurjɨq.[2] The geographic locations of these descent groups are shown in Figure 1. Written genealogies of this sort are to be found here and there among the Yomut of the Gurgan Plain, and are accepted by the local people as authoritative. Ordinary Yomut men, however, do not commit such genealogies to memory. The genealogical knowledge of most Yomut begins with their apical ancestor, Yomut, and traces the descent of various subgroups of the Yomut from this man. Figure 7 gives the genealogy of the larger subdivisions of the Yomut; Figures 8 and 9 show further subdivisions of two of these larger groups, the Datẖ and the Aq-Atabay, the two descent groups represented in Ajī Quī.

It is important to note that the Turkmen do not consider genealogies of

[2] Figure 6 is based on manuscript genealogies found among the Yomut of the Gurgan Plain. However, a similar genealogy can be found in Abul-Ghāzī, 1958:68-72 (Turkmen), 73-74 (Russian).

# POLITICAL STRUCTURE

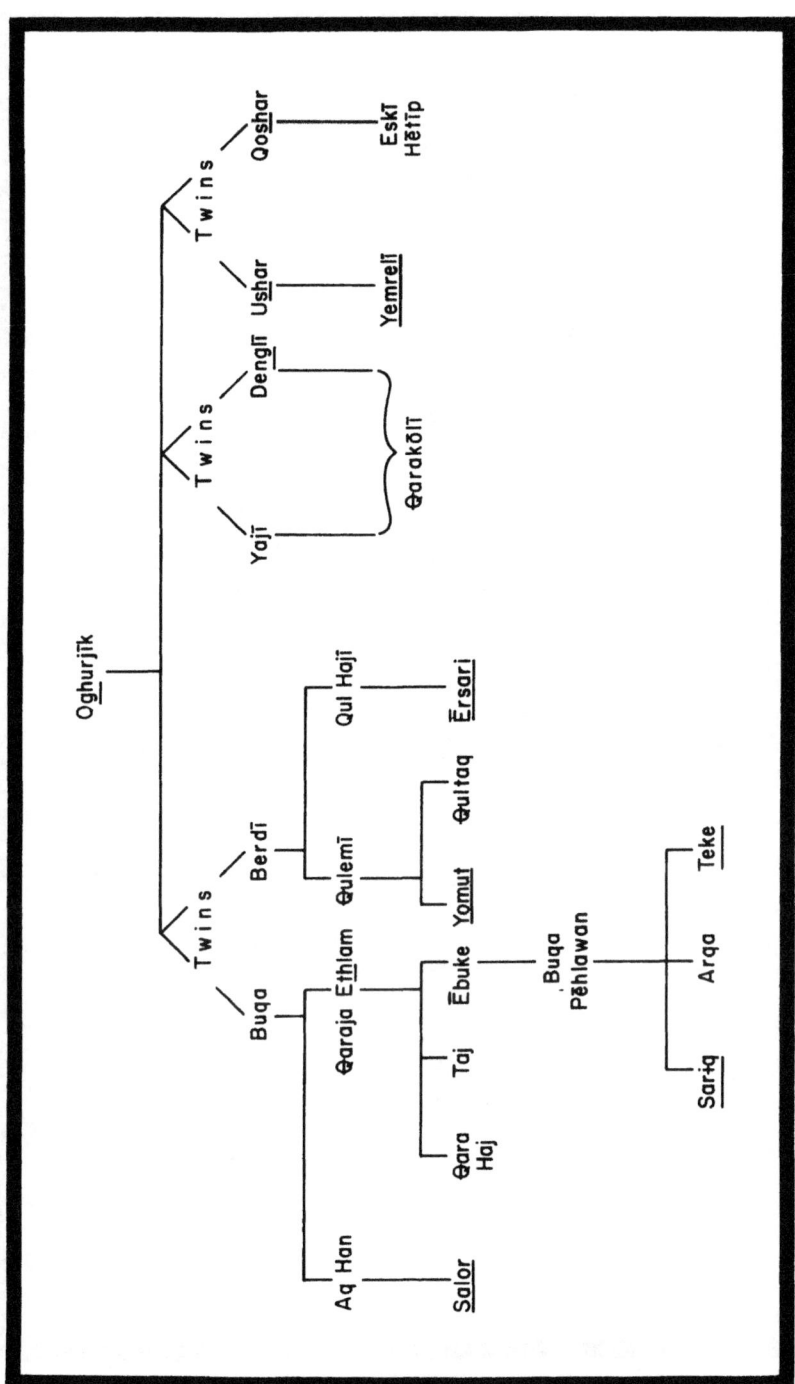

Fig. 6. Descendants of Oghurjik according to written genealogy. Names of extant descent groups are underlined.

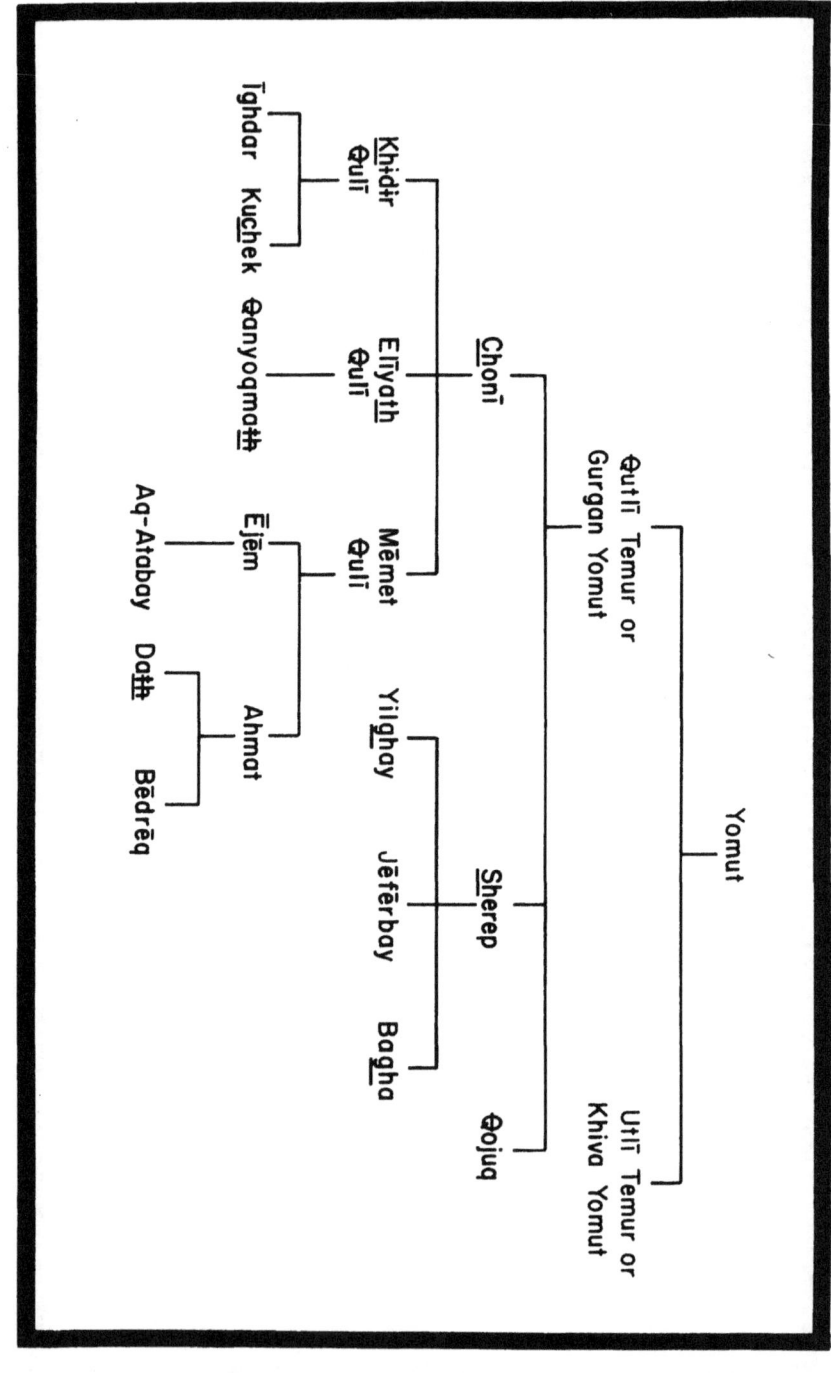

Fig. 7. Genealogy of the Yomut according to a written source.

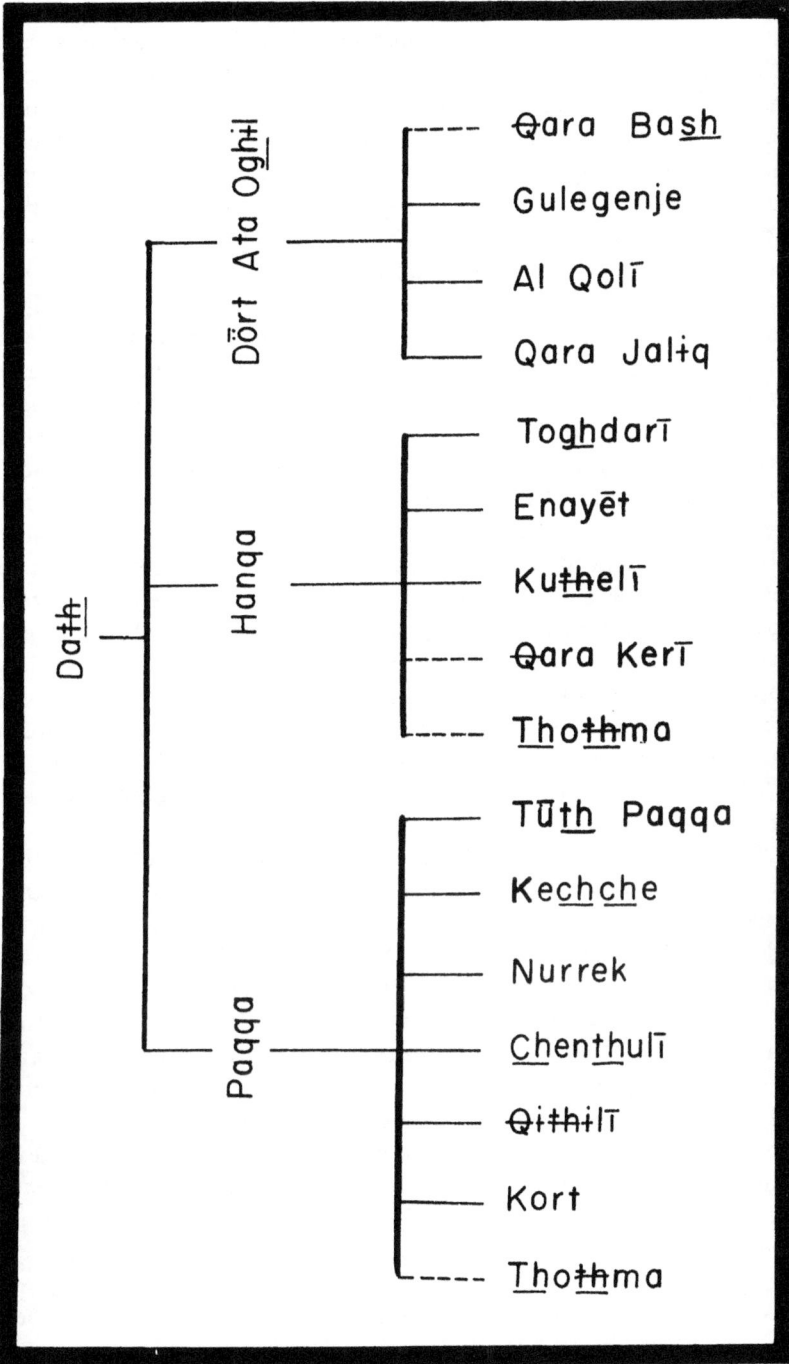

Fig. 8. Genealogy of the Daṯḥ. Dotted lines indicate groups absorbed through co-residence.

the type represented in Figures 6-9 as being complete and precise. For example, consider the genealogy presented in Figure 7: this genealogy is taken from a written source and is more detailed than most genealogies which have been committed to memory. It should also be noted that this genealogy was found among members of the Choni̇̄ descent group and is more detailed for that group than for the Sherep. In fact, several large subdivisions which represent descendants of Sherep, the Behëllke, Düeji̇̄, and Qarawi̇̄, are left out altogether. Most Yomut in reciting their genealogies state that Choni̇̄, Sherep, and Qojuq were sons of Yomut rather than grandsons as stated in the written sources summarized in Figure 7. When the more complete genealogy shown in Figure 7 is presented to informants, they usually are not disturbed by the discrepancy; rather, they nonchalantly point out that the generation of Qulti̇̄ Temur and Utli̇̄ Temur was omitted from the genealogies they have memorized because it is irrelevant. Segmentation at the level represented by this generation explains the relationship of the Gurgan Yomut to the Khiva Yomut, but since contact with the Khiva Yomut is minimal this generation has not been considered important enough to include in the genealogy. Informants will readily admit that in all probability other links in the genealogies which they have committed to memory have been omitted, and that other written genealogies might readily reveal additional lacunae. Although written genealogies are in general more complete than those that have been memorized, it is generally accepted that these too may contain omissions. Occasionally statements to this effect appear in the written genealogies themselves. The Yomut claim that genealogies dealing with more remote generations, whether written or simply committed to memory, are accurate only to the extent that they include those links which are necessary to explain relationships among existing descent groups.

In sharp contrast, the genealogies recording more recent generations are complete and precise. Most informants, if asked to recite their ancestry, will give the names of five to seven ancestors and then stop, stating categorically that further ancestors are not known. After relating his known ancestors an informant can then trace the other descendants of these ancestors, providing a complete genealogy of the male members of an agnatic lineage of five to seven generations in depth.[3] In this study, genealogies of this sort are referred to as accurate or precise genealogies, whereas those of higher generations that are admittedly incomplete are referred to as putative genealogies.

The connection between precise and putative genealogies is based on the knowledge that the apical ancestor of each precisely remembered genealogy was a member of a particular named descent group, although the number of generations separating him from the founder of this named group is not known. Nevertheless, enough is known to provide a link, albeit an imprecise one, between accurate genealogies and putative genealogies of the sort

[3] In the more remote generations of these genealogies, females and males without issue are forgotten.

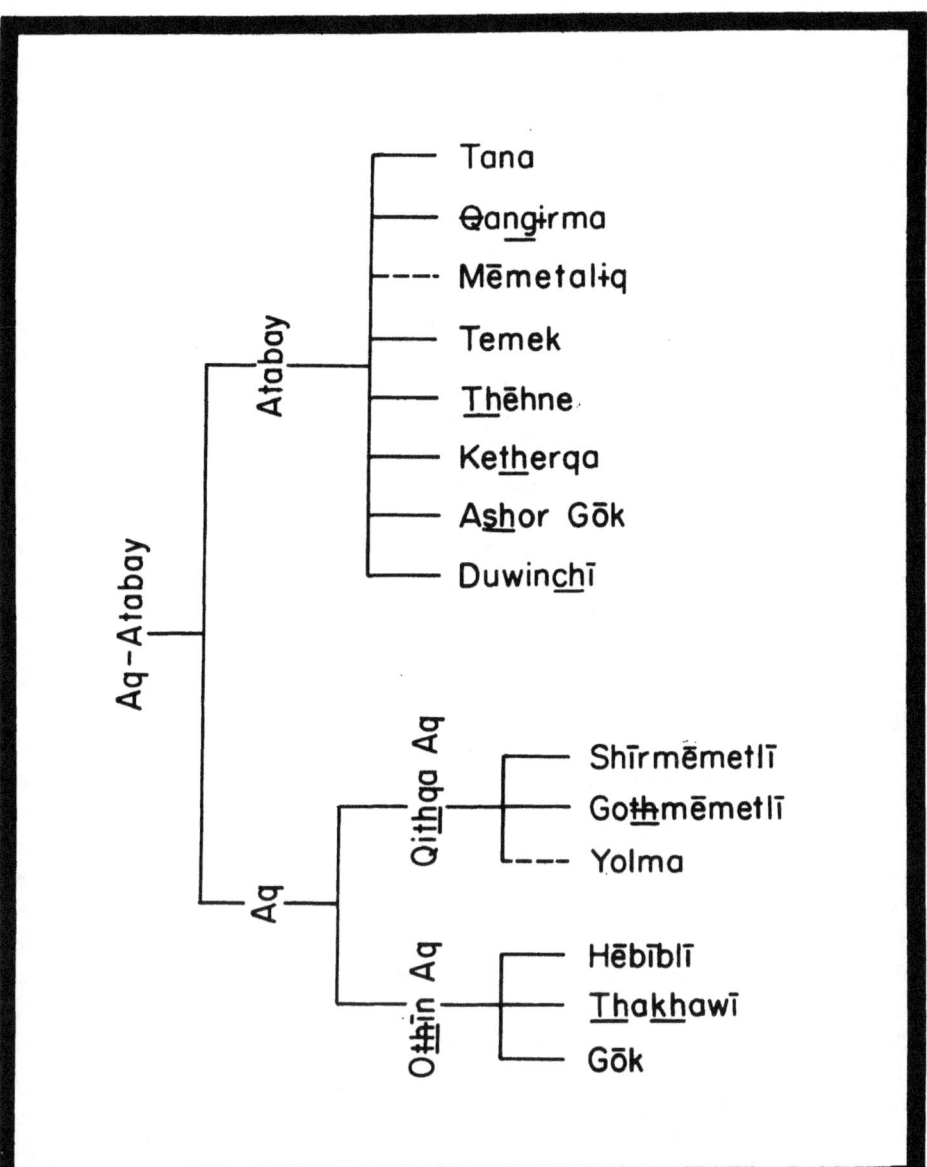

Fig. 9. Genealogy of the Aq-Atabay. Dotted lines indicate groups absorbed through co-residence.

presented in Figures 8 and 9. Thus, each of the smallest groups shown in Figures 8 and 9 divides into a number of lineages with precise genealogies. The founder of each of these lineages is a putative descendant, through an unknown number of generations, of the founder of one of the smallest groups shown. Most of the smallest descent groups contain five to ten lineages with accurate genealogies, usually ranging in size from 20 to 100 households.

## RESIDENCE GROUPS

Before discussing the descent system in greater detail a few remarks about the nature of Yomut residence groups are necessary. Residence groups are contractual in nature, their composition being a matter of mutual consent.

The smallest residence group among the pastoral Yomut, and formerly among all Yomut, is a group of from two to 10 yurts that camp together. Such a group tends to consist of households whose heads are close patrilineal relatives. However, group composition is continually changing. Thus, a father and his independent son usually camp together. A group of brothers whose father is deceased and who are the heads of economically independent households are also likely to camp together. Such closely related groups often join with other similar shallow partrilineages with whom they have no close agnatic ties to form a single camp group. Such a group may camp together for a few months or for several years.

A camp group is very important in terms of the daily activities of Turkmen life. Cooperation and mutual assistance among members of the same camp in economic and domestic labors are extensive. In terms of political affairs such groups are of little importance, but they operate, to a large extent, according to the same principles that apply to larger residence groups which are politically more important.

The contractual nature of camp group composition can best be explained by describing what happens when a household leaves one camp group and joins another. Such a move requires that the head of the household wishing to shift residence first consult with the heads of the other households in his current camp and secure their agreement to his departure. Such permission is readily granted by those campmates who are not close kin. However, since close kin may not be willing to see relatives, on whose support they wish to rely, depart, permission to leave a particular camp is not always granted. It is still possible in such cases for the household wishing to change its camp to move without permission, but sanctions in the form of decreased willingness to cooperate in the future, or even complete estrangement, are likely to follow.

Once a household has permission to leave one camp, the head of that household must next obtain permission to join another camp. This again requires consulting with the heads of the households of the new camp and obtaining their consent. Again, permission is not always granted. Reasons for refusal vary: shortage of water and pasture in the immediate vicinity of the camp is a common reason; a personal dislike of the person requesting permission to join a camp is also a possible reason, although if this is the case some reasons other than the actual one will probably be offered to justify refusal. In general, it can be said that the closer the kinship link between the members of the camp and the household seeking to join the camp, the more readily permission will be granted. Thus, a request from a first or second agnatic cousin would be refused only for very weighty reasons. Refusal of permission to join a camp from such close kin without a convincing justification would lead to estrangement.

A camp group continually faces a number of decisions on which the heads of constituent households must agree: when and where to migrate, which pools of water near a wet season camp are to be used to water livestock and which for household purposes (the same pool cannot be used for both since the water of pools used for livestock is forbidden, haram, to Moslems), and who will pasture livestock in which areas around the camp. If the households are unable to agree on these matters, they can, of course, split up. If, for example, the members of a camp cannot agree where to migrate for spring pasture, they may agree to go separate ways. In such a case, however, they usually make a special point of agreeing to the fissioning of the camp, since to part other than by mutual agreement would be a sign of strong mutual dissatisfaction and a barrier to future cooperation.

The next larger residence group, the oba, consists of a group of households associated with a definite territory to which they share certain common rights. The oba could be described as a group of camps as well as a group of households. However, rights in relation to the oba's territory are vested in individual households, not in camp groups. An oba is a corporate group which shares a joint estate and each constituent household shares equally in the joint estate. The oba's grazing territory is not subdivided into subareas over which either particular camp groups or particular households have a preemptive claim. The way in which constituent households group themselves into camps does not affect the equal rights of each household to exploit the oba's territory. Each camp group which is formed by mutual consent of its members is free to migrate to any spot within the oba's territory so long as it does not crowd a previously located camp. If they wish to camp near enough to a previously located camp to affect that camp's supply of suitable pasture or water they must first obtain permission. If they camp close enough to agricultural land to create a danger that their livestock might accidentally graze a planted field, they must also obtain permission from the owner of the land in question.

Before the establishment of effective government control, the oba had no elaborate executive structure, although each oba had a headman who acted as a spokesman for the group as a whole to outsiders. The office entailed no authority; the headman was chosen by the men of the oba and was authorized to act only on the basis of their consensus. This office was not hereditary, and an incumbent could be removed by consensus, the same process by which he was originally placed in his position.

The principles governing camp group composition also apply to oba composition. In order to leave one oba and join another permission is required, in theory, from all of the household heads of the two obas concerned. In practice, when the number of households wishing to shift residence is small, they consult only those whom they feel will in fact be concerned about their movement. Thus, if one or two households wish to shift to a new oba, the consultation is made as a rule only at the camp level. If a household not consulted feels the matter deserves wider discussion it can demand discussion by the entire oba.

The movement of a large number of households from one oba to another, on the other hand, would be considered the business of the entire oba and permission would be requested from all residents in each of the obas concerned. It should be noted that the size of an oba to some extent determines its ability to defend its territory if necessary. Thus, the departure of a large number of households could have a detrimental effect on those left behind. In general, it is felt by Yomut that shifts of residence of this kind should require the permission of those who will actually be affected by the movement. Who will feel himself affected and who will decide that it is none of his business is sometimes difficult to determine. In such cases, Yomut tend to request permission rather than run the risk of gratuitously offending someone.

Once a person is granted permission to join an oba, he gains full rights in the joint estate of the oba. Each household belonging to an oba has the right to pasture its animals on the oba's territory and the right to use any natural source of water located within this territory. Each household has the right to put any virgin arable land in this territory to plow, but once a household plows up a section of land it becomes their private property. Rights to wells are similar to rights to agricultural land. Any member of an oba can dig a well on the oba's territory, which then becomes his private property.[4]

This is the traditional means of regulating access to natural resources among the Yomut. At the time of my first observation, these matters were regulated ultimately by the Iranian administration. However, among the pastoral Yomut the traditional situation had not been greatly altered in 1965-67. Although technically most of the territory claimed by each pastoral oba was then crown land, the government, except during the period between

---

[4] Although wells are private property, anyone is free to dig a well near an existing well where ground water is known to be present. Therefore, the basic resource of ground water is not effectively monopolized as private property.

1936 and 1941, had not attempted to limit, or regulate, the migrations, either seasonal or permanent, of the pastoralists occupying these territories, nor to regulate the ways in which this territory was exploited. Since 1960, a grazing fee had been occasionally collected from the pastoralists of the Gökcha Hills; the fee was nominal, however, and was not collected regularly. Its purpose seems to have been to demonstrate ownership of the land rather than to raise revenue.

The next largest residence group above the level of the oba is a group known as an īl. The meaning of "īl" in Turkmen cannot always be translated with the same English word. However, when it refers to a contiguous group of obas that have traditionally been on peaceful terms with one another, it is translated for purposes of this study as "tribe." Such groups as the Jeferbay and Aq-Atabay shown on Figures 10 and 11 are designated "tribes." The word "īl" is used in Turkmen both as an adjective and as a noun. As an adjective it means a state of peace between two individuals or groups. As a noun it refers to a group of obas that are on peaceful terms with one another and are united against hostile outsiders in mutual defense. The smallest such groups of politically united obas are geographically contiguous and, therefore, can be described as residence groups. Larger groups that are designated īls are such groups as the Sherep and Chonī (see pages 63-64) and the Gurgan Yomut as a whole. Before effective government control these groups were often internally peaceful and allied in defense. However, they do not always form geographically contiguous groups. Such larger political units are referred to in this study as confederacies.

As will be explained below, the names Sherep and Chonī refer both to descent groups (see Figure 7) and to politically united blocs, confederacies. However, the confederacies include groups that are not members of the Sherep and Chonī descent groups. In Turkmen the Sherep as a descent group is labeled a taypa and consists of the groups descended from Sherep (see Figure 7). The Sherep as an īl (confederacy) is a larger group including in addition the Qojuq, Thalaq, and Düejī descent groups. It should be borne in mind throughout this chapter that an īl (tribe or confederacy) is defined in political terms, while a taypa is defined basically in genealogical terms. Confusion is often possible because of the Turkmen habit of designating an īl with the name of the numerically dominant descent group within the īl.

## THE RELATIONSHIP BETWEEN
## DESCENT GROUPS AND RESIDENCE GROUPS

Despite the fact that residence units and descent units are characterized by different modes of recruitment, there is a tendency for the two to correspond approximately in composition. While there are no categorical

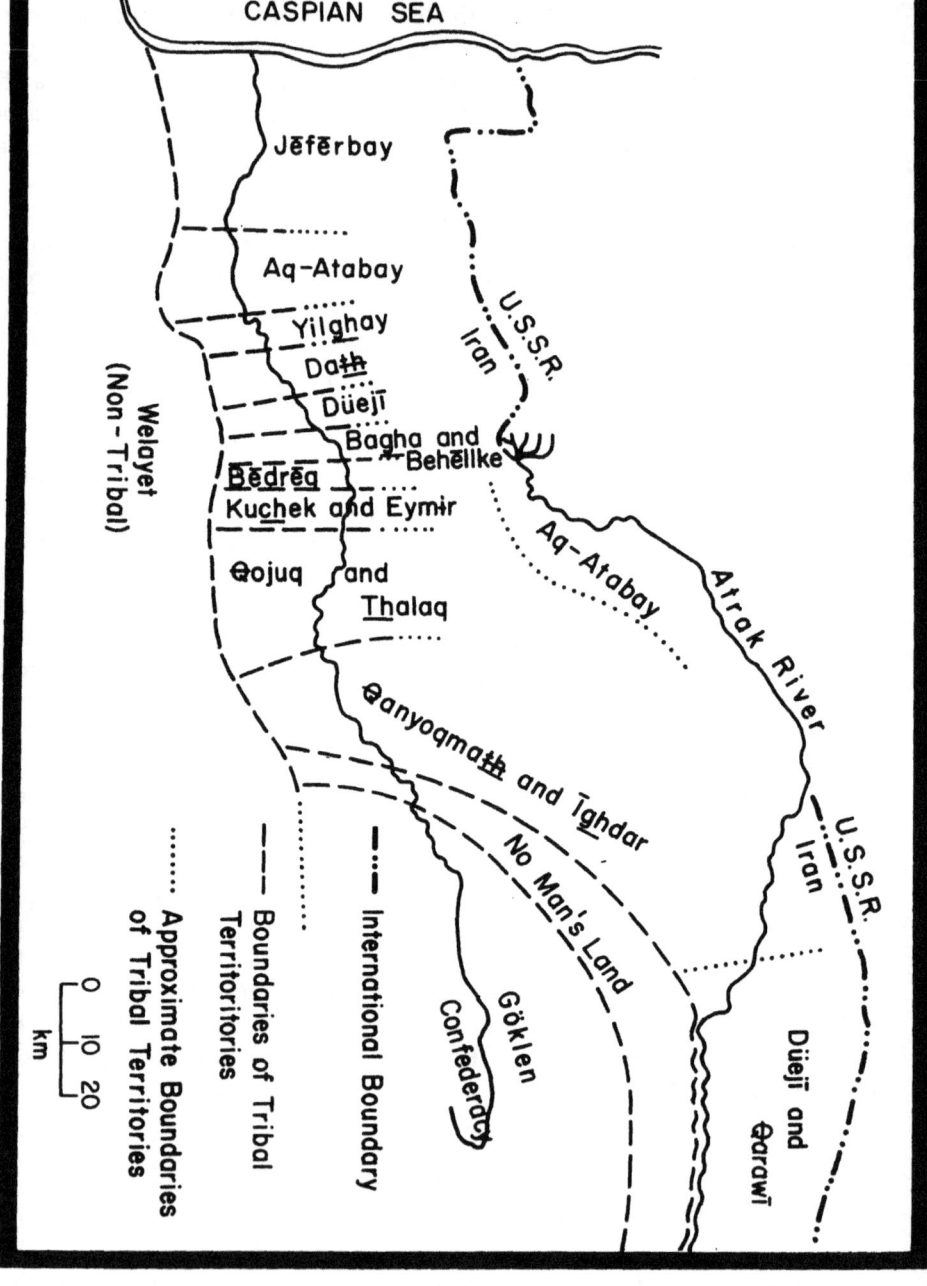

Fig. 10. Locations of tribes in the Gurgan Plain before 1930.

norms dictating co-residence with agnates, there is a strong preference for residence with patrikin. The result is that, as mentioned above, the membership of each oba is predominantly of one descent group. The same generalizations can be made about the composition of tribes and confederacies. In the case of camps, the smallest residence groups, the underlying principles of recruitment are the same, but because of the small size of such groups they often are purely agnatic in composition.

The reasons for preferring residence with agnates are not difficult to understand. Yomut can rely most readily on kinsmen, especially close kinsmen, for support of one form or another and, therefore, it is obviously wise to reside with one's kin. Residing with kin among the Yomut means, for the most part, residing with agnates. Agnatic kinship entails more obligation than uterine or affinal kinship and effective agnatic ties are traced farther than effective uterine or affinal ties. Thus, a man is most secure residing among his patrilineal kinsmen. Also it should be noted that as a result of a preference for marriage with patrikin, uterine and affinal ties extending beyond an individual's patrilineage are limited.

Individuals or small lineages that reside separately from their agnates in residence groups numerically dominated by a descent group other than their own are referred to in Turkmen as gongshī. In general, gongshī do not enjoy the same political advantages as persons who reside with their own agnates. It is true that other members of their residence group will support them in political matters against members of other residence groups as long as such support does not conflict with the obligations of agnatic kinship (see p. 63 below). However, the degree of support they can expect is less than that which close agnates would provide. Also, if a gongshī were to become involved in a dispute with a member of the dominant descent group of his own residence unit, he would be at a disadvantage: he would immediately have numerous opponents nearby, while his own agnates to whom he would have to turn for assistance would be at a distance. The extent of this political disadvantage is limited, however. Co-residence entails a strong obligation of peaceful behavior and careful avoidance of conflict. Hostile behavior between co-resident Yomut, even if they are not kin, is extremely rare. An individual who behaves unjustly toward a gongshī, thus precipitating a dispute, would have difficulty mustering support from his agnates, especially from more distant agnates. The strength of the obligation to support agnates is conditioned both by the closeness of the agnatic tie and the justness of the claim. At the same time a gongshī could expect eventual support from his agnates residing at a distance. Men embroiled in blood feuds with their own close agnates are, however, an exception to this statement (see pp. 71-72 below).

Men occasionally reside away from their close agnates for a time. This is especially true for those employed as shepherds or those studying with a religious teacher. In such cases a man shifts residence for a short period with a

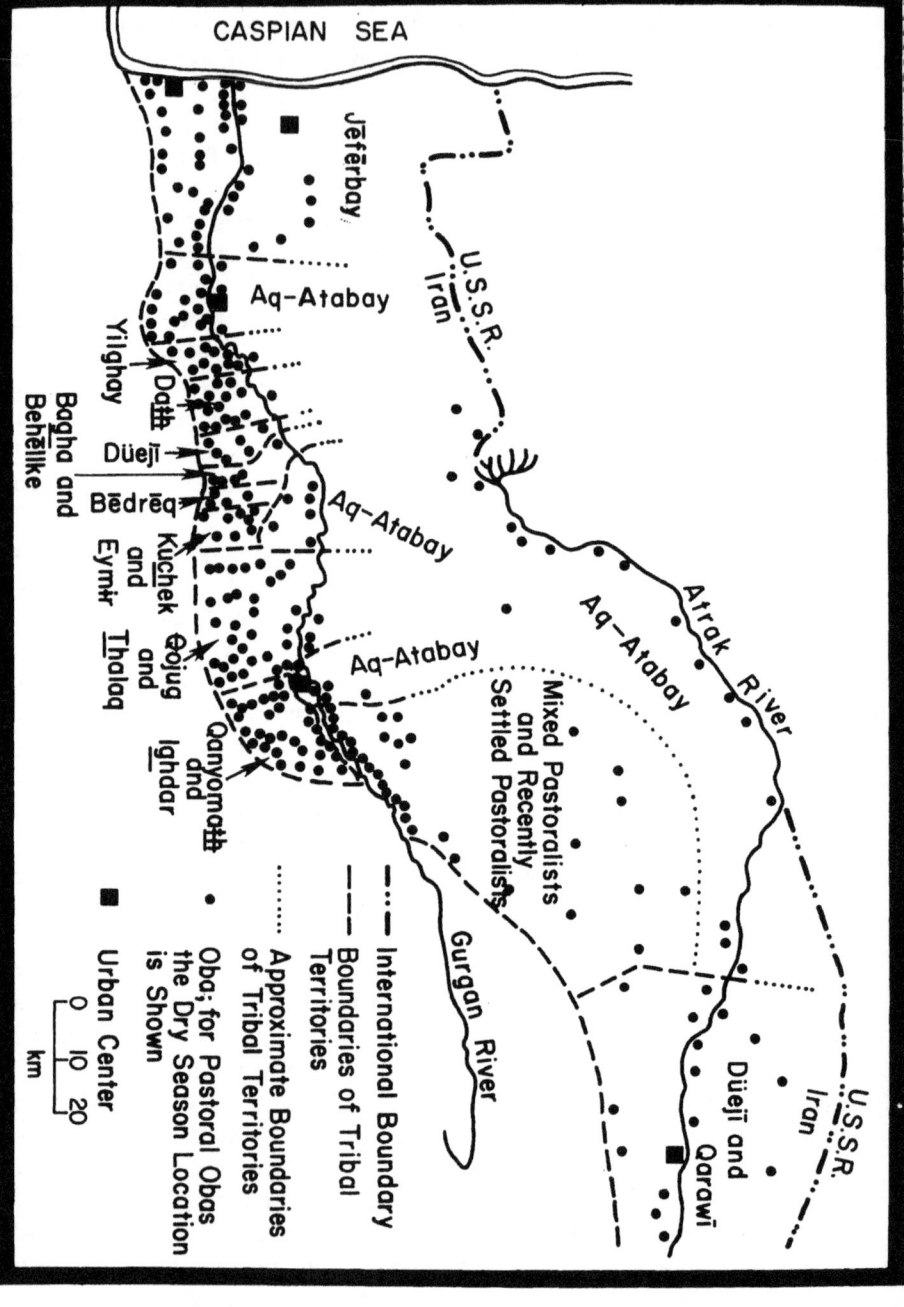

Fig. 11. Distribution of Yomut tribes in 1967.

specific objective in mind and then returns to his own group. Short trips among neighboring obas are also quite common, especially for purposes of trade, and travelers are always offered hospitality, even if complete strangers. The usual expectation is that a traveler who is a complete stranger will be provided with food and lodging for at least one day and night. Because of the readiness with which hospitality is offered, travel is very easy for Yomut throughout not only Yomut territory but also Göklen territory. Most Yomut, however, would hesitate to ask hospitality from non-Turkmen unless some previous social relationship hasd been established. Prior to the cessation of intertribal warfare, travel and residence away from one's agnates was equally possible as long as one stayed among those with whom one was īl (on terms of peace, rather than war).

Brief residence away from one's agnates for some special purpose, or travel for purposes of trade, of course, has little long-term effect on the composition of residence groups. The primary reason for residing permanently at a distance from one's agnates is feud, a matter discussed in greater detail below. There are numerous Turkmen who reside as gongshī in an oba dominated by a different descent group in order to escape a feud in their original oba. Refugees of this sort usually do not reside in complete isolation from close agnates, but rather reside in small groups that constitute shallow patrilineages.

The relationship between descent and residence can best be explained by examining the composition of Ajī Quī by lines of descent. Figure 12 presents the agnatic relationships of households heads in Aji Quī: lineages with precise genealogies are represented by upper case letters. The names of larger lineages based on putative genealogies are given. Putative agnatic links are represented by dotted lines; accurate agnatic links are represented by solid lines. Named groups in Figure 12 can also be found in Figures 8 and 9, with the exception of the Managhar, a subdivision of the Behēllke (see Fig. 7). The only living individuals shown are household heads and the only deceased persons represented, with one exception, are ancestors who explain agnatic relationships between household heads. The one exception occurs in lineage F, where the presence of a widow as the head of a household introduces complications which are not especially relevant to the current discussion. Conditions under which widows become household heads are discussed below in Chapter IV. It should suffice at this point to say that for all practical purposes a widow as household head is basically a surrogate for her deceased husband. To preserve the anonymity of the persons involved, the names of household heads are replaced by numbers. The numbers represent the ranking of each household within Ajī Quī in terms of wealth and these same numbers are used throughout this study to designate particular household heads in Ajī Quī.

A number of things should be noted about the data presented in Figure

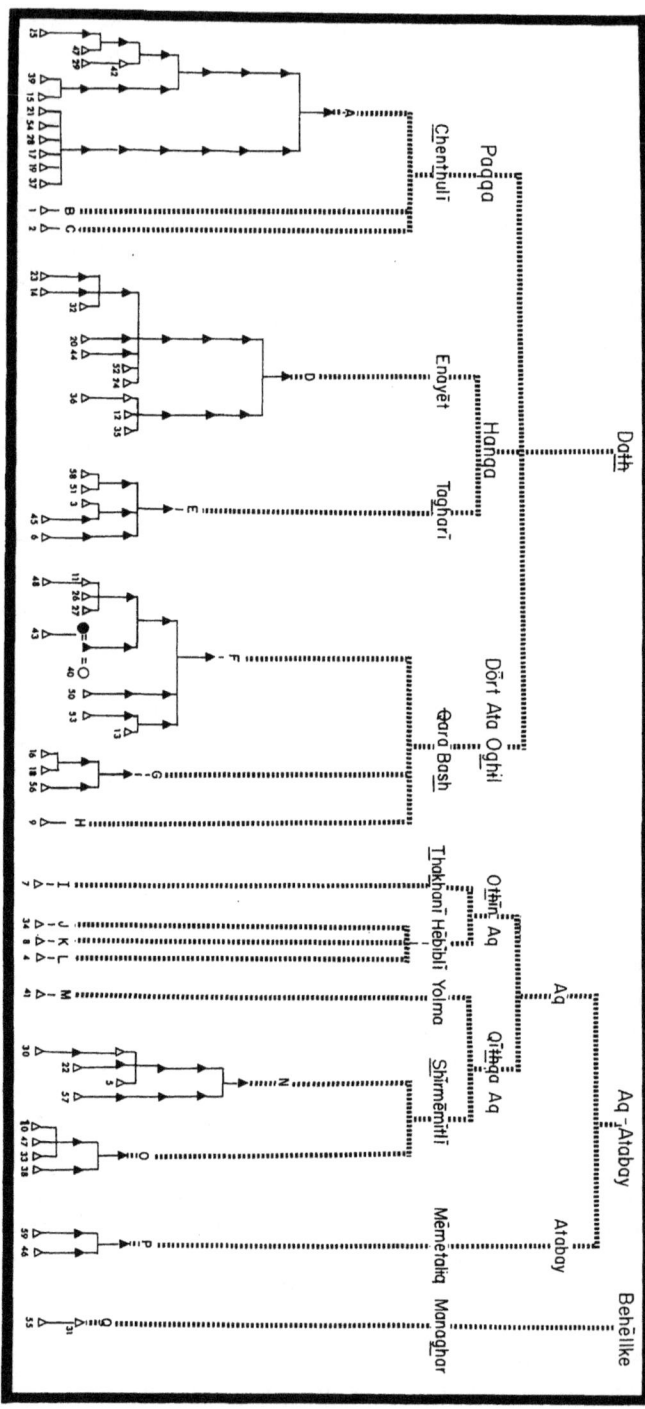

Fig. 12. Agnatic relationships of household heads in Ajī Qui, 1967.

12. First, the dominant lineage is Dath, the gongshī being the Aq-Atabay and Behellke. All lineages in Ajī Quī have additional members residing in other obas. Figure 13 presents a complete genealogy for lineage A, indicating household heads that reside elsewhere (represented by letters). The household heads of lineage A residing outside of Ajī Quī are divided among four other obas, and the oba of residence is indicated in each case by a lower case letter. Two of these obas, those designated "a" and "c" are, like Ajī Quī, dominated by the Dath descent group.

For each of the other lineages represented in Ajī Quī a similar diagram could be drawn showing additional members residing elsewhere. Thus, the relationship between residence and descent is somewhat haphazard whether viewed in terms of the composition of obas, as in Figure 12, or in terms of the distribution of lineage members among obas, as in Figure 13.

If we examine the composition of the next largest residence group, the tribe, a similarly irregular relationship between descent and residence emerges. Figure 14 illustrates the distribution of obas within the īl dominated by the Dath descent group. This is an enlargement of a part of the territory shown in Figure 11. (Ajī Quī falls considerably farther to the east and therefore does not appear on this map.) Each of the obas, with the exception of one newly

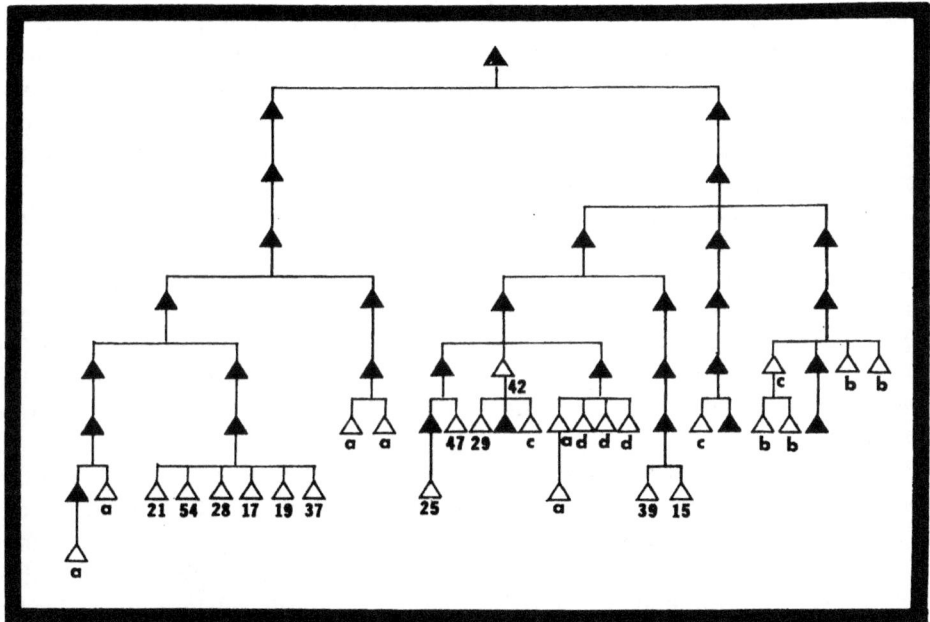

Fig. 13. Lineage A of the Chenthulī. Ajī Quī household heads are indicated by the same numbers used in Figure 12; the remainder of the individuals shown are household heads resident elsewhere, linking ancestors, or recently deceased household heads; those resident elsewhere are divided among four obas represented by the letters 'a,' 'b,' 'c,' and 'd.'

formed oba north of the Gurgan River, is dominated by a descent group of a lower level of segmentation than Daṯh. Figure 14 includes a genealogical breakdown of the Daṯh, the arrows indicating which obas are dominated by which groups. An examination of this data reveals that the genealogical depth of the dominant lineage of each oba varies. Thus, four obas are dominated by lineages of the first level of segmentation below the level of Daṯh (two are dominated by the Paqqa, one by the Dȫrt Ata Oghïl and one by the Hanqa). In each case none of the descent groups representing the second level of segmentation forms a numerical majority. In the case of Ajï Quï it has been noted that no descent group below the level of Daṯh has a numerical majority so that the dominant group represents a still higher level of segmentation. The remainder of the obas in Figure 14 are dominated by groups of a lower level of segmentation, with the exception of one, which is evenly divided between the Nurrek and Keçhçhe lineages. These facts illustrate the generalization that the level of segmentation of the dominant lineage of an oba varies.

Some of the descent groups at the second level of segmentation below the level of Daṯh do not dominate any oba (see Figure 14). These lineages consist entirely of small groups of gongshï scattered among obas dominated by other Daṯh lineages.

An examination of the degree of correspondence between residence and descent at higher levels of segmentation in the descent system reveals an equally irregular relationship. In the particular case of the Daṯh tribe, there are no obas dominated by non-Daṯh descent groups. Among other tribes, however, such obas do exist, and they are referred to as gongshï obas. It is also true that the Daṯh descent group and the Daṯh tribe, which is a residence group, are largely coterminous. Nevertheless, there are four Daṯh obas outside of the Daṯh tribal territory.[5] This degree of correspondence between descent groups and residence groups is not universal. For example, five of the tribes shown in Figures 10 and 11 are in fact composites of two descent groups. The tribes referred to are those labeled Bagha and Behellke, Kuçhek and Eymir, Qojuq and Thalaq, Qanyoqmaṯh and Ighdar, and Düejï and Qarawï. In each of these cases separate descent groups are joined together to form a single tribe, and the smaller of the two groups can be designated the gongshï of the larger group.

There is another factor which further complicates the relationship between descent and residence. Over a long period of time gongshï groups are sometimes gradually absorbed politically into the descent groups among whom they reside. The native explanation of this process is that groups which have taken refuge from feud or intertribal war in their original location and have become gongshï in a tribe dominated by a descent group other than their own

---

[5] These Daṯh obas consist of pastoralists who originally migrated to the territory north of the agricultural Daṯh but who moved farther east after the closing of the Russian border to migration: see Chapter II, pp. 27-28.

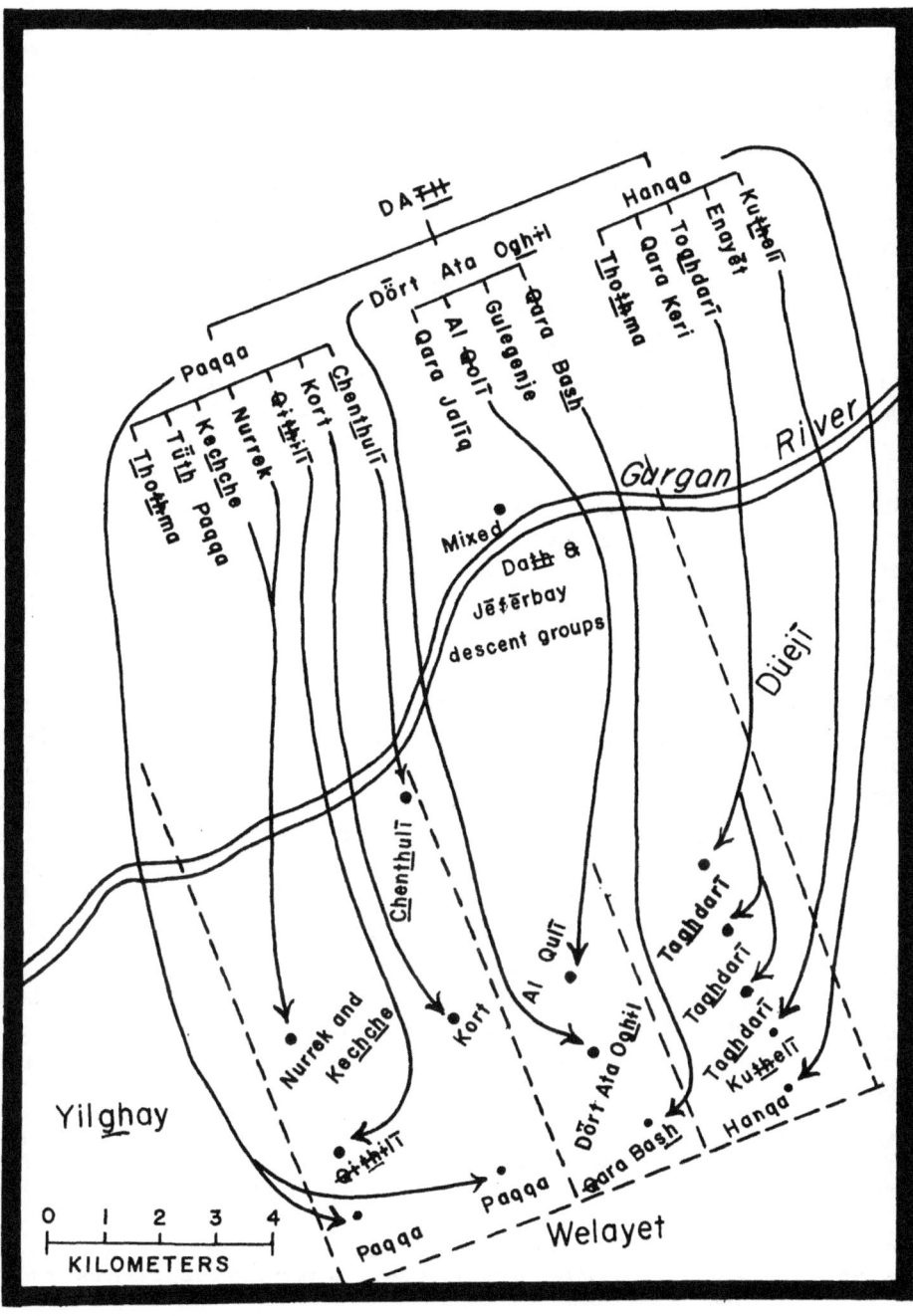

Fig. 14. Distribution of dominant descent groups among Daṭḥ obas.

eventually, for all political purposes, become a subdivision by descent of the dominant group of the tribe. For example, in the genealogy of the Daṭh (Fig. 8), the groups absorbed through long-standing co-residence are indicated by dotted lines. The position they have assumed politically is fully analogous to that of groups which belong to the Daṭh by descent, and thus their position within the segmentary lineage system can be indicated by a diagram of the sort used to relate genealogical connections. The non-Daṭh origin of these groups is not forgotten, however. They are said to have become Daṭh because of their long residence among the Daṭh. In explaining this situation, informants always emphasize that long co-residence is necessary to create a situation of this sort. The notion that a descent group, that is a taypa, could acquire new members through the type of contractual arrangements by which people join a new residence is foreign to the Yomut. Usually, but not always, the position previously occupied by these groups in the descent system is forgotten.

Groups which justify their place in the system of segmentary political alliances by long-standing co-residence are to be found at every level of segmentation above the level of precisely remembered genealogy. The groups incorporated by this process into the Daṭh were all grafted on at a relatively low level. However, an illustration of the above fact emerges from an examination of the segmentary political system[6] of the Yomut. Figure 7 gives the genealogical breakdown of the Yomut, and Figure 15 presents what can be described as the segmentary political system of the Yomut. This consists of a series of named territorial groups and subgroups that is very much like a segmentary lineage system in its political aspects. At each level of segmentation groups can be mobilized in opposition to one another or united into a single coalition against a group on the next higher level of segmentation. The system differs from a segmentary lineage system, however, because it is only partially based on a genealogy.[7]

An examination of the political system of the Yomut at the level of segmentation of the Sherep and Choni̅ confederacies reveals another deviation of the political system from the genealogy, the absorption of the Qojuq into the Sherep confederacy. This is not rationalized by a long history of co-residence, but rather by a myth. The myth states that the three sons of Qutli̅ Temur (see Fig. 7) at one time went on a raid together.[8] During this raid

[6] The term "segmentary political system" is used to distinguish the system of political groups from the system of descent groups. Since the two systems are distinct both in fact and in native conceptualization, it is best to maintain the distinction in ethnographic description.

[7] Pehrson, 1966:18-19; the term "segmentary political system" would seem applicable to the political structure of the Marri, although the term "segmentary lineage system" would not, since the system is not based on a genealogy.

[8] In oral recitation, Sherep, Choni̅, and Quojuq are often referred to in ways which imply that they were sons of Yomut. Note that the word oghil can mean either son or grandson.

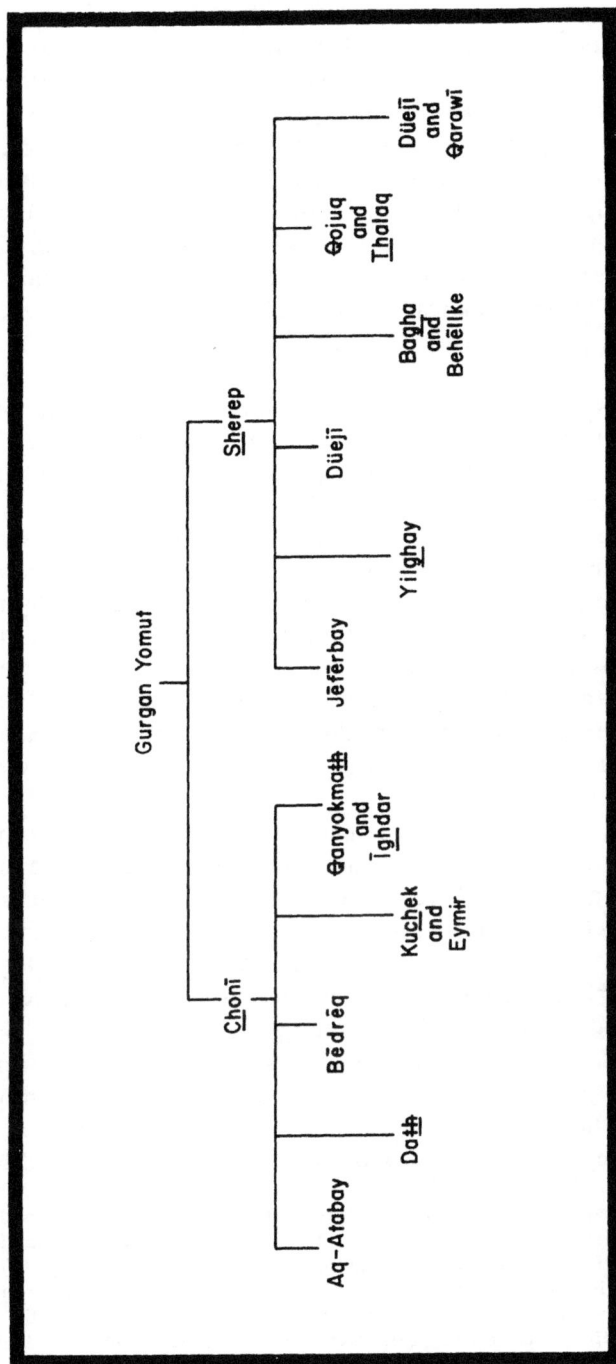

Fig. 15. Segmentary political system of the Gurgan Yomut.

Qojuq's horse was shot and he was left with no means of escape. Qojuq then appealed to Chonī, who was his full brother, to allow him to mount behind Chonī in order to escape. Chonī refused, and Qojuq then appealed to Sherep, who was his patrilateral half-brother. Sherep agreed, and as a result Qojuq has always sided with Sherep in disputes between Sherep and Chonī. The descendants of Sherep and Qojuq have continued this pattern of alliance up to the present. The important fact to note is that this is the only political tie among the Yomut which is not justified by either co-residence or genealogy. A number of observations should be made about this alliance.[9] First, co-residence at this level is basically impossible without disrupting the consistent pattern of interspersed Sherep and Chonī blocs. Second, the Sherep with the addition of the Qojuq (including the Thalaq who are a part of the Qojuq as a result of long co-residence with them) form a political group approximately equal in number to the Chonī. There are 129 Sherep obas and 119 Chonī obas in the Gurgan Plain. Thus, the Qojuq, with 41 obas, clearly play a pivotal role in the local balance of power. (Nine of the Sherep obas, including 7 Qojuq obas, are located in the area labeled "Mixed Pastoralists and Recently Settled Pastoralists" on Fig. 11.) The possibility that this alliance was originally merely an agreement based on expediency is readily suggested by the data, but impossible to substantiate. The myth justifying the alliance emphasizes that the alliance was created in the remote past, in fact, at the time when the apical ancestors of the three groups concerned were still alive. The myth, thus, does little to suggest the notion that the obligations associated with the segmentary political system can be altered in a single stroke by alliances of a contractual nature.

From the above discussion it can be seen that although residence group composition is a flexible matter, most movement between residence groups does not lead to an immediate change in the segmentary political system. In fact, the Yomut claim that readjustment of genealogy to reflect residence arrangements does not occur, and their accounts of their genealogical relationships support this contention. However, readjustment of political obligation to reflect long established residence arrangements does occur. The process, however, begins only after co-residence has been continuous for many generations. Gongshī groups that have been absorbed politically into the groups among whom they reside are always of such remote origin that the time of their initial acceptance by the group into which they are merged is placed at a

---

[9] "Alliance" is used in many anthropological studies to refer only to bonds of solidarity created by affinal ties between exogamous descent groups. Thus alliance almost becomes a synonym for affinal kinship (see for example Levi-Strauss, 1969:98-118). This usage is quite reasonable in societies in which one finds exogamous descent groups, but is not very useful in societies in which marriage preferably occurs within the same descent group. The meaning used throughout this study is taken from *The American College Dictionary*, 1951:34: "any joining of efforts or interests by persons, families, states, or organizations."

point beyond precisely remembered genealogies, that is, more than seven generations ago.

## PEACE, WAR, AND FEUD

The primary obligation implied by co-residence is the obligation to maintain peaceful relations. It has already been pointed out that the name for the largest identifiable residence group, īl, means among other things a relationship of peace. The opposite, a relationship of war, is described as yaghī. In terms of Turkmen notions of right and wrong, it is wrong to steal from or injure someone with whom one is īl, but such behavior is commendable toward someone with whom one is yaghī.

The distinction between īl and yaghī is most carefully defined in reference to the laws of homicide, and a discussion of these laws as practiced before direct administration should clarify the nature of these two political relationships. When a homicide occurred, and both killer and victim were īl, rights of vengeance were limited to a patrilateral kindred of seven generations in depth. This relationship of shared blood responsibility can be expressed in terms of a kin term, "qan dushar," which means "blood reaches." For a person to say that "so-and-so is my qan dushar" means that he and the individual referred to have a common patrilateral ancestor who is not more than seven generations removed from either of them. Rights to avenge homicides among those who were īl were limited to people who were qan dushar with the victim, and suitable targets were limited to individuals who were qan dushar with the killer. One homicide in vengeance erased the blood debt and made friendly relations between the two groups possible again.[10]

Except in cases of accidental homicide, blood money was not used to settle blood debts. According to universally agreed upon norms only vengeance killings could erase blood debts.[11] The usual reaction to homicides was, therefore, for those people who were probable targets for vengeance to take refuge in some distant village. Flight of this sort was the primary reason that residence and descent groups did not correspond perfectly. Thus, the Turkmen, like many other groups, regulated vengeance genealogically. Norms based on genealogy, in addition to defining legitimate victims and legitimate executors of vengeance, also prescribed that those who were genealogically neutral were obligated, when vengeance was imminent, to protect those who were probable targets of vengeance and to assist them in their escape. Once they had found refuge in some distant village, the members of that village were obligated, as neutral parties, to protect them from their pursuers.

---

[10] There is one exception to this rule: see Chapter V, pp. 121-122, and note 7.

[11] In case of accidental homicide a payment called hun is made in compensation. It usually is equivalent to about 100 sheep.

In cases of homicide in which the killer and the victim were related to one another as qan dushar, only the killer himself was a legitimate target for vengeance, and only those closer to the victim than to the killer had the right to take vengeance.

Actually, homicides within a tribe were not frequent, but the possibility of homicide and its consequences were very much a part of the internal politics of a tribe. Whenever a dispute arose—as it frequently did over the ownership of a piece of agricultural land, as a result of livestock grazing a planted field, or over other matters—the agnates of the party who felt himself wronged would confront the supposed culprit with demands that the situation be righted. The agnates of the accused would gather and support his counter-claims. Usually such discussions were only moderately hostile, but not always. Parties genealogically defined as neutral, close to neither disputant, were obligated to play the role of peacemakers between the two groups, and would advocate a form of peaceful settlement. Most differences were talked out in this way and settled peacefully. If, however, peaceful discussion failed to bring about a mutually satisfactory solution to a dispute, violence and usually at least one homicide would result, followed by attempts at vengeance and by flight of those who were legitimate targets of vengeance. However, the general expectation of peaceful relations and the role of neutral parties as peacemakers generally made intra-tribal relations peaceful.

A few additional observations should be made about blood vengeance. The seven generational blood responsibility group defined the strict limits to the right of vengeance, but not the primary responsibility for vengeance. Thus, the immediate kinsmen of the victim were primarily responsible for "taking blood" and they inevitably tried first to execute the killer himself. Only if they felt it would be impossible to do this would they turn to his agnates. Again, if the killer could not be found and executed, they would attempt next to kill the culprit's father, son, or brother before turning to more distant kin. More distant kinsmen of the victim were drawn into the pursuit of vengeance only if the immediate kinsmen needed assistance. Thus, when vengeance was successfully executed, usually it was taken by close agnates of the victim against either the killer himself or a close agnate of the killer.

It should also be noted that the concept of seven generation blood responsibility came into play only if a homicide occurred. The groups confronting one another in the sort of dispute that could potentially lead to a homicide were often either larger or smaller agnatic groups than the seven generational kindreds of the individuals in the groups. A small offense, such as trespassing on a planted field with grazing livestock, would usually involve only a handful of men. A larger disagreement might draw together all of the men of a named descent group of 200 or more families in confrontation with a similar group. Not all the members of such temporarily mobilized groups would be qan dushar to one another. Two members of the same named descent group, whose closest common agnatic ancestor is eight or more generations remote, are said to have "come out of one blood." A descent group all of whose adult members were "not in one blood" might, however, be mobilized over some serious matter. If the confrontation led to violence resulting in a homicide, the vengeance following the homicide was considered a different matter than the original confrontation and was prosecuted in terms of the seven generation kindred of the killer and victim. Thus, if large enough groups were mobilized over some dispute and such a confrontation led to a homicide, it is possible that those involved in the blood-debt might not include the original parties to the dispute. If this happened, it is even possible, though improbable, that the original parties could resolve their differences peacefully. It was common, after a large confrontation resulted in violence, that several people would be killed leading to several different blood debts involving different kindreds.

This was especially true when a dispute occurred between two obas. Such disputes were usually over the boundaries of their respective territories, and the groups mobilized were naturally all of those who shared in the joint estate of each oba. As mentioned above there was often a minority of households within an oba which did not belong to the dominant descent group, but who, nevertheless, shared in the joint estate of the oba. Such people could find themselves caught in a dispute between the oba of their residence and an oba dominated by their own lineage. In such cases agnation was considered more important than co-residence. Thus oba A, dominated by lineage A', but containing a minority of lineage B', might have a disagreement over territory with oba B dominated by lineage B'. In this sort of situation the B' minority in oba A would either not join in the prosecution of the dispute, or if the confrontation became hostile enough they might be forced to resolve their awkward situation by withdrawing from oba A.

If a dispute within a tribe became large enough, drawing in most of the members of the tribe on one side or another according to their agnatic loyalties, the tribe could split up along genealogical lines. Thus, tribe A with subdivisions $A_1$ and $A_2$ would split, and in Turkmen terms the two descent groups $A_1$ and $A_2$ would cease to be īl and become yaghī. If the situation lasted they eventually would be thought of as two separate tribes. This is reported, however, as being rare even when a large confrontation did lead to severe violence.

Such a transition from peace to war, from being īl to being yaghī, was more common among the components of the larger groups which I have called confederacies. The distinction between a tribe and a confederacy for purposes of this study is based on two contrasting characteristics. A tribe was, under traditional conditions, stable as an internally peaceful group whereas a confederacy was not. The component segments of a tribe very rarely became yaghi, whereas the component segments of a confederacy frequently were

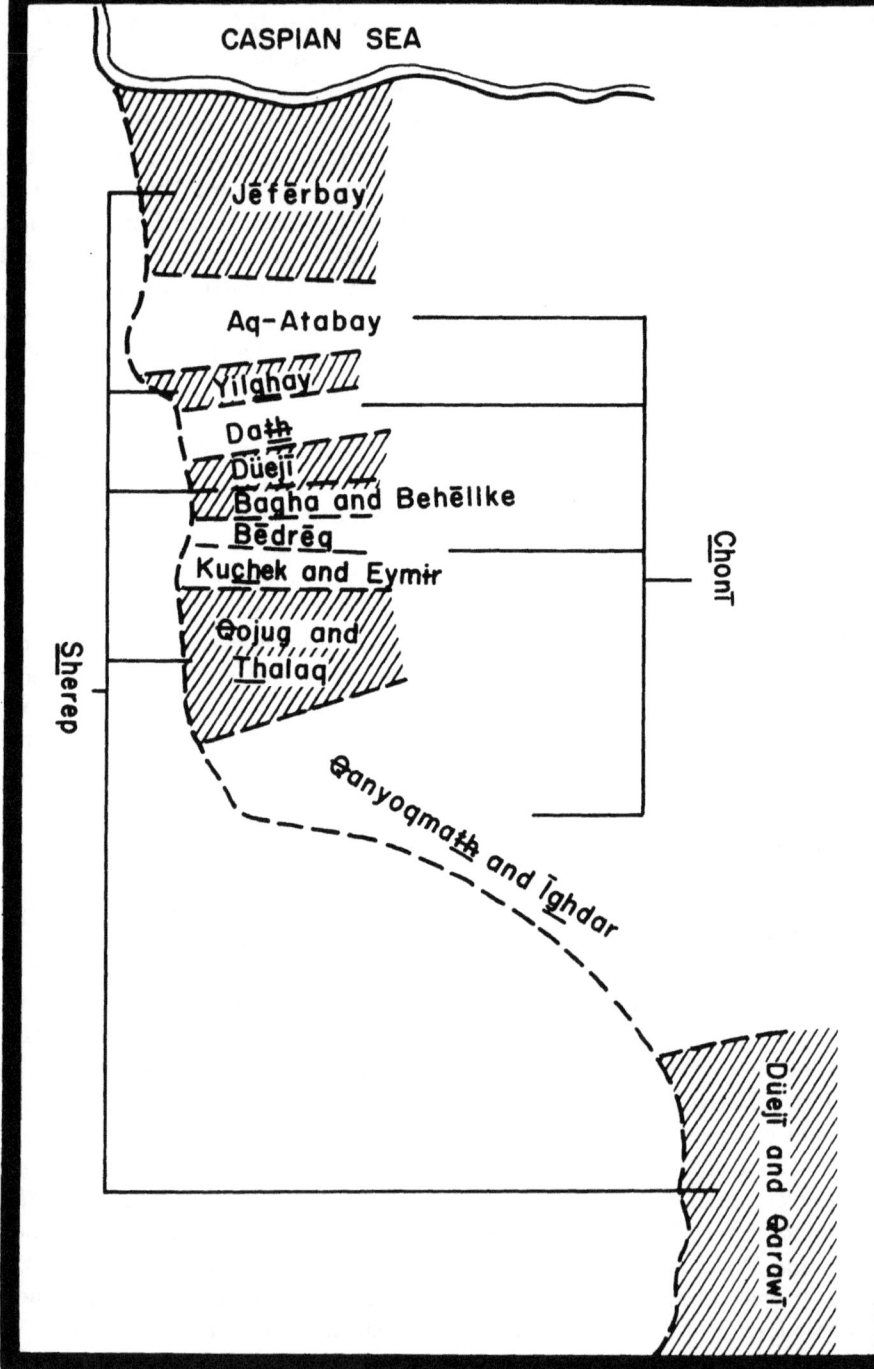

Fig. 16. Location of Sherep and Choni̇̄ tribes.

yaghī. In addition the component obas of a tribe always occupy contiguous territories so that it is possible to identify a compact tribal territory. The component tribes which together form a confederacy, in contrast, often are not contiguous. In Figure 16 the tribes of the Sherep confederacy are hatched to distinguish them from the tribes of the Chonī confederacy. The tribes of each confederacy tend to be interspersed in such a way that each Sherep tribe has one or two Chonī tribes as immediate neighbors. This is a variation of the checkerboard-like alliance pattern that is common in many areas (see, for instance, Barth, 1959:5-21). Usually the tribes of the Sherep confederacy were on peaceful terms with one another, and the same was true of the Chonī. The Sherep and Chonī, however, were usually yaghī. Thus, the basic pattern was for each Sherep tribe, or contiguous group of Sherep tribes, to be hostile with its immediate neighbors and allied with its neighbor's neighbors.

Hostilities between yaghī groups were usually limited to mutual raids for livestock executed by small ad hoc raiding parties. Raids were answered by similar counterraids so that hostilities tended to remain at the same level. Few people were killed in these raids, but when homicides did occur, counterraids with the specific purpose of vengeance killings were often organized. The seven generation rule did not apply between yaghī groups, and any member of the enemy tribe was a suitable victim. The rule that one vengeance killing satisfied a blood debt created by a single homicide and established peace again also did not apply, although a parity of sorts was maintained at one enemy victim for each victim of one's own tribe. Such a parity was expedient as long as an increase in the level of hostility was not desired; it was not a jural rule as it was among groups that were īl.

If hostility between two tribes became intense enough, for instance in a dispute over territory, each tribe would organize a military expedition known as an aq öylī. The aq öylī was constituted as follows: each oba would send one-fifth of their adult males as a fighting contingent and one-fifth of their yurts to house them, while food would be supplied by the people left behind. The total group would elect a leader, known as a beg, and under his direction they would form a highly mobile fighting force. Such military units were also organized on occasion to fight against the Kajar government.

## SACRED LINEAGES

A channel of communication between hostile tribes was maintained and could be used to arrange peace, as well as for other purposes. This channel consisted of a group of small lineages that claimed descent from the first four caliphs. All ordinary Turkmen were perpetually at peace with these lineages of sacred descent: to become yaghī with one of these groups was believed to bring down severe divine retribution. Such retribution was believed to come about not only from becoming yaghī, but from any unjustified act of hostility against any member of one of these sacred descent groups. Numerous tales are still told of people going insane after raiding and robbing members of a sacred lineage who were mistaken for ordinary Turkmen.

Members of the sacred lineages, called Ewlad, were thus able to travel freely between hostile groups for purposes of trade, or to serve as diplomatic messengers. Their special status also required that they act as peacemakers between hostile tribes. This was a role required to some extent of all neutral parties, but it was thought to be even more obligatory for the Ewlad. Informants reported that after they had raided hostile groups, Ewlad would occasionally appear on behalf of the victims, pleading that they were poor and requesting a return of part of the livestock taken. It was further reported that occasionally a part of the booty was actually returned in these cases, but never the entire booty (cf. Irons, 1965:393-414). When hostilities of a larger scale than livestock raids were underway between two tribes, the Ewlad would travel between these groups attempting to arrange peace. They were not always successful in their efforts. Their role as a channel of diplomacy was, however, a valuable one for the Turkmen as a whole, and formed an important part of the traditional political structure of the Turkmen.

Up to this point we have been concerned primarily with the indigenous political institutions of the Turkmen. It is now necessary, in order to give a more complete picture of the forces governing political affairs among them, to explain the relationship of the Yomut to the Persian government. Because this relationship has changed drastically since the establishment of the Pahlavi dynasty in 1925, the discussion must be made in historic perspective.

## RELATIONS WITH THE KAJAR GOVERNMENT

Both the accounts of older informants and written sources agree that during the later Kajar Period (late 1800s through 1925), the Iranian government enjoyed only a very limited ability to control the Yomut (see note 9, Chapter I). The extent of this control varied greatly from time to time and from place to place. Carleton Coon (1958:263-265) has observed that traditional Middle Eastern governments had zones of greater and lesser influence. There were regions in which taxes and conscripts were collected regularly and government decisions in general were not challenged by force. At the opposite extreme there were regions which government representatives dared not enter except in large military units, and from which neither taxes nor conscripts could be collected. Zones of greater or lesser influence of the type described by Coon could readily be identified in the Yomut regions during the Kajar period. Usually the government was able to collect taxes and conscripts from the chomir near the seat of provincial administration, Asterabad (modern Gurgan), but was seldom able to punish offenses by these chomir against Welayet villages or to intervene in the internal wars and feuds of the chomir of this region. As a rule the government had no effective control over the chomir farthest from the seat of administration in the eastern portion of Yomut country, or over the charwa. After the 1870s, when the Czarist government of Russia took control of the region north of the Atrak, the charwa who crossed the Atrak during their yearly movements had to contend with Russian authority while north of the border.

Occasionally the Kajar government sent military expeditions into Yomut territory in an attempt to exercise a degree of control. Battles occasionally occurred between Persian military expeditions and the Turkmen, but they were seldom a serious threat to the Turkmen, and the Persian military was not greatly feared. The Russian government exerted a greater influence on the Turkmen who found themselves on Russian territory and the Turkmen had considerable respect for the Russian military forces. The Russian government intervened and stopped large battles between Turkmen tribes, and was able to punish individual Turkmen for offenses, if they were considered serious enough. However, the Russian government was evidently not interested in closely regulating the internal affairs of the Turkmen, since older informants report that small-scale raiding and blood-feuds did occur among the Turkmen on the Russian side of the border and that such matters were generally ignored by the Russian authorities.

Turkmen slave raiding, which had been a serious problem throughout northeastern Persia during earlier periods, was greatly reduced in scale after the majority of the Turkmen had been brought under Russian control. The Yomut south of the Atrak, who were on Kajar territory, continued their slave raiding on a much smaller scale after the slave markets of Khiva, Bukhara, and Merv were closed. In their raids, conducted mainly against the Kurdish population in the vicinity of Bujnurd, they took only small children. Adult slaves could no longer be sent across the Kara Kum to the slave market in Khiva, and if kept in the Gurgan Plain they could easily run away, given their proximity to their original home. Because of the difficulty of keeping adult slaves in the Gurgan Plain, the Yomut were interested in adult captives only if they could be held for a short period for ransom, not as slaves to be held indefinitely.

## The Office of Thaqlau

Most of the tribes[12] in and around the Iranian Plateau are organized in a hierarchy of chiefs culminating in a paramount chief with considerable

---

[12] In referring to the Basseri and similar groups as a "tribe," I am following established usage. It should be clear from the context whether I am using "tribe" in this way, or in the more restricted sense defined on pp. 46-49.

authority. This chiefly hierarchy exists in addition to a segmentary system of named descent groups, and, to a large extent, the two sets of political institutions are integrated into a single harmonious political structure. Such tribes, thus, have a centralized administrative apparatus which can, at least to some extent, supplement, or even override, segmentary loyalties.

During the Kajar period, the Turkmen had one institution similar to the chiefly offices found among the other tribes in the vicinity of the Iranian Plateau. This office was concerned with the collection of tribute by each of the various Turkmen tribes from the sedentary Welayet villages of the Gurgan Plain. The office was known as thaqlau, or protector. It was not hereditary, but rather fell to the man who was strong enough to hold it. On occasions internal fights broke out in various Yomut tribes over competing claims to this office.

The thaqlau of each tribe collected an annual tribute from the sedentary Welayet villages immediately south of his tribe's territory and in return he agreed not to raid those villages and to protect them from raids by other members of his tribe or by other tribes. In order to prevent raids by his own tribe, he would give a share of the tribute collected to the more successful organizers of raids among his own tribe in return for a promise not to raid the villages protected. To prevent raids by other tribes, he would call on the assistance of those with whom he shared the tribute, and he would also, in some cases, hire armed retainers to act as additional deterrents. The thaqlau would also agree that, if he were unsuccessful in preventing raids, he would compensate the protected villages at an agreed upon rate. The thaqlau, thus, represented the tribe as a whole to the villages protected by his tribe. He also, in effect, represented his tribe to the provincial Persian government. The Persian governor appointed, from among the sedentary population, an official for each Yomut tribe who was responsible, in theory, for collecting taxes from, and guaranteeing the good behavior of, that tribe. These officials, known as sarkardehs,[13] generally dealt with the thaqlau, and the normal channel of communication from the government to the Yomut was through the sarkardeh and the thaqlau. The sarkardehs and the thaqlaus were, in theory, the instruments of indirect rule. Both written and oral sources agree that these officials ordinarily worked together to exploit the sedentary Welayet villages.

In the case of the Yomut tribes closest to the center of local administration, the city of Asterabad (now Gurgan), the thaqlaus were supplied with mounted and armed retainers at government expense in return for a promise to police their tribes. Such attempts to extend government influence over the Yomut seem, however, to have had little success, as can be judged from the limited extent of government control described above.

---

[13] Dārūgheh is a local synonym for sarkardeh.

## Nomadism and Politics

Nomadism played a very important role in the political affairs of the Yomut during the Kajar period, and earlier periods of Persian history as well (see Irons, 1968:49-50; 1969:33-35; 1974). The place of nomadism in Yomut life has changed considerably during the Pahlavi period and the changes will be discussed in a later section. The present section is concerned with the later portion of the Kajar period, a period remembered by older informants and described as well in a number of written sources.

It is clear from the material presented in Chapter II that the Yomut were more mobile than their ecology required. The ecology of the chomïr could easily be combined with a completely sedentary existence, while that of the charwa could easily accommodate a pattern of semi-sedentary residence.

The ecology of the charwa did require migration during the wet season. During this season, camp sites and livestock had to be close together and had to be located where good pasture could be found. Since the location of good pasture varied from year to year a migratory mode of life was required during these seasons. However, during the dry season, the camp site of each oba was approximately the same from year to year. This was natural since there were a limited number of permanent water sources on which they could rely. The same group of households would use the same wells, springs, or river banks for their water each dry season, and would camp within one or two hours walking distance of this source of water. Whether good pasture could be found there or not was irrelevant since the livestock, except beasts of burden, were sent elsewhere with shepherds who lived away from the main camp site. The few beasts of burden kept at the dry season camp site were fed cut fodder where local pasture was inadequate. Thus, there was nothing to prevent the Turkmen from building permanent houses at their dry season location as they, in fact, did in Ajī Quī in 1936.

In the case of the agricultural Turkmen, nomadism provided even less of an ecological advantage. Their migrations were very short and concerned primarily with comfort rather than economic need. Obviously their primary economic activity, agriculture, did not require migration. The care of their small herds, like the livestock of the sedentary villagers, could have been maintained by specialized shepherds without migration by the entire population.

Concerning the chomïr, it is also important to note that their devotion to mobility prevented them from exploiting their habitat more productively by means of irrigation agriculture.[14] The territory they occupied was crossed by numerous streams that could easily be directed for purposes of irrigation.

[14] There is evidence to suggest a general preference in all societies for extensive exploitation of natural resources wherever population densities allow such exploitation. See also Netting, 1965:422-429, 1968:130-143.

Their territory had, in fact, been exploited more productively during earlier historic periods, a fact indicated by both written sources and archaeological evidence (see Petrushevsky, 1968:488; also see Arne, 1945:1-23 for an archaeological survey of the Gurgan Plain). Since the establishment of firm administration, the territory of the chomir has again been made more productive by irrigation. Before the advent of effective government control, however, the Yomut chomir resolutely eschewed such "un-nomadic" practices.

The difference between the economic and political circumstances of the agricultural Turkmen and of the sedentary Welayet peasants before 1925 is very instructive concerning the role of nomadism in traditional Turkmen life. The sedentary peasants exploited their land by the more productive methods of irrigation agriculture. The difference between Welayet and chomir attitudes toward immovable wealth had many readily observable manifestations.

A typical sedentary village consisted of an elaborate complex of buildings surrounded by irrigated fields of rice, cotton, tobacco, and orchards, as well as fields of wheat and barley. A typical settled village included among its amenities a public bath, at least one mosque, a mill, and a number of shops, in addition to the homes of the peasants. A Turkmen oba, in contrast, consisted only of a collection of yurts, a few flocks of sheep and goats, and some fields of wheat and barley.

The contrast in political matters was equally sharp. The sedentary peasants, unlike the Turkmen chomir, were forced to respect the claims of a number of outsiders to a portion of the fruits of their labor. Tax collectors, landlords, and the Turkmen thaqlaus all claimed a share of the peasants' crops. In contrast, the ordinary chomir, although he might not receive a share of the tribute taken by the thaqlau of his tribe, at least paid little or no taxes, and recognized the claims of no landlord to a part of his produce. The ordinary chomir could rely on the combined strength of his agnates to protect his rights of property and person. The ordinary peasant could only turn to the thaqlau, to whom he paid tribute, to the government, to whom he paid taxes, or perhaps to his landlord, to whom he paid rent, for protection of his rights. In return for the price he paid, the peasant enjoyed no more security of property and person than the Turkmen.

It is, therefore, not surprising that the ordinary Turkmen saw his own situation as vastly more desirable than that of the Welayet. He also perceived that his mobility was the factor responsible for his ability to escape the plight of the Welayet. His attitude is summarized in a stereotyped threat which Turkmen nomads occasionally use when they feel seriously offended. The threat is: "I do not have a mill with willow trees. I have a horse and a whip. I will kill you and go." The reference to the mill reflects the notion that immobile wealth could undermine a person's willingness to fight in his own defense, and could lead one to the subservient status of the Welayet peasant. A man with only mobile wealth, "a horse and a whip," was, in contrast, a man to be feared and, therefore, not to be offended. Their association of the willingness to fight with mobility neatly summarizes the role of nomadism in Yomut politics.

Nomadism, for the Turkmen, was more, however, than the result of political calculations; it was a strong cultural tradition. To live in a house, and to invest one's labor and capital in such immobile wealth as irrigation works, orchards, mills, and shops was not just politically unwise; it was unTurkmen. This tradition played a crucial role in the political system of the Turkmen.

## NOMADISM AND FEUD

The threat of violence was an important sanction in the political system of the Turkmen as in most, if not all, political systems. As mentioned above, although most intra-tribal disputes were settled peacefully, the threat of violence always determined the course by which disputes were settled. It is important to observe, in addition, that the possibility of flight was equally important in the process of adjudicating disputes. It was always assumed by all parties involved that, if a peaceful solution to a dispute could not be found, violence would result. It was also assumed that following such violence, blood debts would be reckoned and potential victims of vengeance would protect themselves by taking flight.

Taking flight from political adversaries is, of course, not a habit restricted to the Turkmen. It is familiar in all societies. The Turkmen, under traditional conditions, differed from most societies in the extent to which they relied on this maneuver and, more importantly, in their special adaptation for flight. This was made possible to a large extent because they eschewed immovable wealth, but other factors are equally important. The role prescribed for neutral parties (defined by genealogy) in political matters was equally significant. When a group of Turkmen took flight they knew they could rely on neutral parties to conceal them, protect them from pursuers, give them food and shelter, and, if necessary, assist them in finding means of transport to a more distant place. They knew as well that eventually they could find an oba that would grant them the status of protected neighbors. Such a status would carry with it the right of permanent residence, access to the economic resources of the oba, and the protection of the oba against their adversaries. Thus, flight was encouraged not only by the tradition of maintaining physical mobility, but also by the prescribed role of neutral parties which was built into their segmentary system. The fact that blood debts could only be settled by bloodshed and never by blood money was another aspect of their political system which encouraged mobility. Nomadism and political structure were closely interrelated among the Turkmen and tended to reinforce one another.

## NOMADISM AND RELATIONS WITH THE STATE

Flight, which was so important as a maneuver in intra-tribal politics, could also be resorted to in cases of especially serious intertribal hostilities and in cases of serious conflict with the Persian authorities. When such matters led to the flight of large groups of people, the usual practice among the Gurgan Yomut was to take refuge on the other side of the Kara Kum with the Khiva Yomut.

An appreciation of the role of nomadism in Yomut politics is essential to an understanding of the ability of the Yomut to resist firm government control. The fact that nomadism itself provides excellent military conditioning has long been recognized and needs little elaboration. The Turkmen were fine horsemen and were well supplied with good horses. Raids, both on sedentary villages and on other nomads, were frequent events for them and provided them with extensive military experience. When large Persian military expeditions were sent against them, normally hostile tribes would unite and turn out a large body of cavalry. This seasoned cavalry could usually hold its ground against the Persian forces. Even when confronted with superior strength, the Turkmen did not surrender. Instead, they would retreat into the steppe-desert region north of the Gurgan River, taking their families and livestock with them. Thus, both their mobility and their ability, through their segmentary lineage system, to unite large groups of people enabled them to resist direct conquest.

Another factor contributing to the ability of the Yomut to resist direct conquest was their strategic location on the edge of the arid region north of the Gurgan River. The territory stretching from the Gurgan River north to the Balkhan Mountains was steppe-desert over which the Turkmen could move with relative ease, and over which the armies of sedentary powers, such as the Kajars, could pursue them only with great difficulty. North of the Balkhan Mountains was the uninhabitable Kara Kum desert, and north of this desert lay the territory of the Khiva Yomut. Before the Russian conquest the Khiva Yomut recognized the Khans of Khiva as their suzerains. The Khiva Khans were hostile to the Kajars, and, therefore, their territory formed a potential asylum from the Persian authorities if the Balkhan Mountains did not offer sufficient safety.

It is also important to observe that the effective exploitation of mobility for political purposes was dependent on a social structure which allowed individual households, or larger groups, to shift their residence with ease to distant communities and after doing so to gain access to economic resources in their new location. The role prescribed for neutral parties—as defined by genealogy—in political matters played a very significant role in making this possible. Mobility was also encouraged by the facts that population density was low and economic resources existed in surplus of need throughout Yomut country, and that numerical strength was desirable from a political point of view for each of the various territorial groups into which the Yomut were divided.

The combined factors of their mobility and their strategic location on the edge of the desert are undoubtedly important to an explanation of the Persian government's difficulty in controlling the Yomut. The same factors no doubt account for the ability of other similarly situated Turkmen tribes, such as the Teke, Salor, and Sariq, to resist control by the Persians. Historical records confirm the impression that the Turkmen—in particular the Yomut, Teke, Salor, and Sariq tribes—were much more difficult to control than many of the other tribal groups with which the Kajar government had to deal. Their inability to control Turkmen slave raids is the most obvious case. The four groups most active in slave raiding—the Gurgan Yomut, the Teke, the Salor, and the Sariq—were all similarly situated on the northern border of Kajar Persia and on the southern fringe of the Kara Kum desert.

The difficulties which the Turkmen posed for the Kajar government had plagued earlier Persian dynasties as well. V. V. Barthold observes that:

> Even in the days when Persia under Shāh 'Abbās had acquired great strength, the Persian authorities in Astarābād adopted a defensive policy towards the Turkmans. Although the Persians defeated the Turkmans on the Atrak in A.D. 1598 and rebuilt the fortress on the Gurgan ..., they did not attempt to pursue the Turkmans on their steppe....[15]

This statement indicates that the Turkmen have been militarily exploiting both mobility and the strategic advantage of their arid habitat for a long time in large-scale confrontations with Persian military forces.

There was another pressure, in addition to direct military confrontation, which threatened the independence of the Yomut. The offices of sarkardeh and thaqlau provided a channel of communication between the government and the Yomut. They were also, in theory, institutions for indirect rule of the Yomut. The Kajar attempted to make this theory a practical reality. By supplying armed and mounted retainers to the thaqlaus, they hoped to elevate the thaqlaus to a position of effective authority within their tribes, and at the same time to make them dependent on the government. The Turkmen, however, interpreted attempts on the part of the thaqlaus to assume a position of authority as an infringement of their rights. The reaction was the same as to any other offense; descent groups were mobilized to redress the wrong, and if necessary they resorted to violence and perhaps subsequent flight. The thaqlaus were never in a position to overcome this sort of resistance and put themselves in a position fully analogous to that of the tribal chiefs in other parts of Persia, such as the southern Zagros.

[15] Barthold, 1962:146; the fortress referred to is Mubārakābād, known later as Aq Qal'eh, and still later as Pahlavī Dijh.

One final observation should be made concerning the relationship of the Yomut to the states with which they were in contact. Change in the nature of these states was the factor responsible for the end of their political independence. More modern and more efficient states of the sort that began to appear on their horizons in the nineteenth century were more than they could cope with. The first such modern state—modern in terms of their previous experiences—was the Czarist government of Russia. The expansion of Russia into Central Asia destroyed the independence of the majority of the Turkmen, and indirectly undermined the independence of the remainder. Although the Russian conquests did not directly affect the Yomut of the Gurgan Plain, their incursion into territory north of the Atrak River subverted the strategic position of the Gurgan Yomut. The task of permanently subduing the Gurgan Yomut had been greatly simplified for the Persian authorities by the pacification of the desert to their north. The government had only to maintain a large, permanent military force along the small strip of desert between the Gurgan River and the Russian border. The Kajar government failed to establish such a force, a sign of its own weakness, not the military strength of the Turkmen. Under the reformist government of Riza Shah, the Turkmen of the Gurgan Plain were easily subdued in 1925, and their indigenous political structure never again functioned with complete freedom.[16]

When a large military force was sent against them with instructions to subdue and disarm them, the Yomut initially put up a stiff resistance. But realizing the strength of their opponents, they resorted to their usual strategy of flight and the bulk of the Yomut retreated across the Russian frontier. This tactic, however, was no longer as effective as it had been in the past. The new and more efficient Iranian administration of Riza Shah kept the Turkmen portion of Iran under military control and allowed the Yomut to return only if they surrendered their arms and accepted the authority of the government (Arfa, 1964:177-183).

Naturally, complete pacification could not be accomplished at once, and informants related that a few raiders (baṯhmachīs) continued to evade the government for a while after 1925. However, during the period from 1925 to 1941 the Yomut experienced a gradual tightening of the government's control over their affairs. Raiding and the collection of tribute were eliminated, and measures were taken to suppress feuding. In the mid-1930s a policy of forced sedentarization was instituted to strengthen control over the Yomut (see Chapter II). During the period following the Russian occupation of Iran in 1941, the Yomut watched the government's power collapse and until 1947 many of them were as free of government interference in their affairs as they had been before 1925. After 1947 effective administration returned to the Yomut, but this time more gradually and less dramatically than in 1925.

[16] For descriptions of the military campaign see Arfa, 1964:172-183; and Mu'inī, 1966:74-76.

The return of effective government control after 1947 removed the advantages of nomadism for the Yomut. They could no longer hope to resist the control of the modern Iranian government through mobility. The introduction of mechanized agriculture in the decade of the fifties provided new economic opportunities for most of the Yomut of which they could only take advantage by settling, so that a large number chose to do voluntarily. The effects of these events on indigenous Yomut political institutions can best be related by describing the transition of a single community, that of Ajī Quī.

## THE RECENT POLITICAL HISTORY OF AJĪ QUĪ AND ENVIRONS

The families residing in Ajī Quī at the time of the research on which this study is based (see Fig. 12) had divergent histories. The dominant descent group was the Daṯh. The majority of Daṯh families had originally migrated over territory north of the region of the agricultural Daṯh, crossing the Russian border seasonally (see Fig. 3). Most of them had reestablished this pattern soon after the conquest of 1925. After the closing of the Russian border they moved their grazing grounds to the east, locating their dry season quarters on the Atrak, north of the city of Gunbadi Kāvūs. Later they shifted their grazing grounds and dry season location to the south in the Gökcha Hills where they remain today. This later relocation followed the pattern of population movement out of the Soviet Union and into Iran since the closing of the Soviet border, increasing population density along the Atrak River. The area south of the Gökcha Hills remained underpopulated, forming a no-man's-land between two hostile tribes, the Yomut and Göklen. The result has been a gradual but continuous movement of population from the Atrak River toward the Gurgan River in the eastern portion of Yomut country.

The population of Ajī Quī in 1967 was a composite of people from several areas. Most of the Daṯh of Ajī Quī moved there from the Atrak region as part of the general movement of population described above. Later they were joined by several groups of political refugees, a handful of Daṯh and Aq-Atabay fleeing the Soviet Union and a group of Aq-Ataby fleeing a blood feud in another oba on the Iranian side of the border. Most of these people had gathered in Ajī Quī by 1936.

In 1936, as a part of the government's program of forced sedentarization, the residents of Ajī Quī were forced to build houses at their dry season location. Since they were still allowed to migrate during the wet season, "sedentarization" entailed no ecological change. It did, however, give Ajī Quī the appearance of a settled village and simplify administration in the dry season. According to informants, this was the time when close government administration of their affairs began. Prior to this date government representatives came to the thinly populated Gökcha Hills only occasionally. They came in large armed contingents seeking to collect conscripts or apprehend bandits and otherwise were unconcerned about local affairs. After 1936 contingents of gendarmes began visiting Ajī Quī more frequently, at times weekly. A government headman (kadkhudā) was appointed from among the local population and made responsible for enforcing government decisions in between visits by the gendarmerie. Another official drawn from the local population, known as a bulūkdār, was placed above the headman of every five to ten obas. His job was to oversee the headmen, and, like the headmen, he could call on the gendarmerie to enforce his orders. Many of the bulūkdārs were quite tyrannical, arbitrarily ordering people about and having their orders enforced with beatings if necessary.[17] Many of them also used their power to enrich themselves at the expense of the local population. Above the bulūkdār was the military hierarchy responsible for the governance of the Turkmen regions.

In 1941 when Russian troops entered this region, informants report, the Iranian military and gendarmerie which had been responsible for their administration vanished. Some of the Turkmen who had been bulūkdārs and several headmen who had been especially tyrannical were killed by the local population; others fled from Yomut territory taking refuge in urban areas. A few low ranking gendarmes who were slow in their retreat were also killed and their weapons taken. Several large flocks of sheep belonging to the King had been pastured in the arid northeastern part of the Gurgan Plain under the direction of a Baluch overseer. This overseer was killed and the sheep were divided among the local population. The pastoralists of Ajī Quī destroyed the houses they had been forced to build, using the roof beams for firewood. The ruins of several of these homes can still be seen in the dry season location of Ajī Quī. They had been large, thick-walled homes with two rooms, built in neat rows, decorated here and there with the camel brands of their descent groups.

The collapse of administration in 1941 allowed the pent-up hostility of several years of close and at times arbitrary and exploitative administration to break loose. Free to live again as they pleased, the pastoralists of Ajī Quī and neighboring communities destroyed all evidence of the period of forced settlement. It rapidly became evident to the nomads of the Gökcha Hills that the Russian military was not going to administer them closely and many local Yomut became bandits (bathmachīs), using the Gökcha Hills as their base of operation. (From 1925 to 1936 this region had also been a haven for bandits on a more limited scale.) These bathmachīs were soon joined by Yomut from the Russian side of the border who were interested in asserting their independence from Russian control. A few of the latter included Yomut who were

---

[17] Bulūkdārs in general tended to favor their own close kin, and to direct harsh treatment toward non-kin.

deserters from the Russian military. The Yomut who evaded Soviet authority in this way all had close kinsmen in the Gökcha Hills from whom they could expect assistance. Occasionally the Russian military pursued some of the bathmachīs into the Gökcha Hills, capturing some and killing others. Generally, however, they did not enter the area, and the local population regulated their own affairs along traditional lines.

The Russian army withdrew from northern Iran in 1946 and, according to informants, the Turkmen of the Gökcha Hills were not aware of the return of an Iranian administration for another year and a half. In fact, an ad hoc Iranian administration in the Gurgan Plain had been assembled by former Iranian officials after the invasion in 1941, according to Yomut informants from areas near the city of Gurgan, and this administration was allowed to operate under the direction of a Russian consulate in the city of Gurgan. In 1943 this ad hoc administration was integrated more effectively into the Iranian government in Tehran but the administrative apparatus remained weak. A measure of its strength can be seen in its reaction to a land dispute near the city of Gunbadi Kāvūs in 1947. The territory of two entire obas east of the city was in dispute between Qojuq and Aq-Atabay descent groups, and a rather large battle ensued in which the Aq-Atabay were victorious. Following this, the disputed territory remained in the possession of the Aq-Atabay who still occupy this territory today. The Iranian administration intervened in no way in this intertribal squabble.

The pastoralists of the Gökcha Hills claim that about a year and a half after the Russian withdrawal, the Iranian gendarmerie once again began paying them visits, coming in large groups and seeking men for conscription and occasionally pursuing bandits, but otherwise they left the local Turkmen alone. During the decade of the fifties government patrols gradually became more frequent, and as a result it became more difficult for those engaged in banditry to continue raiding. Numerous bandits were captured or killed, while others, aware of the government's growing power, curtailed their activities.

Local informants relate that by the end of the fifties the government's power in the Gökcha Hills had grown to the point that it was possible to get the government to intervene in local disputes. Although traditionally the Yomut had relied on self-help in disputes, they were quite willing, when they could, to enlist the assistance of the government on their side in pressing some claim. Thus, when in 1959 the residents of one of the Gökcha Hills obas disputed ownership of a tract of agricultural land located in their grazing territory, the dispute was settled by government intervention. The tract of land was a sizeable level valley bottom in which cultivation was possible, and part of which had originally been cultivated by a man who later migrated south to the Gurgan River. The man's lineage, no longer represented in the oba, was small and unable to prosecute the dispute by either traditional means (threats of violence) or modern means (influence with the government's administrative hierarchy). The local residents called on a wealthy and influential merchant who belonged to the dominant descent group of their oba to assist them. He succeeded in purchasing the land under the regulations allowing sale of crown lands, and in quashing the claim of the original owners under the 1941 law making it possible for original owners of crown land acquired by Riza Shah to reclaim their land. The land is now owned jointly by this merchant and the residents of the oba, and, being level and readily accessible, is cultivated with the merchant's machinery. Given the relative power of the two groups involved, the dispute would not probably have been settled by violence even if the government's intervention had not been feared. Nevertheless, settlement of this dispute by government intervention rather than by traditional means marks a transition in the minds of local people. They claim that since about that time it has been possible to enlist the assistance of the government even against groups including the best armed and most successful of bandits. In fact, as a result of the current effectiveness of government control, those who have good Russian rifles and pistols of Second World War vintage have been hiding them. The much less effective flintlocks of local manufacture, though technically illegal, have not been a source of much concern on the part of the gendarmerie because of their general ineffectiveness. Men carrying them can still be seen in the Gökcha Hills, though not in the agricultural areas to the south where government representatives are in much greater evidence.

The transition from a political milieu in which rights were defended only by self-help to one in which they are enforced by government representatives is, however, a process that is not yet complete among the Yomut, at least not among those of the Gökcha Hills, or those in the agricultural regions immediately adjacent to the pastoral region. Whether or not the government will intervene in a particular dispute depends to some extent on its importance. When the government does intervene, the Turkmen themselves may still attempt self-help at the same time. Disputes over large tracts of valuable land are certain to attract the government's intervention. They are, however, frequently preceded by large brawls between groups representing rival claimants. In such brawls, illegal weapons (guns and large knives) are usually not employed because of fear of government reprisal. Occasionally, however, someone is killed. Although the killer may be jailed, such punishment does not prevent the kin of the victim from seeking vengeance clandestinely. A homicide is often punished twice, once by modern means (imprisonment) and once by traditional means (vengeance homicide).

Small disputes are often talked out in the traditional way, and if they do erupt into violence they do not always come to the attention of government representatives, especially if they occur in such a remote area as the Gökcha Hills. A homicide that occurred in one of the Gökcha Hills obas during my study did not occasion government intervention. It resulted from an argument between two men over which of them should water his sheep first at a well. The two men had been on bad terms for years because one had stolen a goat skin filled with mutton fat and brown sugar, a delicacy among the Turkmen, from the other. The original theft led to an exchange of harsh words on a number of occasions. These bad feelings undoubtedly added to the heat of the argument over the watering of their sheep. Ordinarily such a matter would be readily solved by the younger party's deferring to the older party. In this case, however, an argument ensued, followed by a club fight which left one man unconscious. When the victorious party saw that his opponent was badly injured he fled. Fearing a severe beating in reprisal by the agnates of the injured man, he fled to the camp of a group that was defined as neutral by genealogy and asked for protection, which was granted. His protectors hid him and succeeded in deceiving his pursuers by claiming, when they appeared a few hours later, that they had not seen him. The family that had assumed responsibility for protecting the culprit sent one of its young men the next day to call on the family of the victim to inquire about his recovery, still pretending to know nothing of the culprit's whereabouts. The real purpose of the visit was to determine how badly hurt the victim was so that they could appraise the urgency of the situation for the man whom they were protecting. The report this young man brought back was that they feared for the life of the injured man and that if he recovered he would definitely lose his right eye. This convinced them they had best remove the man under their protection to a more distant oba. They arranged to move him that night to an oba 30 miles distant, and the following night he was again moved to another oba, this one 60 miles away. Meanwhile they also, again at night, packed up his tent and belongings and sent them after him, along with his wife and children. A brother and agnatic cousin of the man also joined him in his distant place of refuge since they felt he needed assistance.

Three days later the injured man died of a brain hemorrhage in a hospital in Gunbadi Kāvūs. The killer was a third agnatic cousin (dörtleinjī arqa) of the man he had killed, so only he himself was a legitimate target of vengeance. The son, agnatic nephews, and close agnatic cousins of the victim were intent on vengeance and no one expressed doubt about what they would do if they could locate the man they were after. However, since all those who knew the whereabouts of the killer were defined as neutral by genealogy, they carefully concealed their knowledge of his location from his pursuers.

After several days of frustration in their search for the killer, they decided to file a complaint with the gendarmerie, hoping that after the gendarmerie had captured the man they would be able to kill him. The thought that such a vengeance killing might well mean a prison sentence did not discourage them. The plan at the time of my departure had, however, not borne fruit. The gendarmerie, evidently considering the affair one of minor importance, made no visible effort to pursue the killer.

Political matters among the Yomut at the time of my first study, especially those in remoter areas, as in the affair above often presented a strange interaction between traditional Turkmen institutions and the modern Iranian administration. Another event occurred during my stay among the Yomut that illustrates this point more dramatically. Two Turkmen living in a community near Ajī Quī were caught by the gendarmerie cultivating opium in a remote valley of the Gökcha Hills. They apprehended the men and announced they would each be given eight years in prison. The agnates of the men felt it was their obligation to assist these men in their "dispute" with the government. As always, the importance of the affair determined the size of the group mobilized. In this instance a lineage of six generations in depth mobilized for each of the men. One lineage consisted of 24 households and the other of 46 households. These two lineages, along with three others, form a large descent group of seven generations in depth, but the other three lineages did not feel their assistance was necessary. The two concerned lineages held a council to discuss the affair and then sent representatives to discuss the matter with the gendarmerie. Clearly they could not threaten violence to resolve the "dispute," but there are other means available for dealing with the government. After discussion with the gendarmerie they reached an agreement: the sentence would be reduced to two years and each lineage would raise a consideration of five thousand tumans for the authorities. Situations like this are responsible for the frequent statements to the effect that in the past a lineage's strength depended on the number of riflemen it could muster, whereas today it depends on their collective wealth. It is important to observe that the traditional pattern of alliance still holds even when government intervention is unavoidable, although the means by which traditional obligations must be fulfilled are altered.

Vambery (1865:359) observed of the Turkmen a century ago:

> Every Turkoman—nay, even the child of four years—knows the taife [descent group] and tire [subdivision of a "taife"] to which he belongs, and points with a certain pride to the power or the number of his particular branch, for that is the shield that defends him from the capricious acts of others. . . .

The Yomut of the Gurgan Plain still take pride in the size of their descent group. One literate Aq-Atabay informant, after reading a discussion of the Turkmen written in Persian in which the civilized qualities of the Jēfērbay were lauded and contrasted with the backward qualities of the Aq-Atabay, complained that accounts of the Turkmen written in Persian always praise the Jēfērbay at the expense of the Aq-Atabay because the Jēfērbay have much contact with the government and with influential Iranians. He added with pride, however, that in fact the Jēfērbay are "nothing" in comparison with the Aq-Atabay who outnumber the Jēfērbay and certainly have greater wealth among their total numbers. If there were a war between the Jēfērbay and the Aq-Atabay, the Aq-Atabay would win easily, he added. When I pointed out that intertribal war was no longer possible he said:

> If there were a dispute between the Jeferbay and the Aq-Atabay, all of the Aq-Atabay would gather at the government offices and their power would be felt.

Another Aq-Atabay pastoralist once told me that:

> Before the government came the Aq-Atabay were the government [meaning they were the most powerful], and when the government went away during the World War the Aq-Atabay became the government again. If the government should go away again, the Aq-Atabay would become the government again. No one [meaning no other Turkmen descent group] can control the Aq-Atabay.

It should be emphasized, however, that these views, and the events described above, are representative of the most conservative elements among the Yomut, those that had remained nomadic up to the time of my first study. How the more sophisticated Yomut, long-settled agriculturalists and urban residents, feel about, or behave in regard to, matters of this sort I do not know.

## IV

## DOMESTIC GROUPS[1]

THE Turkmen conceptualize a household as "a group of people who are united in the preparation of bread." Preparing bread means in this context pooling their labor and economic resources for the satisfaction of all their economic needs. This economic unity is indicated by the fact that the bread, which is the staple of the diet, is prepared daily by the same women from the same store of flour. Their unity is indicated in another way as well. They are subject to the authority of a single head, usually the oldest male of the household, who is also, as a rule, the owner of the capital, livestock and land, from which they make their living. Alternately, a household is sometimes described as a group of people who are "united in expenses," or a group of people whose "property is the same." Occasionally the latter group, "people whose property is the same," is somewhat larger than the group of people "whose bread is one." Sometimes a large extended family owns and manages its property as a single unit, but is subdivided into smaller units for purposes of consumption. In these cases the total income of the group is divided among the subgroups which then act independently in spending their share of the larger group's income. This sort of arrangement often involves extended families that are divided into subgroups living in different communities. Occasionally such units reach an impressive size even though the statistical mean for household size is not especially large. The largest such domestic unit observed had 69 members, divided between two communities, one rural and one urban.

Although households are not purely agnatic in composition, the Turkmen think of them as the smallest unit in their hierarchy of agnatic descent groups.[2] Households are grouped into small named lineages, the smallest segments of the lineage system; these segments are in turn grouped

---

[1] The approach used in this chapter is very much influenced by Goody, 1962.

[2] See Chapter III, note 1.

into larger named descent groups, and so on until the largest identifiable descent group is reached.

The household has more functions than any of the larger segments in the system. It organizes economic consumption and production, and the important business of reproduction and child rearing. It is also, in effect, the primary property holding group. Although pasture, natural sources of water, and unused arable land are owned jointly by larger residential groups and each domestic unit gains access to these resources through its membership in such larger groups, livestock and land under cultivation are, for the most part, the property of individual household heads who administer their capital for their own well-being and that of their dependents.

An important feature of the developmental cycle (discussed below) is the fact that it tends to create households which are somewhat larger in terms of adult labor force than those described for other tribal groups in nearby regions (cf. Barth, 1961). This seems to be an adaptation to the fact that households with larger labor pools are economically more viable. The crucial factor, however, seems to be not maximizing productive effectiveness, but rather minimizing the frequency with which completely unviable households are formed.

## THE NORMAL DEVELOPMENTAL CYCLE

The normal developmental cycle of domestic groups is one in which nuclear family households separate off from patrilocal extended family households. Ordinarily a man leaves his father's hearth and establishes an independent domestic unit when his children approach the age at which they can function as adult economic producers. The newly formed household consists of a nuclear family, which, with the passage of time, eventually grows into a patrilocal extended family. The process of growth is regulated by a number of prescriptive norms. These norms, among other things, dictate that a man shall acquire brides for his sons in the order of their birth, using a portion of the household property for each bridal payment, and that later he shall give each son, again in order of birth, a yurt and a portion of his capital with which to establish an independent domestic group. Thus, each nuclear family develops first as part of an extended-family household before becoming economically independent.

The process of developing the core of a new independent household is prolonged by the fact that marriage is customarily followed by a three-year period during which the bride and groom do not live together and are forbidden any contact with one another. This period is then ordinarily followed by a fourth year in which the bride resides only part of the time with her husband. This practice is described more fully in Chapter VI.

One result of this period of wife avoidance is that usually a man does not have children until the fifth year of his marriage. A young man marries between the ages of 14 and 25, and establishes an independent household between the ages of 30 and 40. Before he establishes his economic independence, a man can expect that his father will buy a separate yurt in which he and his wife and children will lead a partly separate existence for several years. Such a yurt is usually referred to as belonging to the son who occupies it in anticipation of his approaching independence. The way in which such a yurt is used, however, clearly indicates whose property it is. It tends to be used as the general work tent for the entire household. Most of the cooking for the household is done in "the son's yurt." Shelter for lambs and kids during the winter and spring is arranged in this second yurt, and all work requiring considerable space, such as carpet weaving, is done there. Occasionally only this second yurt will be moved with some of the younger men of the family to winter and spring pasture while the father of the family remains year-round in a single location.[3] Nevertheless, this period marks a transition toward independence and provides the son who occupies it a degree of privacy that he has not previously enjoyed.

When a man is ready to establish complete independence, he is given a portion of his father's capital in livestock and land. The precise amount is not rigidly defined and ultimately is at the father's discretion. A number of considerations guide the actual division and they are discussed between father and all of his sons over a long period preceding the division. The amount of capital should be sufficient to support the household. An effort is also made to give each son an equal amount. However, the size of a family's herd varies widely over a period of years, so that Turkmen claim it would be meaningless to apply a rigid formula to the division of the herd at a particular point in time. Usually a plan is reached on the basis of discussion among the adult males of a household that allows the oldest son to separate when the family herd has reached a certain size. Thus, a family consisting of a man with three married sons might agree that the oldest son should become independent when the family herd reaches 160 sheep and goats, at which point the oldest son will take 60 animals, leaving 100 for the paternal household. This decision would then imply that the second son should also take 60 animals when he becomes independent, and the exact time of his separation from the paternal household will again be contingent on the size of the herd.

Agricultural land is usually treated differently, since it is no longer an open resource. If the same hypothetical family consisting of a father with three married sons were to have a plot of agricultural land, the usual arrangement would be for the oldest son to take a precise one-third of the land in anticipation of the need to eventually give equal portions to the remaining sons. Giving equal portions to each son, of course, does not exclude the

---

[3] Only a very small portion of older men follow this pattern, and those who do follow it, do not do so every year.

possibility that a particular son will take more of his share in land than in livestock. However, among the pastoral Turkmen, land is definitely secondary in importance to livestock.

Transactions in livestock are a vital part of each step in the developmental cycle. A family of average wealth spends several years building up its herd in preparation for the marriage of a son, or the establishment of an independent household for one of its sons. Conversely, the marriage of a daughter brings with it a large compensation, which can speed up this process.

The establishment of an independent household (ayrlashmaq) does not dissolve the close relationship between father and son. An independent son generally camps near his father, and cooperation between their households is extensive. Labor, tools, and beasts of burden are shared freely between the two households and, to conserve labor, they may continue to herd their livestock together. The close tie between these two independent hearths is symbolized by a practice known as dadishiq. Dadishiq can best be translated as "mutual feeding." According to this practice, each time a meal, other than simple bread and tea, is prepared at either hearth, a small portion of the food prepared is sent to the other household and is there consumed by one of the women or children of the household. The symbolism implied by women and children habitually consuming food cooked in another household is especially significant. Men travel frequently, visiting and receiving hospitality from a number of hearths. Women and children, in contrast, rarely visit households other than those of immediate neighbors and close relatives. If they consume a meal prepared at a hearth other than their own, it is usually the hearth of some close kin. Feasts, particularly wedding feasts, are the primary exception. Thus, continually providing food for the women and children of another household implies a close kinship tie with that household.

The close tie between father and an independent son also carries with it obligations of economic assistance in times of special need. Once a man has separated from his father he may experience a very different economic fate from that of his father. If, as sometimes happens, one household suffers serious economic losses, while the other prospers, generous aid will flow from the more fortunate to the less fortunate party. Occasionally one or the other becomes completely impoverished. The usual response to this situation is for the two domestic units to merge again.

Extensive economic assistance is often provided between households that are more distantly related as well. Assistance of this sort between brothers, paternal uncles and nephews, agnatic first cousins, and also between close affinal and uterine kin is expected when needed. However, the obligation between a father and an independent son is much greater. This fact is indicated indirectly by the Islamic law, as the Turkmen interpret it, regarding the obligation to give alms, thakat.[4] The amount to be given annually is rigidly divided in terms of a set portion of an individual's property in livestock and income from land. Roughly the proportion required to be given is one-fortieth of one's capital in livestock, and one-tenth of one's agricultural income (see Coon, 1958:109-11 and Lane, 1908:92-93). The law also defines those who may receive such obligatory charitable offerings as paupers, full-time students of religion, and full-time teachers of religion. These offerings are most often given to the closest kinsman who fits one of these designations. The recipient must be a member of another household since a gift within the same household would be economically meaningless. It is also stipulated that the recipient be neither father nor son of the donor. The obligation between father and son in these matters is considered to go beyond the giving of thakat, while, in a strict interpretation of the law, obligation of assistance to other relatives need not go beyond this limit. In point of fact, charity beyond thakat frequently is given to close kin, especially to economically independent brothers, but the implication of the law, as the Turkmen interpret it, is clearly that financial assistance need not go beyond thakat.

The importance of the father-son relationship is reflected strongly in two other institutions relevant to the domestic cycle: the practices of ultimogeniture and adoption. Ultimogeniture is the obligation of a youngest son to remain in his father's household as long as his father lives. This practice assures each man who is fortunate enough to have sons that he will not be left without the service of an able-bodied man in his old age. The youngest son, in effect, is barred from assuming control of his patrimony until after his father's death. His older brothers may each establish an independent hearth, in the order of his birth, each taking with him an equal patrimony, but the youngest son assumes independence only after his father's death, at which time he inherits all of the property that has remained in his father's hands. A special kinship term, korfe, can be, and often is, applied to the youngest son, especially in address, that denotes his special status. This term is used most frequently by his older brothers, although it can be used by the father himself.

Adoption is resorted to when a man has only daughters, or no children at all. A man in this situation is recognized as being at a definite disadvantage. His daughters, if he has any, will eventually marry and live with their husbands, leaving him with only his own and his wife's labor to support himself. The remedy is the adoption of a boy from a close agnate, usually from a man who has a large number of sons. Only close agnates are adopted, and the decision to give someone a son in adoption is considered, to some

---

[4] Thakat appears in most English sources as zakāt or zaka; the rendering used here reflects Yomut pronunciation. Thakat is used both as a generic term for alms and also as a specific term for alms based on livestock ownership as opposed to those based on agricultural income, which are called üshür.

extent, to rest with the entire lineage involved. Ordinarily a lineage of five or six generations in depth is involved in the discussion leading up to the actual decision.

An adopted son assumes, for most purposes, the same role as an actual son in his adoptive father's household. His original genealogical position for political purposes is not changed, however, which is reflected by the fact that he is still referred to as the son (oghil) of his original father, and at the same time, as the adopted son (oghilliq) of his adoptive father. His economic status is the same as that of an actual son of his adoptive father. He loses any right to claim a portion of his genetic father's estate, and instead gains an eventual claim to his adoptive father's property. However, being in the position of an only son, he does not have a right to establish an independent household during his adoptive father's lifetime. An adopted son can, and often does, marry a daughter of his adoptive father, although this is not a necessary consequence of adoption. In cases of such marriage, no bridewealth is necessary, or even possible, since the adoptive father, who stands economically in the position of father of the groom, as well as father of the bride, would have to pay himself. In addition to the bridewealth of 100 sheep and goats customarily given to the father of the bride, 10 sheep and goats are customarily given to the mother of the bride, and a nominal payment, equivalent to about one sheep, is given to a close agnate, usually a paternal uncle of the bride. When an adopted son marries a daughter of his adoptive father, these latter payments are considered especially important, since no marriage can be valid unless some kind of payment is made to some one.

In Yomut society, a man ordinarily profits considerably from the labors of his sons. The practice of adoption is a way of compensating those unfortunate enough to have no sons. The economic importance of sons is a topic which deserves further investigation, which can best be done by comparing the composition of particular households with their economic status. However, it will first be necessary to discuss a few exceptions to the normal developmental cycle.

## EXCEPTIONAL PATTERNS OF HOUSEHOLD DEVELOPMENT

The majority of households follow the ideal pattern of nuclear families breaking off from patrilocal extended families. This means that the majority of households in any particular community contain either a nuclear family headed by a young man, or a patrilocal extended family headed by an older man (see Table 1, p. 91). Most exceptions to this pattern are the result of the premature death of the head of the household. When a man dies leaving behind several sons, none of whom are ready to establish independent households, the surviving sons, as a rule, continue to form a single domestic group, with the oldest brother in the role of household head. Such a group of brothers continues the cycle of household growth and separation much as they would have had their father survived.[5] The oldest brother, acting as head of the family, arranges marriages for any of his brothers who have not yet acquired brides, using part of the family livestock for each bridal payment. The birth order among brothers is still followed to determine the order of marriage and establishing independence. If a widowed mother of such a group of brothers survives, she usually remains with the youngest son, although if convenient she may move to the household of an older son. Such a widow is in no sense considered the head of a household.

A much more awkward situation occurs when a deceased man leaves behind a widow and several immature sons. A boy under the age of about 14 is not considered fully adult, and, therefore, is not capable of assuming the role of head of a household. In such cases the surviving widow often becomes head of the household until one of her sons is mature enough to assume the role. This arrangement is thought of as a means by which a widow can hold her deceased husband's estate in trust for her immature sons. The household and its property are never referred to as belonging to the widow, but rather as belonging to her deceased husband.

Such a situation is difficult in a society in which women ordinarily play only subordinate roles. The awkwardness of having a woman as head of a household arises not only from the inferior status of women, but also from the fact that women are not supposed to have contact with men beyond the sphere of kinship. Contact with non-kin is considered the proper business of men. Still further difficulties arise from the lack of male labor which is necessary to the economic well-being of the household. These problems can be resolved only be calling on the assistance of male relatives of the widow's husband. A widow who heads an independent domestic unit must camp near a brother, or other close agnate, of her deceased husband, who assumes some of the duties of household head on her behalf. This man, with the assistance of his own sons, supplies the male labor necessary to maintain the family's livestock and to cultivate its land. He also acts as a representative of the household in all dealings beyond the sphere of kinship. Such transactions as selling or buying in the bazaar of the nearby city, or arranging a marriage for a daughter require that a man act on the widow's behalf. In these matters, the widow is recognized as having the final say in decisions; her husband's agnate merely plays the role of spokesman and advisor.

An alternate solution to the difficulty arising when a deceased man leaves behind a widow with only immature children is the dissolution of his household. This is most frequently done when only daughters are left behind. When such a household is dissolved, the children usually take up residence

---

[5] The oldest brother, who acts as the head of such a fratrilocal household, unlike the head of a patrilocal extended family unit, cannot disinherit younger male members of the household.

with collateral agnates. The widow herself stays with her children unless she is married off elsewhere. The complicated matter of the disposition of widows is discussed in Chapter VI.

Another variation of the normal domestic cycle is the development of polygynous households. The primary factor militating against polygyny is the high bridal payment required for a polygynous union. The bridewealth for a married man seeking an additional wife is generally three times the amount the same girl would fetch if she were to marry a previously unmarried man. Such a bridal payment is difficult for most families to gather together, and makes little sense in terms of the developmental cycle of domestic households. The capital a man would use to acquire a second wife for himself could be used instead to acquire brides for three of his sons. Only exceptionally affluent fathers would consider such a luxury.

## HOUSEHOLD TYPES IN A PARTICULAR OBA

Now that the developmental cycle of domestic groups has been outlined, it will be useful to examine briefly the composition of the households in the community which formed the focus of my research. The usual definitions of joint and simple households will not be especially useful for this purpose. Rather, the nature of the domestic cycle will be more clearly delineated if households are classified in terms of two criteria: the kinship relations of dependent males to the head of the household, and the marital statuses of dependent males. This emphasis on males in classifying household types is not usual among anthropologists, but it makes sense in terms of Turkmen social structure. Among the Turkmen, the fate of a household is ultimately determined by its male members. A household can grow only by having sons. The marriage of a son is an important step in the process by which a household grows into a lineage; the marriage of a daughter is not. Men are the heads of households, and, as such, are the property holders of Turkmen society. The dependent males of a household will eventually become independent and claim a share of the family property; dependent women have no similar potential claim on their family's property. Turkmen are quick to point out that although wives are essential to the growth of a family, they can be replaced. If a wife dies, a second wife can be found. If a son dies he cannot be replaced. This fact is reflected in the common statement that if one has sons, one can find daughters. It makes sense then to concentrate on the essential male core of a family rather than the female appendages. It also makes sense to classify married men and widowers together since the status of each within a household is very much the same and most widowers under 50 eventually remarry.

The composition of each of the 59 households of Ajī Quī is summarized in Table 1. The table demonstrates that the majority of households in this

## TABLE 1
## COMPOSITION OF AJÏ QUÏ HOUSEHOLDS

| Age of Oldest Male in Household | Part of Ideal Domestic Cycle | | Less Frequent Types | | Unusual Household Composition (premature death of father of family) | | | |
|---|---|---|---|---|---|---|---|---|
| | Nuclear Family | Patrilocal Extended Family | Polygynous and Patrilocal Extended Family | Married Man, Married Patrilateral Nephew | Widow, Immature Sons | Unmarried Brothers | Married Man, Unmarried Brothers | Two or More Married Brothers |
| 60+ | 2 | 9* | 2 | 1 | | | | |
| 50-59 | 5 | 1 | | | | | | 1 |
| 40-49 | 15 | 4 | | | | | 1 | 1 |
| 30-39 | 8 | | | | | | 2 | 1 |
| 20-29 | 4 | | | | | 1 | | |
| 10-19 | | | | | 1 | | | |
| 0-9 | | | | | | | | |
| Total of Each Type | 34 | 14 | 2 | 1 | 1 | 1 | 3 | 3 |
| Number of Individuals in Each Type | 187 | 134 | 29 | 10 | 7 | 4 | 19 | 29 |

*Includes one household consisting of a man with a married adopted son.

community represent stages in the normal developmental cycle of domestic groups.

A few observations should be made about the data in Table 1. There are four nuclear family households headed by men under 30 years of age. Three of these men are in this position because their fathers are deceased and they have no brothers. Their situation is similar to that of the fratrilocal household; the normal domestic cycle has been altered by the premature death of their fathers. The fourth man in this category was thrown out of his father's household with very little property because of differences of opinion. As is typical in such cases, the disinherited son, nevertheless, camps next to his father and receives some economic assistance from his father.

The seven men over 50 whose households have not yet grown into patrilocal extended families have suffered what the Turkmen view as misfortunes. One man has no children; this is the only case of completely sterility in Ajī Quī. Two men had the misfortune of having several daughters, before having any sons, so that the age difference between father and oldest son is unusually great. Three men married late because of poverty, with the same result; two now have sons with brides that have not yet joined their husbands and, therefore, are not yet married by any demographically realistic definition. One man has several daughters and only two sons, who are 13 years apart in age. This has resulted in the oldest son establishing his independence before the youngest son has married. (The youngest son in this case also has a bride who has not yet joined him.)

Another household unusual in its composition is that of an uncle and nephew: an impoverished man who has no brothers and whose father is deceased has been taken into a patrilateral uncle's household. This uncle also has no married sons in his household for reasons similar to those above. His first wife died at a time when he was impoverished and unable to care for his immature son. He placed his son with the boy's matrilateral grandparents in whose household the son then grew up. The son is now in his productive years, but it would be considered wrong for his father to expect that he return now. It is felt in cases of this sort that those who raise a child during his economically unproductive years have a right to claim his labor once he has reached his productive years. Because of his poverty, this man did not take a second wife until long after his first wife's death, and, as a result, his second son is still only 12 years old.

Despite the vagaries of demography and poverty, however, the majority of households fall into the two types expected in terms of the ideal developmental cycle.

## INHERITANCE

The normal developmental cycle of domestic households vastly simplifies matters of inheritance: all but the youngest of a group of brothers receive a patrimony during their father's lifetime, and the youngest brother receives the entirety of the father's residual estate after the father's death. This practice obviously deviates from Islamic inheritance law. Yomut custom and Islamic law are reconciled by the practice of giving shares inherited under Islamic law to the heir designated by Yomut custom. Consider, for example, the case of a deceased man who leaves behind a widow, several independent sons, several dependent sons, and several daughters. According to Islamic law, the widow has a right to one-eighth of her husband's estate, and the remainder is to be divided among the children, giving each son an equal share and each daughter a share equal to one-half of a son's share (Lane, 1908:105-107). According to normal Yomut practices, all of the estate should go to the dependent sons who can either divide it equally among themselves, establishing independent households, or—as is more probable—remain together in a single joint domestic unit. The usual procedure in such a case would be for the widow, the daughters, and the independent sons to give their shares to the dependent sons.

This procedure is not always followed, however. On rare occasions an independent son refuses to grant his share to his brothers who have remained in their father's household. When this happens, it becomes a source of estrangement between the independent son who insists on taking his share under Islamic law and the dependent sons who, as a result, receive a smaller inheritance. Often such an act is an expression of earlier differences between brothers. This estrangement takes the form of reduced willingness to cooperate; usually it does not bring about a complete rupture of friendly relations or assumption of residence in different camps.

When a daughter of a deceased man refuses to grant her share of her father's estate to her brothers a complete rupture of all social relations results. This break in social relations extends to more distant agnates as well, so that a woman who holds to Islamic inheritance law cuts herself off completely from her agnates. In case of serious mistreatment by her husband, a woman can only turn to her brothers, father, and more distant male agnates for assistance; being completely cut off from them is therefore a serious matter. A woman who does not give her patrimony to her brothers also faces the possibility that, if she were widowed, her brothers would insist on reclaiming her and, if possible, marrying her off elsewhere. Such a procedure would separate her from her children, who, if they were no longer nursing, would usually remain with their agnates. Because of these difficulties it is rare for a woman to insist on taking her inheritance, and when a woman does, it is usually a result of strong coercion from her husband.

Most Turkmen women own very little property. When a woman marries, her father usually gives her a small dowry (thep) consisting of clothing, jewelry, carpets, and household utensils. Wealthy men also give their daughters a dowry in livestock (minit), usually either a camel or a cow. The minit can grow to considerable value through natural increase. On a woman's death these items are normally divided among those of her children who are living with her at the time of her death. Her husband generally gives his share to her children, and daughters generally grant their claims to a portion of the minit—if there is one—to their brothers. The majority of married women, however, do not have a minit and their thep is ordinarily of little value.

In general it can be said that Islamic rules of inheritance are bypassed, in effect, through the practice of giving shares prescribed by Islamic law to the heirs designated by Turkmen custom. When Islamic rules are followed at the expense of Turkmen custom it is an expression of unfriendly relations among close kin.

## V

## KINSHIP NORMS AND CATEGORIES

KINSHIP is by far the most important factor regulating the social life of the pastoral Turkmen. Most of their lives are passed in small camps, the majority of which include only close kin among their residents. Frequently when households that are not closely related camp together, a distant, and at times tenuous, kinship tie is discovered and used as the basis of interaction among camp members. Following is a description of the norms, attitudes, and sentiments regulating kinship behavior, beginning with those kinship relations which are most important in determining the form of Turkmen society.

A relationship can easily be suggested between the norms described here and the fact that, in the normal course of the developmental cycle of domestic groups, extended families remain united for purposes of economic production for long periods of time. In any society in which such families are held together, there is a tendency for conflicts to emerge which pull the domestic unit apart. Adult sons do not always accept easily the authority of their fathers and older brothers, and daughters-in-law tend to place the interest of their own children and their relationship with their own husbands above those of the household as a whole. The forms of deference and avoidance described below appear to be significant in reducing the possibilities that such conflicts will actually disrupt extended families.

### PARENT–CHILD

The relationship of a father to his younger sons has a distinct master-servant quality. As a son matures, however, unquestioning obedience gives way gradually to a somewhat different relationship. By the age of 14 a boy is able to perform any form of male labor under the supervision of his father or an older brother. From about this age on a young man begins to share in the decisions of his family. Although the father is the ultimate authority within the domestic circle, other members of the family are consulted before important decisions are made. A boy of 14 is likely to be consulted only in matters especially relevant to his own life, such as the choice of his bride. Older dependent males are considered to have competence in matters relevant to general household affairs. If a man has sons over the age of about 25, he will include these sons in a discussion concerning where and when to migrate, when to sell livestock, and so on. Thus, the transition to the status of an economically independent son is a gradual one.

Father and independent son usually camp together and they have strong obligations of mutual assistance. Once a son has established economic independence the extent of his deference to his father naturally diminishes, but he is nevertheless expected to confer with his father and seek his approval in all important decisions. There are many ways in which those of junior status must defer to those of senior status in all Turkmen social relations, and these matters are most stringently followed in the behavior of sons toward their fathers. Numerous actions which might seem trivial to a foreign visitor in Turkmen country are taken very seriously by the Turkmen themselves as means of expressing senior and junior status in general. A senior individual must always be allowed to speak first and to pass through a door first. The senior of several individuals eating together must reach into the common tray first and must be allowed the choicest portions of the food. His hand must be the last, as well as the first, to reach into the common dish. After eating, the senior person has the prerogative of saying the after-meal prayer and the privilege of performing the after-meal ablutions first. The most junior of several individuals sharing a meal has the obligation of pouring water for the rest while they carry out their ablutions. When two individuals meet, the junior party must give the first greeting (thalom ēleyk) and the senior party must give the second greeting (waleyk). If they have not seen one another for some time (roughly a day or more) inquiries concerning well-being are expected, and in such cases the senior individual must begin the pleasantries. Only after he has finished his inquiries does the junior party ask about the senior's health and well-being. In all matters of this sort it is considered especially important that a son defer to his father.

Only a sober and reserved demeanor is appropriate for a son in the presence of his father. Light conversation and conviviality, which includes smoking and singing, are improper, and joking is strictly prohibited. References to sex are stringently forbidden in the presence of one's father. This prohibition extends to a host of matters that are in some way related to sex. Thus, mentioning one's wife's name or talking to one's wife except to give simple and brief orders is improper in one's father's presence. Bathing is also an improper subject of conversation in the presence of one's father since Islam prescribes a bath after sexual intercourse to restore the ritual purity necessary for saying one's namath, the special prayers that a Moslem must say five times a day. Heating water for a bath and slipping away from the camp site to bathe must be done furtively lest one's father be offended.

Until a separate yurt is bought for a son he sleeps next to his wife in his father's yurt. The impropriety of visible or audible sexual activities complicates marital life for a young man. A man can only have sexual relations with his wife after he is reasonably assured his father and mother, and older brothers as well, are asleep. Once certain of this, intercourse must be accomplished silently lest he awaken and offend his father as well as others from whom he must conceal his sexuality. Young men often confided in me that the whole business was very trying.

The attitudes typical of Turkmen fathers toward their sons combine the expectation of subordination and deference with considerable affection. In addition to their emotional attachment to their sons, there is an awareness that the labor a son performs is of considerable economic value. In his sons lies a man's hope that he may eventually head a prosperous household and his assurance that he will be cared for in his old age. "Sons are the source of wealth" (oghïl dōlēting bashï) is a meaningful proverb among the Turkmen.

The relationship of a young and unmarried daughter to her father is likewise deferent and entails an even stronger obligation of obedience. The prescription of reserved conduct and the prohibitions on joking and reference to sex, direct or indirect, apply as well. The decision as to when and whom a girl should marry is ultimately in her father's hands. This is rationalized in terms of both a girl's obligation to obedience and her inability to bring good judgment to bear on such important matters as marriage. Despite their expectation of subservience, fathers are very affectionate toward their daughters. Because of this bond of affection, the giving of a daughter in marriage is emotionally very difficult for Turkmen fathers, as well as for other members of the domestic group.

It is considered highly improper for a man to discuss his daughter with anyone other than close kin. A man in a circle of people with whom he has had long acquaintance might make brief mention of his daughter. For example, he might observe that his son has gone to fetch his married daughter for a visit. An acquaintance might make a few equally matter-of-fact statements about a man's daughter in his presence, but the range of acceptable comments is very limited. A vague hint of interest in her as a sexual being is extremely offensive. This includes any reference to her physical appearance, or to her qualities as a wife. Extended discussion of a daughter is possible only with close kin. Even with close relatives a daughter's sexuality is a subject to be avoided. Consultation with near relatives concerning giving a daughter in marriage must be circumspect and must be phrased euphemistically.

A father is responsible in a special way for the purity of his daughter.[1]

---

[1] The responsibility of fathers for the purity of their daughters among the Turkmen is similar to that found throughout the Middle East and Mediterranean regions. See, for example, Peristiany, 1965. This responsibility extends to collateral male agnates, and to a woman's husband and his agnates.

A father has the obligation to kill a daughter, even a long-married daughter, if he discovers her in a voluntary act of illicit sexual intercourse. He also has the obligation to kill the male partner to such an illicit act. A father's responsibility in such cases depends on the degree of his daughter's guilt. A daughter who is a victim of rape would not be killed, although the man who raped her would be, if caught.

A society's norms are reflected not only in the way people behave when they wish to be inoffensive and respectful, but also in the way they behave when they choose to be offensive. One of the strongest curses among the Turkmen is the statement, "I should take your daughter." ("Take" has a sexual implication in this context.) Given a man's responsibility for his daughter's purity, it is easy to see why this curse is an especially effective one.

A father's attitude toward his daughter changes in some ways after she is married. After her marriage her father-in-law and, to a lesser extent, her husband assume the position of authority in her life which was previously occupied by her father. For instance, after she is married her father becomes hesitant to apply any form of corporal punishment. Such hesitance stems, so Turkmen say, from the fact that she is now another man's daughter-in-law (gelin). Thus, a girl's status in her father's household during the three-year period of husband and wife avoidance following her wedding is somewhat different from her previous status. However, the general docility of a Turkmen girl in the presence of senior male agnates, especially her father, prevents any great changes in her behavior.

After a young woman has taken up permanent residence with her husband, she returns once or twice a year to her father's household to visit for a week or two. During such visits, a father is extremely hesitant to discipline his daughter in any way and especially indulgent to the grandchildren she brings with her. A married Turkmen woman is much freer in her father's household than she could ever be in her husband's household but, even so, while visiting her father she keeps to the portion of the yurt reserved for women and for most of her waking hours keeps her hands busy with spinning, sewing, the preparation of food, or some other activity thought proper for women. Her greater freedom in her father's household is a relative matter.

The prescriptions that a daughter be reserved in her father's presence and avoid reference to sex do not diminish after she is married. Her father's obligation to avoid discussing her with strangers or distant relatives, and the prohibition on oblique reference to her sexuality, even to close relatives, also remain in effect.

A son's attitude toward his mother, in contrast to that toward his father, entails less deference and greater affection. Thus, while it is thought that a man's obligations to his father are stronger than those to his mother, it is generally expected that his sentimental attachment to his mother will be stronger. Mothers are more indulgent than fathers, and a mother often serves as an effective channel through which a young man can influence his father. Thus, if a young man has any preferences concerning his bride, he will express them to his mother rather than to his father. Obligations to be reserved in one's mother's presence are less stringent, although references to sex are definitely forbidden. It is also important to note that a mother's authority over a son diminishes more rapidly than a father's as he matures. Adult men are expected to be respectful and deferent to their mothers, but not obedient. The relationship of mother to daughter is similarly less reserved and more indulgent than that of father to daughter.

## GRANDPARENT-GRANDCHILD

The norms applying to relations between parents and their children are extended to relations between paternal grandparents and grandchildren. Respect for paternal grandparents should be greater than respect for parents since the former are more senior. The similarity of parent-child and paternal grandparent-paternal grandchild relations are reflected in kinship terminology (see Fig. 17). The term for paternal grandfather, qaqa, is often used, especially in address, to one's own father. The usual terms for agnatic grandchildren in both address and reference are the same as those used for children, although an alternate term meaning grandchild is sometimes used in reference. The most common term for paternal grandmother in both reference and address is eje, the same term used for mother. Occasionally an alternate and more honorific term, oqqaje, is used. As mentioned above relations between maternal grandparents and grandchildren are indulgent and lack the disciplinary and reserved attitudes associated with parent-child relations. This difference is reflected in the use of different kinship terminology (see Fig. 18).

## SIBLINGS

Seniority is the basic factor governing relations among brothers. A younger brother's relationship with an older brother can realistically be described as a more dilute version of his relationship with his father. The dyads, father's brother-brother's son and older brother-younger brother, are the same in terminology and norms. The greater the difference in age, the more closely the relationship approximates that between father and son. Between brothers of approximately equal age there is little deference or expectation of formal respect, but the prohibitions on mention of sex, joking, and convivial demeanor still apply. Competition in sports, such as horse racing or wrestling, is also forbidden among brothers, whatever their relative ages. Even in the case of twins some distinction of seniority is made. The older twin, for example, will be the first to marry and to establish an independent

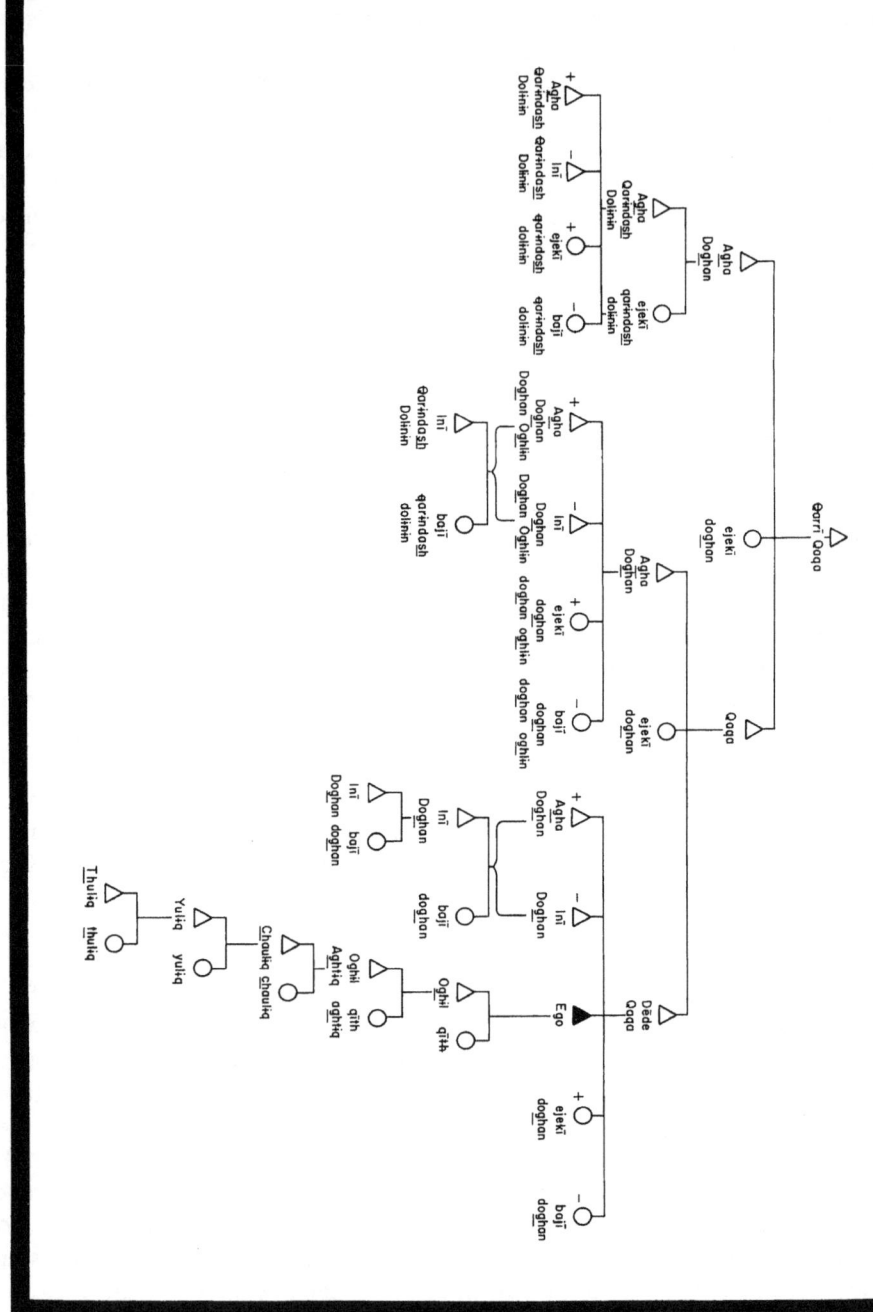

Fig. 17. Agnatic kinship terms. Terms for female ego differ only in one way: the term inī is never used. Lineal descendants of females are, of course, not necessarily agnates, but they are referred to by the terms shown in this diagram. Terms written in different horizontal lines represent alternate terms.

# KINSHIP NORMS AND CATEGORIES

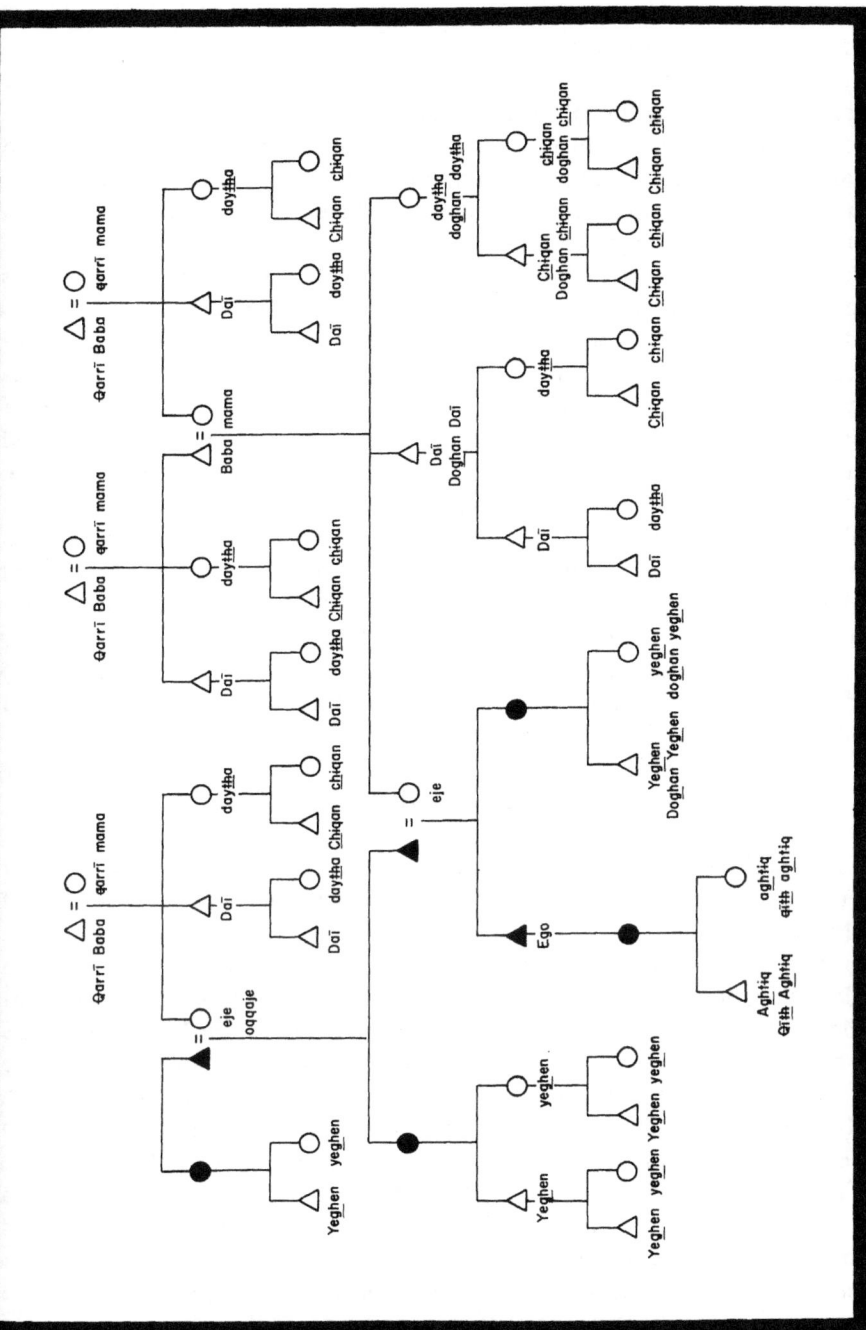

Fig. 18. Uterine kinship terms. Terms are the same for female ego; symbols for linking agnates are shaded. Terms written in different horizontal lines represent alternate terms.

household, and in terms of reference one will be designated "older brother" (agha) and the other "younger brother" (ini).

Relations among sisters follow the same pattern, emphasizing seniority and reserved conduct although the prerogatives attached to senior status are weaker. Relations between brother and sister, like that between parent and daughter, change sharply when a girl marries. While brother and sister are still living in the same household, the elder of whatever sex tends to act as a parental surrogate, as might readily be expected, and as such has the right to discipline younger siblings of both sexes. This is primarily true when there is a considerable difference in age between siblings. However, after a girl is married it is thought improper for her to discipline a younger brother or for an older brother to discipline her. Reserved conduct and complete avoidance of joking and mention of sex are still expected, but the prerogative of discipline is replaced by an emphasis on congeniality. Brother and married sister are expected to speak to each other only in a pleasant tone of voice, and orders must be replaced by requests.

The brother-sister relationship is similar to the father-daughter relationship in that discussing a sister with distant relatives or non-kin is prohibited and reference to her sexuality to anyone is strictly forbidden. These prohibitions lose none of their force after a girl marries. Brothers share with their fathers the responsibility for a sister's purity. The brother-sister relationship also parallels that of father-daughter in providing material for curses: "I should take your sister" is a very potent insult.

## HUSBAND-WIFE

The relationship of husband and wife in Turkmen society can scarcely be discussed without reference to third parties. The relationship is somewhat unusual in that it combines avoidance with sexual access and permitted joking. Which of these seemingly contradictory modes of behavior obtains at a particular time depends completely on whether a third individual is present and who that individual is. If anyone senior to a man is in his presence, he avoids conversation with his wife other than simple, brief orders. The wife herself avoids all those in her husband's household senior to her husband, including guests, by veiling her face and not speaking to them. When such senior individuals are present she avoids her husband as well in the same way.

Turkmen justify avoidance of affines by saying that it is necessary as a way of showing respect, or at times by saying that one feels shame in relation to affines. These are very common justifications for affine avoidance in other societies in which it has been described. The justification for spouse avoidance is different, however. Turkmen say that one avoids one's wife out of respect for, and a feeling of shame in relation to, her senior agnates, not because of feelings relating directly to one's wife herself. A woman's avoidance of her husband likewise is not justified in terms of feelings relating directly to her husband.

When no third party senior to a husband is present, the relationship between spouses is quite free. However, even in this situation husband and wife avoid using one another's name or the reference terms for husband and wife in addressing one another. Grunts and hisses are generally used to gain one another's attention. When individuals senior to a husband are absent, joking between husband and wife is permitted. Though not strictly obligatory, joking of one sort or another is in fact extensive between husband and wife; to a large extent it consists of mild teasing on the part of the husband. When joking with their wives, men often address them as dōth (friend) or eltī (co-wife, or husband's brother's wife) instead of using the usual grunts and hisses. Oblique references to sex are permitted and supply much of the spice for the joking that does take place.

Attempts to fool their wives in one way or another are a favorite form of entertainment among Turkmen men, who enjoy telling other men, provided they are not close relatives and are of approximately the same age, about the ways in which they have deceived their wives. The more fantastic the tale, the better. Of course, some wives are more gullible than others, and some manage to turn the tables on their husbands, all of which is part of the fun. It must be noted that men of approximately equal age who are well acquainted and not closely related can also joke with one another and frequently do. Humor, of course, is relative to cultural context, and what amuses Turkmen is not likely to amuse non-Turkmen. A frequent touch of humor is introduced into conversation between men who can joke with one another by indirect reference to a man's relationship with his wife. A statement such as "You will see Jume Gul [Friday Flower] tonight, won't you?" usually brings a knowing grin from a husband, and such banter is considered good fun in the proper context. When Turkmen indulge in such humor they must always be careful that their senior agnates are not within earshot and also that no agnates of the wife to whom one is referring are present. The prohibition against discussing female agnates diminishes as the relationship becomes more distant. The feeling against discussing female agnates is still quite strong with reference to third agnatic cousins, and is present in milder forms with reference to all agnates that are in one blood. The better acquainted two men are, the weaker the feelings become about discussing more distant female agnates. Norms of this variety are one of several reasons why Turkmen must be aware of the genealogies of people with whom they deal.

Although husbands are free to discuss their wives and even indulge in jokes with sexual implications about them, a man is nevertheless responsible for his wife's sexual morality. A husband must kill both his wife and her partner if he catches her in the act of adultery. Responsibility for a woman's purity and prohibition of references to her sexuality are not the same thing.

Responsibility for a woman's purity concerns only illicit sexual behavior and the responsibility falls on both her agnates and her husband. Prohibition of reference to a woman's sexuality concerns both licit and illicit aspects of sexuality, a prohibition that falls on her agnates, not on her husband.

Husbands have considerable authority over their wives and the right to use corporal punishment to enforce their authority. When a husband is especially displeased with his wife's behavior, the usual reaction is an immediate slap or two across her face. Occasionally a few blows with a piece of firewood or a shepherd's crook serve the same purpose. The behavior of wives is in fact quite subservient and incidents calling for such mild corporal punishment are not common. Prolonged or severe beatings are very rare. Although a husband's authority over his wife is extensive there are conventional limits beyond which he cannot go without arousing the objections of her agnates. He is expected to feed and clothe her adequately as well as to refrain from excessive punishment. It is also considered desirable that affection develop between husband and wife, and in fact it usually does. Often a girl is given in marriage to a boy with whom she is not well acquainted, but this seldom prevents a bond of affection from developing between them, especially if a wife proves a hard worker and a good bearer of children.

The role of wife in Turkmen society, like all social roles, is subject to manipulation. The idea of subservience does not preclude a woman from influencing her husband, and it is generally recognized, though with disapproval, that many women have great influence over their husbands.

## AFFINES

Distinctions of senior and junior status are as important in affinal relations as they are in agnatic relations. Both husbands and wives avoid all who stand in the relation of senior agnate to their spouse. The more senior a particular individual is to one's spouse, and the closer the relationship of that individual to one's spouse, the more obligatory avoidance becomes. Thus, avoiding parents-in-law is more imperative than avoiding siblings-in-law, avoiding a brother-in-law is more important than avoiding a sister-in-law, and avoiding a father-in-law is more obligatory than avoiding a mother-in-law.

The obligation to avoid affines weighs more heavily on women since a woman usually joins her husband while he is still a part of his father's household and spends at least the first decade of her married life in her father-in-law's yurt. A man, in contrast, never lives in his father-in-law's household and usually finds himself in a separate camp group throughout most of his married life.[2] For this reason it can be said that the father-in-law

---

[2] An adoptive son (oghillïq) who marries his adoptive father's daughter is, of course, an exception to this statement.

daughter-in-law bond is structurally the most critical affinal tie. The status of daughter-in-law, like most kinship and affinal ties, can best be explained not as a single status, but as a series of statuses through which a married woman passes. The norms relating to a woman's behavior toward her affines are extremely elaborate. A married woman's obligation to avoid her father-in-law is strongest in the earliest part of her marriage. During her earliest contacts with her father-in-law she throws a cloth over her head completely covering her face. Ordinary female Turkmen garb leaves only the face, neck, hands, and feet visible. Thus, a single large cloth added to the usual female garb leaves nothing visible except her hands and feet. While veiled in this way a girl cannot see and needs someone to guide her. At her wedding an older brother's wife (or a wife of some other older male agnate)—that is, a woman defined as her yenge—leads her. During the year in which she alternates between her father's and her father-in-law's yurts, and for about the first month after permanently joining her husband, her guide is a younger sister of her husband (or a more distant younger female agnate of her husband). In the early period of residence in her father-in-law's household, she must veil herself in this manner from all members of the household senior to, or equal with, her husband including wives of older brothers, and from her husband as well when any of her husband's seniors are present.

During this early period of married life a gaily decorated curtain, known as a tuti, is hung across the northwestern portion of the yurt behind which the bride can sit with her face uncovered. (Yurts are always placed with their doors facing south, and the various internal divisions of the yurt, which have highly conventionalized social uses, are often designated in terms of compass directions). At night she sleeps with her husband behind this curtain, and while the two of them are alone behind this curtain they can talk to one another in whispers. During the daytime, the new bride occupies herself with visiting and with sewing, the only sort of work that can easily be performed behind a tutī. Members of her husband's household and camp who are junior to her husband make a special point of visiting with a new bride during this period since it is recognized that this can be a difficult and lonely time in a woman's life. Residents of nearby camps who are junior to her husband also emphasize visiting the new bride. Although both males and females junior to her husband make these visits, the majority of the visitors are female.

The process by which a bride adopts less restrictive forms of affine avoidance is a very gradual one which can be traced through many stages. In a sense, her return to her husband's household three years after the wedding marks the first transition, the abandonment of complete spouse avoidance. A new bride spends the fourth year following the wedding alternating between her natal and affinal households, and at the end of the fourth year she joins her husband permanently. The tutī is used continuously during the fourth year while the bride is in her affinal household and for about the first month after she joins her husband permanently. After this the tutī is used only at night when the bride and groom sleep behind it, and when the bride changes clothing or combs her hair. The rest of the time affinal avoidance takes a less restrictive form known as bürünmek. Bürünmek refers specifically to a manner of veiling which consists of covering the face below the eyes with a cloth, and then pulling one's head cloth down over one's forehead in such a way that only a slit is left open for the eyes. A new bride who is practicing bürünmek also tries not to let anyone senior to her husband see her eyes. She does this by sitting close to and facing the wall of the yurt while sitting indoors and by holding her head cloth with her hand in such a way as to block the view of individuals she is avoiding while she is moving about.

The next transition occurs, as a rule, after the first child is born. (In cases of sterility, the same transition occurs somewhat later.) After giving birth to a child, a woman ceases the practice of bürünmek, and adopts a less confining form of affinal avoidance called yashmaq. Yashmaq refers to a type of veiling in which only the mouth is covered.[3] The degree of avoidance associated with yashmaq entails concealing one's mouth and not speaking to, or eating from the same dish, as the person avoided. The sort of avoidance associated with yashmaq is not reciprocal. A father-in-law and a mother-in-law can speak to their daughter-in-law in order to direct labors and frequently do so. If necessary for her work a daughter-in-law can respond with hand motions, nods of her head, or by whispering to a junior individual who can relay her communications. After reaching this stage in her marital career, a wife gradually relaxes and eventually abandons her avoidance of co-wives of her husband's older brothers, and also her avoidance of husband's older sisters who pay occasional visits to their natal yurt. Avoidance of husband's older brothers and of husband's more distant senior agnates is relaxed but rarely abandoned. Thus, a woman who has been married many years usually practices a very sloppy yashmaq toward her husband's older brothers which consists simply of holding the corner of her head cloth between her lips, not speaking to them, and concealing her mouth more fully when she speaks to someone else in their presence, or when she is eating. Yashmaq in regard to a mother-in-law similarly reaches this relaxed form without ever being fully abandoned. A woman's avoidance of her father-in-law follows a similar pattern

---

[3] The Turkish cognate yaşmak also refers to veiling, but in this case the sort of veiling prescribed by Islam (see Lane, 1908:181-183 and Arberry, n.d.:49-50). Despite the similarity of form, the veiling of women prescribed by Islam and that prescribed by Turkmen custom are quite different. Roughly speaking, Islam prescribes that a woman should veil herself from all men except those whom she cannot marry according to the incest prohibitions. Turkmen custom prescribes that a woman veil herself, and in other ways avoid, all men and women who are both senior to her husband and socially close to her husband. The Islamic prescription is based on modesty, the Turkmen on "respect" for affines.

without becoming quite as careless. A Turkmen woman who has been long married usually is continually readjusting her yashmaq, tucking it carelessly between her lips while her mother-in-law is on the other side of the yurt, pulling it up a bit as she approaches, pulling it fully across her mouth as her father-in-law enters the tent, and so on.

A woman's relationship to her husband's juniors contrasts sharply with her relationship to his seniors. The visiting mentioned above between a wife and her husband's junior agnates during the early stages of a marriage is the beginning of social ties that are indulgent and affectionate. The relationship that develops with the females of this category tends to be an especially affectionate one. This relationship, designated by the kinship terms yenge and baldith (see Figs. 19 and 20), is especially associated with the early stages of marriage in two ways. When a girl is taken to her husband-to-be's household on the day of her wedding, none of her agnates can accompany her. It is, however, obligatory that she be accompanied by two women who stand in the relationship of yenge to her. These yenges stay with her during the two or three days that she spends in her husband's household and then return with her to her father's domestic group. Three years later when she rejoins her husband, again her yenge will ride with her on the bridal litter, although this time her agnates as well will accompany her. After rejoining her husband, during the first one to three years of her life with her affinal group, most of her social contact will be with young girls of her husband's domestic circle to whom she herself stands in the relation of yenge.

After avoidance of wives of husband's older brothers has ceased, a woman gradually develops a relationship with these women which is reserved and deferent, but less so, for example, than the relationship between brothers. The term of reference used for this category of affine, eltī, is the same as that used between two wives of the same husband. However, the relationship between wives of the same husband tends, not surprisingly, to be more deferent than that between wives of brothers.

Affine avoidance is much less burdensome for men, because as mentioned earlier they usually reside in different camps from their affines, and also because it is more easily relaxed and even completely abandoned with the passage of years. A married man's avoidance of affines is usually described with the verb qachmaq, meaning "to escape," and this word conveys fairly accurately what is involved. Accidental encounters with a father-in-law—except in cases where avoidance has been abandoned—cause a man to turn and run in a state that one could easily interpret as fear. The actual emotion involved is occasionally described as fear, more frequently as shame. While he is maintaining avoidance, it is out of the question for a man to be in the same yurt as his father-in-law or to pass within speaking range on the road; it is possible, though somewhat unusual, for a man to be in the same large crowd, as at a wedding, with his father-in-law so long as he does not come

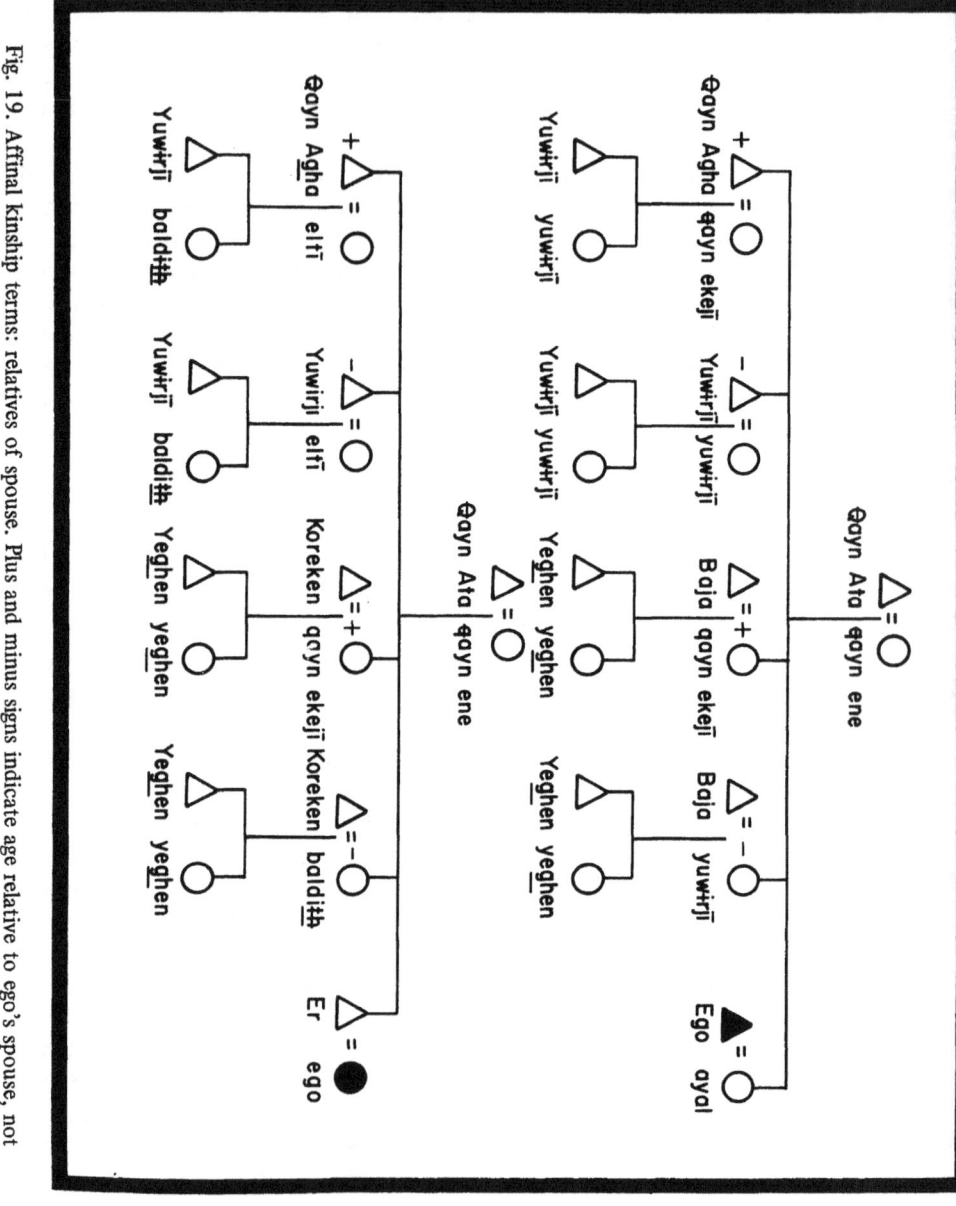

Fig. 19. Affinal kinship terms: relatives of spouse. Plus and minus signs indicate age relative to ego's spouse, not relative to ego.

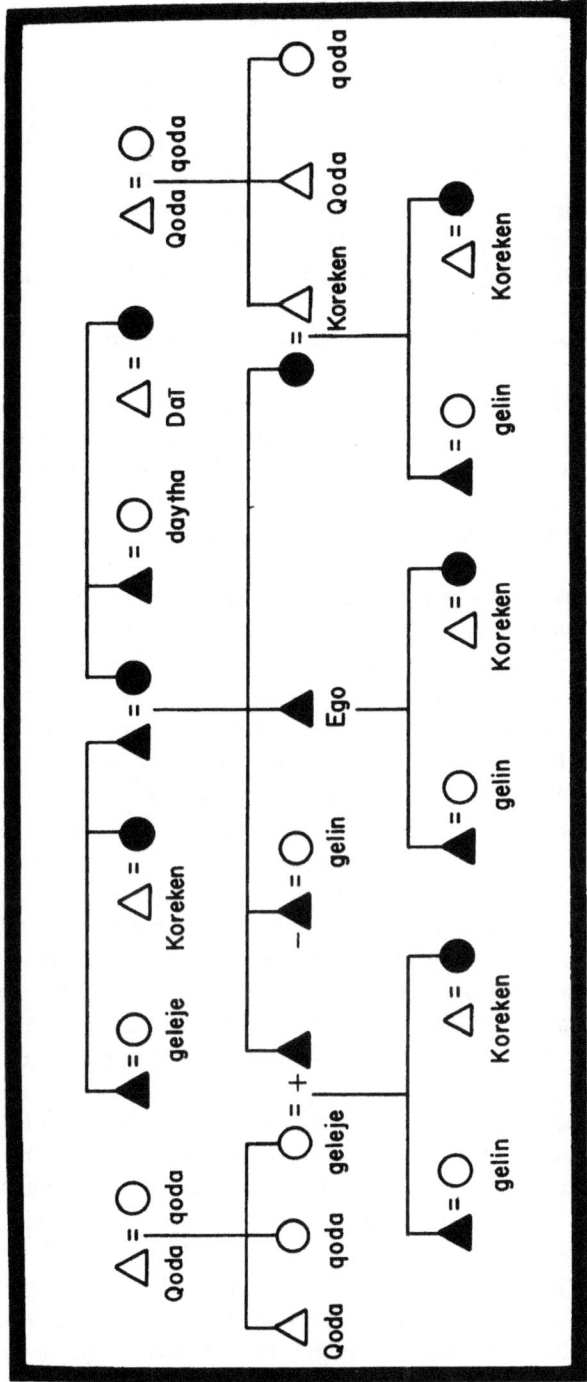

Fig. 20. Affinal kinship terms: affines of consanguineal kin. For female ego, the terms shown differ only in that geleje is replaced by yenge; symbols for linking cognates are shaded.

within the range that would ordinarily require a greeting between kin or acquaintances that do not avoid one another.

Most men avoid both father-in-law and mother-in-law in this way as long as these affines live. Avoidance of sisters-in-law and brothers-in-law is usually abandoned after a number of years of marriage. The variables of sex and seniority play an important role in these matters as in most Turkmen affairs. Cessation of avoidance of women and of men closer to one's own age occurs earlier than that of more senior men. Most affines when they encounter a man married to their sister invite him "not to escape from them." Such invitations are usually proffered for several years before being accepted. A man or woman makes similar invitations to a daughter's husband, but these are very rarely accepted.

Affine avoidance as practiced by Turkmen men also enjoins avoiding one's father-in-law's tent whether one's father-in-law, or any other affine who must be avoided, is in it or not. A number of Turkmen behavioral norms are justified in terms of "respect for yurts." (Among settled Turkmen one respects houses as readily as yurts. It is clear that it is not yurts in particular, but domiciles, that are respect-worthy.) It is frequently said that one cannot argue with someone as freely in a yurt as in the open or in an urban bazaar because such behavior is disrespectful to the yurt. Thus, it is not surprising that Turkmen claim that one must respect not only affines, but also affinal tents; in both cases respect is expressed by avoidance.

Avoidance of affinal yurts can actually be observed most frequently in relation to grandfather-in-law's yurt. The consistent emphasis on greater respect for more senior individuals is naturally manifested in the notion that greater respect for agnatic grandfather-in-law is required than for father-in-law. Greater respect in this instance means greater obligation of avoidance. This fact is combined with the fact that after a man dies, the yurt he passes on to his youngest son is still considered in some sense his yurt and is occasionally referred to as such. It is also at times referred to as the old yurt (qarrī öy) of the small lineage consisting of the descendants of the original owner of the yurt. Thus, a man avoids the qarrī öy of his wife's lineage even though it may be inhabited by a younger brother of his wife who need not himself be avoided.

A father-in-law has the option of putting an end to his son-in-law's "escaping" from him by sending—through a third party—an invitation that his son-in-law come to his tent to join him for tea or for a meal. A formal invitation of this sort is taken more seriously than a casual invitation not to flee after a chance encounter. After receiving this type of invitation, all avoidance of one's father-in-law and his tent, as well as avoidance of mother-in-law and brothers-in-law, ceases. (Avoidance of grandfather-in-law's tent might, however, continue for a while.) In the vast majority of cases of first-cousin marriage (agnatic or uterine), the father-in-law eventually does send such an invitation. As the consanguineal tie of husband and wife becomes more distant, the propensity of fathers-in-law to exercise this option decreases so that in the overwhelming majority of cases in which husband and wife have no close consanguineal relationship the option is not exercised. The prerogative of putting aside avoidance also exists in relation to a daughter-in-law, but in such relationships, its exercise is extremely rare, even in cases of first-cousin marriage.

In those instances in which a son-in-law has been formally invited to his father-in-law's tent and all avoidance has ceased, he must, as with his own father, be especially reserved in his father-in-law's presence and must avoid scrupulously any reference to sex. After avoidance has ceased, it is possible that a man might be in the presence of both his father-in-law and his wife at the same time. In these instances it is obligatory for husband and wife to avoid each other. The wife must veil herself from her husband (ya<u>sh</u>maq), not speak to him, nor eat from the same dish as he. He must similarly avoid talking to, or referring to, his wife. This practice parallels a young man's avoidance of his wife in his father's presence.

A man's relations with his wife's junior agnates is an indulgent and friendly one. In contrast to a woman's situation, however, a man has much less contact with this category of affine and attaches less importance to his relations with them.

An affinal relationship is recognized between a man and his wife's sister's husband. Men who have taken their wives from the same household refer to one another as "baja." Relatively little importance is attached to this relationship, although it is expected that the two men will be amiable with one another. Joking and reference to sex are permitted between men in this category. Like distant relatives or non-kin these men can compete with one another in wrestling or horse racing.

The two persons primarily responsible for arranging a marriage are the father of the groom and the father of the bride. The final decision concerning the formation of a marriage rests with these two, although both consult with and are usually influenced by their own wives and sons, and to some extent by their brothers. There are, of course, exceptions: when one of the prospective spouse's fathers is deceased an older brother, or another older agnate, acts as surrogate; older men, usually widowers, conduct marriage negotiations on their own behalf. The normal situation, however, is that described above. The affinal category of qoda (see Fig. 20) includes all relatives of the groom and all relatives of the bride who conceivably might be consulted concerning the decision to form a marriage. Thus, all senior agnates of both spouses and the mothers of both spouses are qoda to one another. Those linked to one another in this way are obligated always to be pleasant and hospitable toward one another. References to sex and joking are prohibited between them, but there is no special need for great reserve in one another's presence. Rather emphasis is on all avoidance of hostility, sharp words, blunt commands, and similar actions.

A number of formal rituals between qodas are described below under the heading of ceremonies surrounding marriage. In addition informal visiting between qodas is frequent. This relationship is one aspect of an alliance between two households formed by marriage. In many ways it parallels other ties uniting the same two households. The relationship between brother and married sister carries with it the same emphasis on congeniality. Eventually, if the marriage bears fruit these same two households will contain individuals united by uterine ties. Uterine kinship is likewise characterized by congeniality.

## UTERINE RELATIVES[4]

The amicable nature of relations with mother's family and with sister's children contrasts sharply with the reserve required in relations with agnates. This is because authority and seniority, which are so important in agnatic relations, play a very small role in uterine kinship. A child first becomes acquainted with his mother's family when he, as a child, accompanies his mother on visits to her natal home. As stated earlier, his maternal grandparents treat him very indulgently although they do at times have the prerogative of exercising moderate authority over him. Relations with mother's brothers are equally indulgent and when a sister's child reaches adulthood his relationship to his mother's brother lacks the shadow of authority found in the tie to uterine grandparents. Prohibitions on joking and references to sex which play such a large role in Turkmen kinship also apply to kinship ties traced through females. However, reserve and subordinate conduct required in the presence of senior agnates is replaced by a relationship emphasizing mutual congeniality. In the numerous situations mentioned above requiring recognition of one party or the other as senior, a man does defer to older uterine kin, especially to grandparents. Mother's brothers, however, do not wield authority and are not apt to issue sharp, blunt orders to her children.

The consanguineal tie with mother's brother and the reciprocal link with sister's son are very close relations and most individuals throughout their lifetime maintain the habit of periodically visiting relatives of these categories even if they live at a considerable distance. This pattern of visiting ordinarily does not extend to mother's sisters who are usually married into households of different camp groups, and often of different obas, than mother's brothers. The same is true of sister's daughters once they leave their natal households to live with their husbands. In general, it can be said that Turkmen make little

---

[4] Uterine is often used to designate kinship traced *only* through females. In this book, however, it means any form of kinship traced through *at least one* female link.

effort to maintain contact with uterine kin other than male agnates of one's own mother and sons of one's own sister. Often contact is maintained because of proximity. However, if such relatives do not live nearby, contact is usually not maintained by periodic visiting.

In the light of this fact it is not surprising that the relationship between sons of sisters is not considered an especially close one. A special effort to maintain an active relationship with individuals of this kinship category who live at a distance is rare. If individuals related in this way live near one another, they are likely to visit one another frequently and to be willing to assist one another in numerous ways. If not, the relationship tends to fall into abeyance.

## THE CONTRAST BETWEEN AGNATIC AND NON-AGNATIC KINSHIP

There is a sharp contrast in the obligations entailed by agnatic and non-agnatic ties. Turkmen make a sharp distinction between two sorts of assistance. One variety of assistance expresses friendly relations with another individual without expressing hostile relations toward any third party. Frequent assistance of this sort constitutes an alliance with someone but not an alliance of two individuals against a third individual. The giving of women in marriage, of economic aid in times of need, of hospitality, honoring another person by attending his wedding or funeral, all are examples of this type of assistance, which might be labeled economic and social aid.

The second variety of assistance, which can be characterized as political aid, involves assisting someone in a dispute against a third party. Assistance in disputes, whether large or small, is a strict obligation among agnates. The closer the agnatic tie and the more important the matter under dispute the greater the obligation to assist. The extent of the obligation to assist is to some extent influenced by the rightness or wrongness of the claim one's agnate is pressing in his dispute. When one's rights, as Turkmen conceptualize them, have clearly been violated it is easier to muster support among agnates than when one's complaint against another is less clearly justified.

Uterine and affinal kin are not obligated to assist one another in disputes, and in general it is thought most proper that they not assist lest they drag their own agnatic group into the conflict. In the case of very close uterine kin there is sometimes a conflict between norms and sentiments in these matters. Instances in which a mother's brother or sister's son attempts to aid someone clandestinely in prosecuting a dispute are not infrequent. This seems much less often to be the case among close affines.

In disputes it is possible that close uterine or affinal kin might be obligated by virtue of the agnatic tie to take opposite sides in a dispute. In such cases, the person in a situation of conflict between sentiment and formal obligation often reacts by advocating a peaceful solution to the dispute among his own agnates. Another common reaction in such cases is to refuse to take an active part in the dispute at all.

To explain fully the contrast between these two types of kinship ties, it is useful to speak of social alliance and political alliance.[5] The first can be defined as an obligation of assistance that does not involve conflict and that cannot be described as assistance against some third party. The second can be defined as assistance of one person in prosecuting a dispute—by peaceful or violent means—against a third party. The first includes only cooperation; the second, both cooperation and conflict, both allies and opponents.

In Turkmen society, close agnatic ties require both types of alliance, whereas distant agnatic ties call only for political alliance. Close uterine and affinal ties entail only social alliance, while more distant ties of these varieties incur no obligations at all.

These two types of alliance are distinct in another way. Social alliances can be weakened or even fall into abeyance because of disagreements or disputes between the parties involved. Political alliances cannot be diminished by such disagreements. Thus, if two brothers or a father and son argue violently and afterwards are no longer on speaking terms, their social obligations—hospitality, economic aid, dadishiq, and so on—will cease. If the disagreement is serious enough it may never be repaired. However, their political obligations to one another are not altered. One informant related an experience which illustrates this point nicely:

> I had a violent argument with my father and he threw me out of his house with nothing at all. Two days later my father had a dispute with someone. I went and found that person and beat him. I beat him furiously. After I had done this, I was still on bad terms with my father. But, I had to fight for him; he's my father, after all.

The statement is one reflection of the fact that Turkmen social structure allows very little room for choice in matters of political alliance, as opposed to those of social alliance. The fact that options are limited in the political sphere is reflected in the careful reckoning of degrees of agnatic kinship. Distinctions of closeness and distance in the sphere of patrilineal kinship correspond to political obligations. One must ally with one's father against a brother, with a brother against a cousin, and so on, corresponding to degrees of kinship. Choice to the extent that it is observable relates to the degree of support, rather than to who is supported. One can refuse to support a brother against a cousin because one's cousin is in the right; one can in such a situation advocate privately to one's brother that he desist from his dispute, but one cannot openly ally with a cousin against a brother.

---

[5] See Chapter III, note 9.

It is also important to note that there are only two acceptable reasons for offering limited, or no, support to an agnate involved in a dispute: the proposition that the claim the disputant is pursuing is not justified, or that the matter is of too little importance to demand one's assistance. Thus, the fact that one has fought violently with an agnate does not diminish one's obligation to support him in a disagreement with more distant agnates, or strangers. As mentioned above genealogy also defines certain individuals as neutrals in a dispute, and as, therefore, having an obligation to minimize the conflict in whatever way possible. These political positions are not influenced by social alliances, which inevitably follow a different pattern.

In order not to be misleading it must be emphasized that open conflict is not a part of daily camp life. The Turkmen place great emphasis on avoiding all actions or discussions that might lead to conflict. When hints of conflict arise, those who are neutral by genealogy take their obligation to preserve the peace very seriously. The general impression the Turkmen make on an outside visitor is one of remarkable harmony. This impression is all the more remarkable in light of the ruthlessness with which they do pursue their political obligations once violent conflict has broken out.

## THE EXTENSION OF KINSHIP

The above discussion has been primarily concerned with relations among close relatives. The manner in which more distant kin are treated deserves some elaboration. Agnatic kinship entails detailed reckoning of degrees of closeness, but the full method of reckoning degrees is quite complex. Lineal kin, as alluded to above, are considered closer than all collaterals. This is reflected in the fact that the terms for lineal kinsmen are never extended to collaterals, although the terms for lineal agnates can be shifted up and down the generations (see Fig. 17). Collaterals removed from lineal kin by only one generation are prohibited as marital partners and constitute the next degree of agnatic kinship (represented by the term doghan). This category includes siblings, father's siblings, and brother's children. Within this category of kin one's own siblings are to some extent recognized as closer than parent's siblings and brother's children, and can be distinguished as "own siblings" (öth doghan) from "father's-sibling siblings" (dēdeming doghanī doghan). It is common to make these distinctions when introducing kinsmen to someone who does not know their genealogical position. The remainder of categories of collaterals can be distinguished simply by counting generations. When two agnates wish to reckon their degree of patrilateral kinship they do so by reckoning the number of ancestors linking them to their common ancestor. If they have a common grandfather they are doghan oghlin; if they have a common great grandfather they are dolinin; the next degree is simply dörtleinjī arqa ("fourth generation"), and more distant agnates are designated simply as "my fifth generation," "my sixth generation," and so on. Frequently the number of generations linking two individuals to their common ancestor is different in their respective lines of descent. In such cases, the relationship is that designated by the more distant line (see the relationship of ego to his dolinins in Fig. 17). The significance of the seventh generation is defining rights of blood vengeance has been discussed above.

Responsibility for the purity of female agnates extends in attenuated form over a wide range. The obligation to kill a woman guilty of sexual transgressions falls primarily on those closest to her, and strong sentiments about such transgressions extend only to second or third cousins. However, a right to act as surrogate in executing a female offender against the code of purity extends to all agnates in one blood with the woman.

Because of the possibility of falling victim to blood vengeance for the homicide of a distant agnate, many Turkmen are secretive about their genealogies above the fifth generation. This is especially true if they reside separately from their distant agnates and there is some hope of actually succeeding in obscuring their genealogical position. It is often only with considerable difficulty that an anthropologist can pry loose details concerning the remoter generation of precisely remembered genealogies. Individuals who are in positions of considerable political power—because of their influence with the government—are often conspicuous exceptions and are quite willing to broadcast their seven ancestors. Specific ancestors beyond the seventh generation are usually not remembered. What is remembered is that one's seventh-generation ancestor was a member of a particular named descent group. How many generations separate the last remembered ancestor from the founder of this named group is not known. However, this named group is part of a hierarchy of larger and larger descent groups based on a theory of descent but an admittedly incomplete genealogy. Genealogical information on these larger groups is never sensitive. These larger groups and the precise nature of the genealogy on which they are based has already been discussed (see Chapter III).

Affinal kinship tends to be recognized only over a very short range. Usually the first or second cousins of a man's spouse are the most distant ones with whom he will recognize any affinal tie. During the first few years of married life, he may avoid these relatives of his spouse, but as a rule, he will quickly accept their inevitable invitation that he not "escape" from them. Afterwards his recognition of an affinal tie will be reflected when he is in their presence by reserved conduct and by avoidance of references to sex or to his wife. A woman extends avoidance farther and continues the practice over a longer period of her married life. In general a woman avoids all people who enter her husband's camp group who are of approximately equal status with or are senior to her husband, unless they are more closely related to her than her husband. Thus, she avoids temporary guests in her husband's household, or other households in his camp group, who have no kin tie to her husband, if they are approximately the same age as, or older than, her husband. Similar treatment is given to non-kin residing permanently in her husband's camp group. In other contexts—in her natal household, or while visiting other camp groups for feasts—she avoids only those who have some more permanent tie to her husband, his agnates, current residents of his camp group, and close associates of any sort of her husband. Again avoidance of men associated with her husband is more important than avoidance of women. After many years of marriage, among women a wife ordinarily avoids only her mother-in-law and close agnates, or camp-mates, of her husband who are of her mother-in-law's generation.

Uterine ties as mentioned above are more active if only a single female link is involved rather than two. Among mother's agnates effective ties, or links which are cultivated through frequent visiting and which can serve as a basis of substantial assistance, usually do not extend beyond mother's brothers and mother's brother's sons. The term daī and its female counterpart daytha are extended to all collaterals of uterine ancestors (see Fig. 18), but distinctions of a closeness can and sometimes are made. Thus, mother's actual brother can be called doghan daī ("sibling mother's brother"),[6] while mother's brother's sons, and father's mother's brother can be labeled yaqin daī ("close mother's brother"). More distant relatives of this category tend to be designated as dashkī daī ("distant mother's brother"), when distinctions of this sort are made. However, the dividing line between "close" and "distant" mother's brothers is in no way precise. Only the designation doghan daī has a precise, generally-agreed-upon meaning. The terms doghan yeghen ("sibling sister's child"), yaqin yeghen ("close sister's child"), and dashkī yeghen ("distant sister's child") follow the the logical pattern as reciprocals of the terms above (see Fig. 18).

The term chiqin is used for all descendants of a woman defined as daytha. Distinctions of the kind discussed above are rarely made since the relationship is not very important. However, the term doghan chiqin can be used to designate the closest relative of this category, mother's sister's child. The adjectives yaqin (near) and dashkī (distant) can be used in a way similar to those for the more important categories of "mother's brother" and "sister's child."

Recognition of uterine kinship of any real consequence tends to extend, like that of affinal kinship and in contrast to agnatic kinship, over only a small range of close relatives. This would not, however, be immediately obvious to a newcomer among the Turkmen. Uterine kinship terms are used in address over the widest conceivable range as a means of politeness in dealing

---

[6] The terms included in parentheses are literal translations of the Turkmen phrases, intended to illustrate the use of word doghan ("sibling," or "born") to designate close kinship ties.

with people who are in fact considered either distant agnates or not relatives at all. If one's mother belongs to a descent group that is distant from one's own, all people agnatically closer to one's mother can be called daī or daytha. Thus, many Yomut can count all of the members of one of the large subdivisions of the Yomut as his classificatory mother's brothers or mother's sisters. Such a descent group may include as many as 10,000 members. When two Yomut who do not know one another meet for the first time, they inevitably inquire about one another's descent groups. In such cases it is not unusual for two strangers to discover that they stand in the relationship of mother's brother and sister's child or in the relationship of sisters' children to one another. After this discovery they address each other by the appropriate terms. However, this is only politeness and entails no obligations beyond those extended to any other Yomut without such a relationship. Affinal terms which would imply reserved conduct are not extended beyond the narrow range in which actual obligations of an affinal variety are recognized.

When unrelated individuals, or distant agnates, are in frequent contact with one another, they attempt to find any tenuous uterine tie they can which they then use as a term of address. Thus, one frequently hears uterine kin terms in address. If one inquires of a Turkmen what his relationship is to the numerous people he addresses as uterine kin, he will often answer that there is no kinship tie at all. If then asked why the uterine term is used in address, some distant and tenuous connection is produced to justify the term. Such an answer is likely to be followed by a statement to the effect that the relationship is too distant to have any real importance.

## THE PLACE OF DECEASED ANCESTORS IN THE KINSHIP SYSTEM

Among the Turkmen, a number of practices tend to keep the memory of deceased ancestors alive among their descendants. Death among the Yomut is followed by a number of ceremonies expressing mourning. Many of these rituals are also believed in some way to serve the welfare of the deceased. Among these is the practice of commemorating a person's death with a special feast (ölen gun thadagha). This practice, known as "keeping death days," is most elaborate during the first year after death. A feast is given on each of the first seven days after death, while mourners are coming to pay their respects. Again the tenth day, the day marking one month (in the Islamic calendar) after death, and the fortieth day* after an individual's death are marked by similar feasts. Each following day which marks the passage of a month since death is commemorated in the same way until the anniversary of the person's death is reached. Thereafter the anniversary of that individual's death is commemorated each year by a feast. The obligation to perform these expressions of respect for the deceased falls on the next of kin, for practical purposes, on the sons of the deceased. A son or a group of sons continues these feasts for a deceased father or mother throughout the remainder of their own lives.

A second practice has a greater effect, however, in keeping the memory of the deceased alive. This is the custom of giving the deceased's name to the next child of the appropriate sex born in that family. This child is then addressed in the manner appropriate to the deceased. Thus, after a man dies, the next male child born to one of his sons will be given his name. All of the deceased man's sons will then address this boy as dēdem, "my father." Their wives, including the boy's own mother, will address the boy as kēbem, a term meaning parent-in-law which is restricted in usage to persons with inherited names. Similar usages are extended to other kinsmen and even to outsiders. Thus, the boy's siblings and first agnatic cousins will call him qaqam, "my father's father." Grandchildren of the deceased through the female line will call him babam, "my mother's father." Distant agnates will address him by name, but will add the honorific dēde (father) to the end of his name as they would have in addressing the deceased.

This usage is extended to kin terms of reference as well. Inquiries as to kinship relations in cases of persons with inherited names yield such responses as so-and-so is "my brother and my grandfather's name." In situations where such precision is not called for, the referent appropriate to the deceased alone is usually used. Thus, a man asking a third party to fetch his son who bears his father's name would say, for example: "Tell my father to come here." Since all names are passed on as soon as the opportunity arises, a fairly large portion of Turkmen bear such names, and daily discourse is liberally sprinkled with what appears to be references to, and address of, deceased ancestors.

These usages of address and reference are not reciprocal. Thus, a man who bears his grandfather's name and who is addressed by his brothers as qaqam ("my father's father") does not respond with oghlim or aghtighim ("my son," or "my grandchild") but rather with terms appropriate to their actual relationship to him.

Names of remoter ancestors also survive as a result of repeated inheritance, and such names are then referred to as "ancient names." Men, or boys, bearing the names of remote ancestors are addressed as qarrī qaqa by the agnatic descendants of the original bearer of the name. This is the kin term appropriate to an agnatic ancestor more remote than a grandfather. Names of women are similarly passed on by their sons to one of their granddaughters, and because of repeated inheritance female names can belong to remoter ancestors than grandparents of the name bearer. However, the remoter histories of female names are forgotten, in sharp contrast to the treatment of names of male ancestors. This is not surprising since remote female ancestry, unlike remote agnatic ancestry, has no social significance.

Names of those who do not have direct descendants are passed on by their collaterals, with the exception of those who die in infancy. However, little importance is attached to them, and people bearing such names are usually not addressed by kinship terms.

One exception exists to the practice of addressing bearers of inherited names in the manner appropriate to the original bearers of their names. This applies to spouses of the deceased. Husband and wife are forbidden to address each other either by name or by the kinship terms for husband and wife. Hisses and grunts are the usual ways of gaining a spouse's attention. When a person's spouse dies, and his, or her, name is inherited, the manner of address described above is not used in addressing the new possessor of the name. Rather the forms of address and reference appropriate to the actual relationship are used.

The two practices described above are related to individual ancestors and have the effect of keeping alive the memory of such ancestors, and of social links through that ancestor to other living people. There are, in addition, a few practices which are related to all ancestors in general. The most formalized of these is a practice known as petir kethmek. Petir is a kind of thin hard bread, and kethmek means simply "to cut." The custom of "cutting petir" consists of cutting several loaves of this bread, which are round and flat like all Turkmen bread, into eight equal sections each, and then sending pairs of wedge-shaped pieces of bread to the houses of nearby kinsmen, and other neighbors. This is done after sunset on Thursday, which in Turkmen reckoning is the beginning of Friday, a day of special religious significance for Moslems. The beliefs behind this practice exist in two forms which can be described as the ordinary and the intellectual version of the same belief. The ordinary version is that repeated by most Turkmen which maintains that at sunset on Thursday, that is, at the beginning of Friday, all of one's ancestors are hungry and have their eyes on the road awaiting the sending of petir to kinsmen and neighbors by their descendants. The custom of cutting and giving paired wedges of petir somehow satisfies the hunger of awaiting ancestors. The intellectual version is that repeated by religious teachers which states that the dead cannot be hungry for food, but rather are desirous of religious merit. Giving of any kind earns merit which the giver can keep for his own benefit, or can give to the deceased. The merit accrued by giving petir is, according to this more intellectual rationalization, given to awaiting ancestors.

One effect, at any rate, is again to remind the living of their ancestors, and, as in the custom of dadishiq described above, the practice defines a radius of close kith and kin surrounding each household. The circle of households included in petir kethmek, which many households practice weekly, is slightly larger than the circle of households included in the more frequent practice of dadishiq.

One other practice is believed to have the same effect of satisfying the hunger—or desire for religious merit—of deceased ancestors. After meals a prayer in Arabic is always recited, by men at least, and following the prayer the statement "we give" (bēkhsh etdik) is added in Turkmen. Saying this prayer satisfies hungry ancestors who have been watching their descendants eat. A similar prayer which is believed to have a similar effect is said each time a Turkmen sees a gravestone, although in this case the occupant of the grave rather than the ancestor of the person praying receives the benefit of the prayer.

These practices are seldom associated with any fear of ancestors, but rather a simple concern for their well-being, although most Turkmen will agree that gross neglect of these duties might arouse their ancestors to some sort of harrassment of their descendants.

## SLAVERY AND KINSHIP

Slave raids, directed primarily against the Kurdish population in the vicinity of Bujnurd, continued until the pacification of the Yomut in 1925. Only children were captured in these raids, and those so taken were either kept by their captors or sold to other Yomut. Thus, numerous individuals currently living among the Yomut were slaves in their youth, and the general social status of slaves is still well remembered. Slaves assumed a position in their owners' households which might be described as that of second-class sons or daughters. Slaves performed the same labor as ordinary sons and daughters and a bond of affection developed between slave and master. Female slaves were given in marriage for the same brideprice as other brides and once married were treated much the same as any other wife. A man could, if he chose, provide a male slave who had reached adulthood with the means for an independent existence and set him free, a process similar to that of establishing an independent household for an acutal son. If his master did not do this, a slave gained his freedom after his master's death. The slave, however, did not have a position among actual sons of his owner rigidly determined by age. It was not necessary that he assume a position ahead of younger sons of his owner in being provided with a bride, or that he be granted independence ahead of younger actual sons. Usually he received a smaller "patrimony" than ordinary sons. Thus, his position was similar in terms of duties, but somewhat less advantageous in terms of privileges. For political purposes he assumed a position similar to that of an actual son. His owner and sons of his owner, as well as more distant agnates of his owner, would defend him in disputes against outsiders, and he was expected to reciprocate. Descendants of slaves assumed a position in the system of political alliance analogous to one they would occupy had their slave ancestor been an actual son of his master. The social alliances implied by agnatic bonds also extended to slaves, although in an attenuated form. Thus, Yomut of slave origin were accorded a place in the kinship system, although not one precisely the same as that of other Yomut. The descendants of slaves, either in the male or female lines, are defined as a distinct social category, designated "qul," in contrast to "īgh," Yomut having no slave ancestry. (The female counterpart of qul is qirniq and that of īgh is bīke.) The status of qul is said to be inherited indefinitely, although it is hard to know for certain whether or not large and powerful descent groups of slave origin have insinuated themselves into īgh status. There are, however, large descent groups whose genealogies stretch beyond the range of precisely remembered genealogies (beyond seven generations) who are reported to be of slave origin and all of whom are defined as qul. Like men of slave origin, or their recent descendants, these descent groups have a precise position in the segmentary lineage system. This position is based on the assumption that the founding ancestor of the group was a slave of a man belonging to some named descent group on a level higher in the hierarchy of descent groups.

Among the Yomut the categories of slave origin and non-Yomut origin are merged. In the days of slaving and at present as well, Yomut occasionally take wives from neighboring Welayet or Göklen villages. Such wives are defined as qirniq and their children, and remoter descendants, are defined as qul or qirniq.

These two social categories, qul and īgh, are relevant to the rules governing choice of marriage partners, which will be discussed in the next chapter, and also to rules regulating blood vengeance. The rule regarding vengeance is basically that in reckoning blood debts, two quls equal one īgh. Thus, two men of qul status must be killed to satisfy the blood debt created by killing one īgh.[7]

## THE PROMINENCE OF THE FATHER-SON RELATIONSHIP

Some of the ideas developed by Francis Hsu (1965:638-661) provide insight into the kinship system of the Yomut. In this article, Hsu points out that different kinship systems give prominence to particular dyads within the nuclear family, and that "when a relationship is thus elevated above others it tends to modify, magnify, reduce or even eliminate other relationships in the kinship group." Relationships of special prominence are labeled "dominant relationships" by Hsu and the characteristics of these relationships are designated as "dominant attributes." Using this terminology Hsu proposes the following hypothesis: "the dominant attributes of the dominant relationship in a given kinship system tend to determine the attributes and action patterns

---

[7] The data gathered on blood feuds indicate that the rule equating two quls with one igh for purposes of vengeance is in fact seldom followed. The rule concerning marriage between those of pure Turkmen descent and those of slave origin is, in contrast, largely adhered to; data on marriage between these two groups is presented in Chapter VI.

which the individual in such a system develops towards other relationships in this system as well as towards his relationships outside of the system" (1965:641). In father-son dominated kinship systems, other kinship dyads tend to take on the attributes of the father-son dyad, which Hsu describes as continuity, inclusiveness, authority, and asexuality (*ibid.*:642-645). By continuity Hsu simply means a tendency to preserve kinship ties over a long period of time. Concern about ancestors and accurately remembered genealogies are manifestations of this attribute. The concomitant ramification of social relations is the attribute which Hsu labels inclusiveness. Authority and asexuality need no explanation. After discussing these attributes, Hsu provides a more specific description of the characteristics of a father-son dominated kinship system:

> The parents will have more to say about their son's future wife than the son himself .... married partners in this system seem aloof to each other, for they often place their duties and obligations towards parents before those towards each other. Custom will strongly disapprove of any sign of public intimacy between spouses. Instead it enjoins them to exhibit ardent signs of devotion to their (especially his) elders. In case of a quarrel between the wife and the mother-in-law, the husband must take the side of the latter against the former, especially in public. Polygyny with the ostensible aim of begetting male heirs to continue the father-son line is a structural necessity.
>
> Yet in spite of all this the marital bond in a father-son dominated system tends to endure. Divorce is possible but rare. The attribute of continuity and the attribute of authority militate against the dissolution of the marital bond. Continuity means that all bonds including the marital bond are likely to last once they are formed. Authority, with all that it implies toward the past and the superiors, means that the pleasures or displeasures of the married partners are less important considerations for staying together than those of their elders or of the kinship group as a whole according to tradition.
>
> This form of kinship is likely to be associated with a strong cult of ancestors and a maximum tendency for the development of the clan (*ibid.*:648-649).

It is obvious without detailed discussion that the kinship system described in the present study conforms closely to the pattern Hsu outlines. One word of warning, however, does seem necessary. Hsu has been strongly influenced in his description of father-son dominated kinship systems by the characteristics of the Chinese kinship system. Similarities between Chinese kinship and the kinship systems of Altaic-speaking peoples may be a result of common historical influence rather than of an inherent tendency flowing from the prominence of the father-son dyad within the kinship system.

A detailed test of Hsu's hypothesis is beyond the scope of this study. Hsu traces the characteristics of kinship systems to the process of enculturation within a nuclear family which gives prominence to one particular dyad. Because of the prominence of a particular kinship relation to an individual during the period of his life in which he is enculturated, he extends the behavior patterns associated with that dyad to other kinship dyads. A hypothesis of this sort will inevitably provoke controversy since it offers psychological explanations for social phenomena. However, it does seem possible to separate Hsu's method of classifying kinship systems from his hypothesis for explaining these systems. Without either accepting or refuting the portion of Hsu's hypothesis conerned with enculturation, it does seem useful to observe that particular kinship systems, such as the Yomut kinship system, do have the complex of characteristics described by Hsu for father-son dominated systems and to recognize that these characteristics are closely interrelated.

The primary virtue of Hsu's characterization of kinship systems, assuming that most systems can be classified in terms of a dominant dyad, is that it characterizes a kinship system in terms of the predominant mode of interpersonal behavior associated with it. Thus, in the case of the Yomut, obedience to lineal ascendants and respect for senior collaterals, especially agnatic collaterals, occupy a central position in the kinship system. More particularly, a dependent son's most basic duties are those to his father; his other social ties, in particular his relationship with his wife, are in no way allowed to interfere with his obligations to his father. Whatever else one may see in the elaborate requirements that a son conceal his sexuality from his father and that a daughter-in-law conceal her person from her father-in-law, these forms of behavior do prevent a man's wife from distracting him from his obligations to his father. In his father's presence, a son must be attentive and must not only ignore his wife but also avoid any suggestion that he has the attribute of sexuality that might lead to some form of devotion to her. His wife must cooperate by concealing her face and avoiding conversation with either her husband or her father-in-law. In a similar fashion a man's duties to his mother and older brothers are placed above his devotion to his wife. Seen in these terms the association of respect for seniors with concealment of sexuality makes sense as a way of elevating a man's obligations to his seniors above his concern for his wife. The Yomut seem to overemphasize what Hsu has referred to as disapproval "of any public intimacy between spouses."

A man's avoidance of his father-in-law prevents him from intruding into the affairs of his affinal household. Avoidance of not only a father-in-law, but also of his tent, seems significant in this way. Thus, affine avoidance as practiced by men has a similar effect of preventing the marriage bond from disrupting the internal discipline of domestic groups.

One point not suggested in Hsu's article of 1965 should be observed about the prominence of the father-son relationship in the Yomut kinship system. The qualities Hsu describes as authority and asexuality are significant primarily in the domestic sphere, whereas those described as continuity and inclusiveness are significant primarily in the political sphere and hence are more relevant to a discussion of the corporate structure of Yomut society. Since this study is concerned primarily with domestic groups and the network of kinship ties uniting individuals, it is more concerned with the attributes Hsu has designated authority and asexuality. The interpretive aspect of this study is concerned with the economic functions of the kinship system, and in discussing these functions, considerable attention is focused on the division of Yomut society into independent property holders and dependents. The modes of behavior associated with authority and asexuality can be seen as means of supporting the division of society into independent household heads and dependents. In evaluating the effect of these modes of behavior, it must be borne in mind that authority, other than that recently imposed by the government, does not exist among Yomut pastoralists above the household level. The point was made above that a man owed respect, but not obedience, to senior collaterals. Such respect entails the same prohibitions concerning evidence of sexuality as does the obligation of obedience to one's father. Nevertheless, the respect shown senior collaterals has very different consequences than the obedience of a son to his father, or of a daughter-in-law to her father-in-law. These differences reflect the division of Yomut society into economically autonomous households.

## KINSHIP NORMS AND DOMESTIC GROUPS

Among the Yomut, each domestic household regulates its own affairs with a high degree of autonomy. It is true that closely related households often cooperate in their economic labors, especially in herding. However, such cooperation is arranged between household heads on the basis of mutual agreement, and any head of a domestic unit who is not satisfied with some cooperative arrangement can withdraw and make an alternate agreement with different households. It is also true that there are obligations of assistance toward kinsmen who find themselves in economic or other difficulties. Strictly obligatory assistance is, however, limited in extent and does not greatly curtail the right of each household head to dispose of his property as he sees fit. Assistance beyond what is strictly obligatory is common between close kin, but such assistance is ultimately voluntary and is based on the expectation of a continuing relationship of mutual support. This again implies mutual satisfaction. When, for one reason or another, estrangement develops between heads of domestic units who are close kin, each is free to withdraw any or all forms of cooperation other than the political obligations entailed by the agnatic bond. Such estrangement is not common, but the possibility of such alienation and withdrawal of support is an important consideration in all interaction between members of different domestic groups, whether household heads or dependents.

This fact is reflected in the rules regulating behavior between kin. Within the domestic household there is an emphasis on discipline. Discipline is a strong component of both the parent-child and the husband-wife relationships. Between a father and an economically independent son there is still a measure of authority. However, with the exception of father and independent son, it is only possible for separate domestic groups to cooperate on the basis of mutual consent, implying again a strong need for mutual satisfaction in dealings between separate households. This need is expressed in the norms governing social ties that cut across households. Senior collateral agnates are accorded respect, but not obedience. A man respects his father-in-law in a way that allows little room for conflict. The relations of father to married daughter, and brother to married sister, as well as uterine ties, emphasize congeniality and willingness to cooperate without authority.

There are two basically different varieties of social relations involved in the distinctions pointed out here. The difference stands out most clearly in the contrast between a man's relationship to his wife and to his married sisters (see Levi-Strauss, 1963:41-49).

One informant summarized this contrast as follows:

> If I want my wife to do something I simply tell her to do it. Whether she wants to or not does not matter. After all, a wife has no business other than serving her husband. If my wife annoys me, I hit her. It is no one else's business to ask me why I hit my wife. If she is dissatisfied with the way I treat her, it is no fault. But with my sister it could never be this way. She must always be satisfied with the way I treat her. If I want her to do something, I must ask with a pleasant tongue. I must always speak to her with a pleasant tongue. A man's sister is very dear to him.

One thing reflected in this contrast is the fact tht the husband-wife relationship falls within a single household, whereas the relationship between brother and married sister falls between two autonomous households. In all personal ties cutting across households, it is felt that each party must be satisfied with the way the other treats him, or her. Any action that offends one party must be compensated for in some way, perhaps by some extra favor, if friendly relations are to be preserved. The tie of father and independent son is, of course, a partial exception. Relations within the household are predicated on authority rather than mutual cooperation; there is no requirement that subordinates be satisfied with the treatment they receive from their superiors. The relationships of father to dependent son and husband to wife clearly fall in this category.

# VI

# MARRIAGE

AMONG the Yomut, the ties created by marriage have little social significance beyond the range of two closely related groups of households. In many societies which anthropologists have studied, marriage plays an important role as a form of alliance between two lineages. Among the Yomut this is conspicuously not the case. As pointed out above, marriage does not form a political alliance between the groups involved. Marriage does create a very important social alliance, but one involving only very shallow lineages, lineages whose household heads are united by a common father or grandfather.[1] Its greatest significance lies at the household level. Decisions concerning marriage rest ultimately with the heads of two households, although close kinsmen in other households are, as a rule, consulted. The bridewealth is usually raised entirely by the groom's household and the bulk of the wealth given remains in the bride's household. The bridewealth itself creates an economic burden for poorer families leading to delays in marriage. The possibility that such delays are a form of population regulation is discussed at the end of this chapter.

## CHOICE OF MARRIAGE PARTNER

Proscriptions concerning marital partners are precisely those defined by Islam: parents, parent's siblings, siblings (including both matrilateral and patrilateral half siblings), and siblings' children. Although of little practical importance the prohibited degrees also include all ascendants and their siblings, all descendants, all descendants of siblings, and father's and son's wives. Marriage is also forbidden with one's wet nurse, or with anyone who would be forbidden if the wet nurse were one's actual mother.

Among the Yomut, marriage is not prescribed with any category of kin, although there are generally agreed-upon preferences. These preferences are different for wife takers and wife givers. Giving a daughter or sister in marriage is difficult emotionally both because of the loss of the girl and

---
[1] See the distinction between social and political alliance made earlier (pp. 113-114).

because of concern for her welfare in her husband's household. Therefore, it is not surprising that Yomut would rather give their women to close kin on the assumption that in a case of marriage to close kin a girl would find the adjustment to married life easier. The generally stated preference is for any category of kin, with closer kin being preferred to more distant kin. They also prefer to give a daughter to a husband who is approximately the girl's age. The older the husband in relation to the girl the less desirable the match. Previously unmarried boys are much more suitable than widowers, and both are more desirable than married men. Giving daughters to distant agnates or unrelated neighbors and acquaintances is not disapproved of and is quite common. Giving daughters to complete strangers is highly disapproved of, although such matches do occur. When a girl is given to a complete stranger there must be a mutual acquaintance of the two parties to act as go-between and to vouch for each party to the other. Marriages of this sort usually involve poor families as wife givers, families in dire and immediate need of the bridewealth offered. Frequently the wife seekers in these cases are looking for a bride for a boy who has some disability—lameness, blindness, or some other less desirable quality. Child marriage is allowed, though not especially approved, and when a man seeks a child bride for an infant son he often takes her from strangers. In such cases the period of husband and wife avoidance extends until both partners reach puberty.

Men seeking brides for their sons state somewhat different preferences. They are primarily concerned about acquiring a girl who will be healthy, a hard worker, and a good bearer of children. Taking a bride from a family one knows well is, therefore, preferable since one has a better chance of appraising a girl's probable qualities as a wife. Fertility and a propensity to produce more sons than daughters are thought to be hereditary and are given consideration in seeking a bride. Physical characteristics are thought to be inherited equally from both parents and, therefore, large, strong females are preferred as wives since they will produce better sons. Plumpness is also a desirable quality since it is a sign of good health. A child is believed to derive much of his character from his mother, and for this reason girls believed to be of good character are also preferred.

From the wife taker's point of view the ideal age for a bride is in the range of 12 to 14, whatever the age of the husband. In seeking brides for previously unmarried boys, Yomut consider only previously unmarried girls, except in cases of leviratic marriages, which are discussed below. When seeking a second bride for a widower or a second wife for a married man, preference is also given to previously unmarried girls, although considerations of bridewealth often overcome these preferences.

In discussing these matters, Turkmen are quick to point out that there is a large personal element in any choice of marital partner. Turkmen do not simply seek the closest kinswoman of the appropriate age. Efforts to appraise a girl's qualities as a wife and purely individual likes and dislikes play an important role in these choices.

Young men have some say in the selection of their brides. Occasionally a young man forms a romantic attachment to a particular girl and tries to persuade his father to seek that girl as his bride. Such attachments are not, however, always a prelude to marriage, nor is a young man's preference of this sort always respected by his father.

Preferences for close kin on the part of wife givers are stated to apply primarily to a daughter's or sister's first marriage. These considerations are given little weight in accepting or refusing requests for a widowed daughter or sister in marriage. Table 2 summarizes the consanguineal relations between bride and groom for all existing marriages and most of the recently terminated marriages in Ajī Quī which represent first marriages for both partners. Table 3 summarizes the same data for current and recently terminated marriages in Ajī Quī which represent second, or later, marriages for at least one of the partners.

A distinction is made between Yomut of foreign or partly foreign origin, which usually means slave origin, and Yomut who putatively have only Yomut

TABLE 2
CONSANGUINEAL RELATIONSHIPS OF WIVES TO HUSBANDS
IN AJĪ QUĪ FOR FIRST MARRIAGES

| Kinship Category (Actual or Classificatory) | Consanguineal Kin of Known Genealogical Connection Degree of Kinship | | Putative Agnatic Kin[2] | Non-Kin (Yomut) |
|---|---|---|---|---|
| | First Cousin | Second, or More Distant, Cousin[1] | | |
| Father's Brother's Daughter | 11 | 25 | | |
| Mother's Brother's Daughter | 12 | 1 | 21 (14%) | 64 (44%) |
| Father's Sister's Daughter | 7 | 2 | | |
| Mother's Sister's Daughter | 1 | 1 | | |
| Totals | 31 (21%) | 29 (20%) | | |

[1] The high frequency of marriages with agnatic cousins is largely an artifact of the practice of tracing kinship links much farther through the male line.
[2] This category consists of women who have no genealogically demonstrable tie to their husbands, but to whom their husbands would apply agnatic kin terms of reference because they share membership in a named descent group throughout which agnatic kinship terms are extended in reference. Agnatic terms of reference are usually extended only among members of the smallest descent group above the level of precisely remembered genealogy; such groups vary greatly in size, with most of them falling in the range of 500-2000 people.

## TABLE 3
### CONSANGUINEAL RELATIONSHIPS OF WIVES TO HUSBANDS IN AJĪ QUĪ FOR SECOND MARRIAGES

| Kinship Category (Actual or Classificatory) | Consanguineal Kin of Known Genealogical Connection | | Putative Agnatic Kin* | Non-Kin, Non-Yomut | Non-Yomut |
|---|---|---|---|---|---|
| | Degree of Kinship | | | | |
| | First Cousin | Second, or More Distant, Cousin | | | |
| Father's Brother's Daughter | 1 | 2 | | | |
| Mother's Brother's Daughter | | | 4 (10%) | 27 (69%) | 5 (13%) |
| Father's Sister's Daughter | | | | | |
| Mother's Sister's Daughter | | | | | |
| Totals | 1 (3%) | 2 (5%) | | | |

*See note 2, Table 2.

## TABLE 4
### FIRST MARRIAGES AND NON-YOMUT DESCENT IN AJĪ QUĪ

| Female Partner | Male Partner | |
|---|---|---|
| | Īgh (Pure Yomut Ancestry) | Qul (Non-Yomut Ancestry) |
| Bīke (Pure Yomut Ancestry) | 38 | 3 |
| Qirniq (Non-Yomut Ancestry) | 2 | 107 |

ancestors. The norms are different for wife givers and wife takers. It is preferable for igh men, men of pure Yomut ancestry, to take only bike wives, that is wives of pure Yomut ancestry, and those of mixed ancestry to seek wives of equivalent status. Bike daughters and sisters, however, should never be given to men who are not of pure Yomut origin. An examination of actual marriages in Aji Qui reveals that the preference for endogamy is largely followed, but that the theory of hypergamy, in Aji Qui at least, is not reflected in actual marriage choices: marriages between those of pure Yomut origin and those of mixed origin violate the norm as frequently as they conform to it (see Tables 4 and 5). The small number of such marriages recorded makes it

TABLE 5
SECOND MARRIAGE AND NON-YOMUT
DESCENT IN AJĪ QUĪ

| Female Partner | Male Partner | |
|---|---|---|
| | Īgh (Pure Yomut Ancestry) | Qul (Non-Yomut Ancestry) |
| Bīke (Pure Yomut Ancestry) | 9 | 4 |
| Qirniq (Non-Yomut Ancestry) | 1 | 19 |
| Göklen Turkmen | 2 | 2 |
| Welayet | | 1 |
| Unidentified | 1 | |

difficult to draw general conclusions concerning the frequency of marriages between pure and mixed Yomut. However, that occasional violations of the norm of hypergamy do occur is quite clear.

Similar norms of preferred endogamy and permitted hypergamy are stated for the Yomut as a whole in relation to what are seen as inferior groups, Göklen Turkmen, and Welayet. Among the Welayet, those whose mother tongue is a Turkic dialect are preferred because they are able to adjust to life in a Turkmen household more readily. The evidence available indicates that these norms are followed more rigorously than those regarding marriage between pure and mixed Yomut. All marriages recorded in Ajī Quī between Yomut and non-Yomut are hypergamous (see Table 5), as are those recorded elsewhere (see Table 6). Inquiries over a wide area concerning such marriages indicate that most Yomut can readily point to marriages that violate the rule of hypergamy between īgh and qul Yomut, but that most are unaware of any violation of the norms regarding marriage with non-Yomut. Giving Yomut women to Welayet is even more strongly disapproved of and only one instance of such a marriage came to my attention. This was a case of a Yomut girl marrying an Azerbaijani Turk: the daughter of a Turkmen member of the Iranian parliament eloped while studying at the University of Teheran, and as a consequence was disowned by her father. The fact that this occurred among a family that represents the extreme movement away from traditional Yomut

TABLE 6
MARRIAGE AND SACRED DESCENT: THE CASE OF THE QARA MAKHTUM

| | Both Partners Qara Makhtum | One Partner Qara Makhtum and One Partner Ewlad Other than Qara Makhtum | One Partner Qara Makhtum and One Partner Ordinary Yomut | Male Partner Qara Makhtum and Female Partner Göklen or Welayet |
|---|---|---|---|---|
| First Marriage for Both Partners | 53 | 8 | 10 | |
| Second Marriage for One or Both Partners | 4 | 4 | 10 | 8 |

life, and the severity of reaction to the marriage, reveals the strength of feeling regarding these marriage rules.

There are also special marriage preferences concerning the sacred descent groups (Ewlad) mentioned in Chapter II. The Ewlad prefer to marry among themselves, and this preference finds expression in the fact that bridewealth in marriages between Ewlad equals only three-tenths of the bridal payment customary among ordinary Yomut. Marriages between ordinary Yomut and Ewlad of the Yomut are not forbidden, however, and when they do occur entail the usual bridal payment of 100 sheep and goats. Table 6 summarizes data concerning 97 marriages occurring among a lineage of Ewlad, the Qara Makhtum,[2] who live on the Gurgan River 20 miles to the south of Aji Qui. Among the Ewlad, as among ordinary Yomut, the distinction is made between īgh and qul. The lineage represented in Table 6 was founded by a qul who is either six or seven generations removed from most living adults of the lineage. Thus, they are all defined as qul and all of the marriages recorded in Table 6 are marriages in which both parties are qul. As is also evident in Tables 2 through 6, preferences for endogamy influence first marriages more than later marriages.

## ENDOGAMY AND AGNATION

The preference of various tribal groups in the Islamic world for lineage endogamy has puzzled a number of anthropologists who have assumed that unilineal descent groups are by their very nature exogamous (see Murphy and Kasdan, 1959:17-29 and 1967:1-14; Patai, 1965:325-350). This particular

---

[2] Qara Makhtum is a fictitious name.

characteristic of the Yomut, and most other Islamic tribal groups, may appear less unusual if cognizance is taken of the fact that societies vary extensively in the degree of their reliance on affinity as a mechanism of social integration. Robin Fox (1967:228-230) has observed that kinship systems can be arranged along a continuum in terms of the degree of their reliance on marriage as a means of integration. Some systems, notably in Australia, Oceania, Southeast Asia, and South America, rely very heavily on the affinal bond as a basis of social solidarity. Other societies, notably in Africa, the Middle East, and Central Asia, place greater emphasis on descent as a means of creating social solidarity.[3] Among the first group of societies, a description of the marriage system often comes close to being a complete description of the kinship system. Among the second, those societies that emphasize descent, a description of the descent system often provides the main part of any description of the kinship system. Marshall Sahlins (1968:63) has observed that among some societies that emphasize lineage as a means of social integration, or more particularly political integration, there is a prohibition on parallel marriage, that is on more than one marriage between the same lineages. Sahlins interprets this as a means of diffusing the affinal ties of lineage members so that when a dispute arises with another descent group, not more than one member of the lineage will have his aggressiveness dampened by affinal or cognatic ties with the other group. Such a prohibition tends to eliminate marriage as a basis of social and political integration and tends to elevate the importance of descent (Sahlins, 1968:62). "As a mode of alliance it is the next thing to lineage endogamy...." (*ibid.*:63). Sahlins' interpretation suggests that kinship systems with a prohibition on parallel marriage fall near the descent-emphasizing extreme of the continuum suggested by Fox, and further implies that societies practicing lineage endogamy fall still closer to that extreme. Such a view has much to recommend it since it places lineage endogamy on a continuum of social types which includes forms more familiar to anthropologists, rather than setting it apart as an oddity. Such an interpretation also suggests that the endogamous habits of the Turkmen represent only a shift in emphasis from the lineage exogamy of the Kazakh, Kirghiz, and various Mongol groups, a shift in the direction of greater emphasis on agnation.

It should, however, be noted that there is room for subtle variation in the implications of endogamy. Among various Arabic-speaking tribal groups, lineage endogamy does not completely discount the political significance of affinal ties. In this regard it is important to note that among Arabic-speaking

---

[3] To some extent this may be a function of the size of the groups defined by the kinship system. In societies with elaborate lineage systems containing numerous levels of segmentation, marriage can only operate as a bond creating solidarity at one level of segmentation; solidarity at other levels must be based on descent, a fact which necessarily leads to some extent to an emphasis on descent over affinity as a basis of solidarity.

tribal groups, as among the Yomut, endogamy is preferred but not prescribed. Thus, the result is a situation of flexibility: one can create extra-lineage ties or one can forego them (Cunnison, 1966:86-96). Also one can use lineage endogamous ties to emphasize some and de-emphasize other internal bonds of solidarity (Peters, 1960:48-52; Aswad, 1968:140-143). Among the Yomut, and probably among other Turkmen groups, the distinction between social and political alliance makes this impossible and, in effect, completely removes affinal and uterine ties from the domain of politics.

## MARRIAGE NEGOTIATIONS

Proposals of marriage and negotiations of bridewealth among the Yomut are conducted by go-betweens representing the father of the prospective groom, on the one hand, and the father of the prospective bride, on the other. A visit by such a group of representatives of a man seeking a bride for his son and a girl's father is known in Turkmen as a qodaliq. It is not unusual for a man to arrange several qodaliqs on behalf of a son before getting a positive response. A man usually requests that several important men act on his behalf in such matters since the impressiveness of the qodaliq party is a measure of his own status. A man seeking a daughter-in-law cannot himself accompany the qodaliq party, nor can he send members of his own household. Such behavior would be considered extremely indelicate.

Under ordinary circumstances, marriage is referred to in terms that imply wife purchase. However, during a formal proposal, a qodaliq, such expressions are assiduously avoided. Such expressions as "So-and-so (the proposed father-in-law) has sent us to request that he become your kinsman," are used instead. If the proposal is between kinsmen such expressions as "So-and-so wishes to renew his kinship tie with you" are used. Further details are usually not offered. It is not necessary to mention either the proposed groom's or the proposed bride's names. Since marriage of both sons and daughters follow the birth order, it is clear what match is being proposed.

A father receiving such a proposal may give an answer immediately, or, as is more common, say that he needs time to consult with kin and give a date when he will give a definite answer. In the latter case the same party returns on the date given to hear the answer to their request. After a proposal has been accepted, another date is set to discuss the bridal payment, again between representatives of the groom's father and the bride's father himself.

Conventions regarding bridal payments set relatively rigid limits within which to negotiate, and there is no relationship between the wealth of the bride's family and the size of the bridal payment. Bridewealth conventions are stated in terms of livestock. The customary marriage payment when both partners have not previously been married is usually said to be 10 mal. Mal in this context means one large domestic animal, either a camel, a horse, or a cow. Not infrequently the payment is referred to as "10 beasts" (on olagh). It is understood that 10 sheep or 10 goats can be substituted for one mal. In addition to the 10 mal paid to the bride's father, an additional payment of one mal called "inner money" (icher pul) is paid to the bride's mother.

Negotiations concerning marital payments settle the question of precisely what sorts of livestock, or equivalent values in money, will be paid: how many ewes, yearlings, lambs, she-goats, yearling goats, or kids will in fact be given to satisfy the equivalent of 10 mal. Occasionally a part of the payment is also actually made with larger livestock—camels, horses, or cows— and frequently a part is paid in money. These too are matters to be settled by negotiation. When money is paid the current market value of mature animals is used to convert mal into cash. Sometimes a small part of the payment, usually about one mal to be paid in the form of 10 lambs or kids, is deferred until after the next lambing season, and this too is a matter for negotiation. The equivalent cash value of a bridal payment of ten mal plus one mal icher pul usually fell between 10,000 and 12,000 tumans ($1,250 to $1,500) at the time of my research. Although the basic amount is fixed by custom, the market value of the animals used to make up the equivalent of 10 mal plus one mal icher pul varies so that the precise value of individual payments does vary. For marriages that represent the first marriage for both bride and groom, however, the range of variation is small.

On the other hand there is a substantial variation based on the marital histories of the parties involved. Here again the amount is set more by convention then by negotiations reflecting the desirability of the match. The customary marital payments are summarized in Table 7.

The data summarized in Table 7 represent what a bride's father has a right to ask. As pointed out above various combinations of wealth can be construed as the equivalent of one mal. An additional element of variation is introduced by reductions which the father of a bride can make if he chooses. In the case of marriage between close kin—first or second agnatic cousins, or

TABLE 7
CUSTOMARY BRIDAL PAYMENTS

| Marital History of Partners | Bridewealth | "Inner Money" |
|---|---|---|
| Both partners previously unmarried | 10 mal | 1 mal |
| Widower-virgin bride | 20 mal | 1 mal |
| Married man-virgin bride | 30 mal | 1 mal |
| Widower-widow | Variable | None paid |
| Married man-widow | Variable | None paid |

first uterine cousins—a reduced bridal payment is sometimes agreed upon. Reductions are most common in the case of first agnatic cousins. In marriages involving a virgin bride and a widower or a man who has a living wife, reductions from the customary payments (20-30 mal) are common, though by no means universal. The lure of a large bridal payment is the primary motive for giving women to such men despite the preference for giving daughters and sisters to previously unmarried boys. However, a family in a difficult economic situation is often willing to accept less than the maximum in these situations rather than wait an unknown period for another proposal which in all probability will bring in the most common payment of 11 mal.

In cases involving a boy or girl with an obvious defect, such as lameness or partial blindness, an adjustment in bridewealth is usually made. If the bride has the defect, the payment is usually reduced by one-half; if the boy has the defect, it is raised by one-half.

An alternate arrangement is the exchange of one girl for another. This is commonly referred to as chalshiq. In marriages of this sort, the two weddings take place a few days apart, and on the day of each wedding a nominal payment, usually about 100 tumans, is made. Without such a nominal payment the marriage is not thought to be valid. Roughly 15 percent of the marriages recorded in Ajī Quī were transacted in this way (29 out of 194 marriages).

## THE DEVELOPMENT OF A MARRIAGE

Usually several years separate the acceptance of a proposal of marriage and the beginning of the bride's permanent residence in her husband's household. The process leading from one event to the other is punctuated by a number of ceremonies. The first such ceremony consists of a formal visit by all of the women of the groom's household and of closely related or neighboring households to the women of the bride's household. The women associated with the groom prepare a special kind of sweet bread, called ekmek,[4] which is closely associated with rituals surrounding marriage. Women from neighboring households, or closely tied by kinship to the bride's household, gather to receive the women associated with the groom. The mother of the groom, after arriving, presents the ekmek to the mother of the bride, who then distributes it in pairs of loaves to all present. (The loaves consist of extremely thin discs about a foot in diameter.) The name of the ceremony, duth dadishmaq, "mutual feeding of salt," reflects the act of giving ekmek (salt [duth] is often used to mean nourishment in general). The groom's

[4] The word "ekmek" is obviously related to the Turkish word "ekmek" meaning bread in general. In Turkmen the word refers only to a type of thin bread cooked in butter and sprinkled with sugar. The word for bread in general is "chorek."

mother also gives the bride's mother a necklace, an alajayup, which is to be worn by the bride. This sort of necklace, especially associated with marriage, consists of two threads, one black and one white, twisted together, on which some silver coins have been hung. The bread distributed is consumed and before people depart, the mother of the bride gives each woman present two loaves of ekmek to take home. The duṯẖ dadiṣẖmaq occurs generally a few days after the acceptance of a request for a girl in marriage, and usually before the negotiations of the bridal payment.

Ordinarily after the bridewealth is agreed upon the date of the wedding itself is set. Usually the groom's father requests a month or so to gather together the money portion of the bridal payment and to make preparations for the wedding celebration itself.

The selection of the precise date of the wedding by the groom's father is a matter of considerable importance, certain dates being considered auspicious and others inauspicious. Weddings never take place during two lunar months, Ṯẖēpēr Ay and Boṣẖ Ay (the second and eleventh months of the Islamic calendar). The ninth month of the Islamic calendar, Araṯẖ Ay, is the month during which Moslems are required to fast and, as a consequence, is inconvenient for weddings although not inauspicious. Any of the other lunar months is satisfactory for weddings. The precise day of the wedding must be selected in conjunction with beliefs that hold certain days inauspicious for movement and others auspicious. It is felt that if one travels on an inauspicious day the business in pursuit of which the journey is undertaken will suffer. Thus, a bride's journey to her husband's household for her wedding, if made on an inauspicious day, bodes ill for the marriage. The fourth, seventh, fourteenth, seventeenth, twenty-fourth and twenty-seventh days of the Islamic month are most auspicious. The second, fifth, twelfth, fifteenth, twenty-second, and twenty-fifth days are acceptable, while the remainder are distinctly inauspicious.

A second set of beliefs must also be consulted. On the first day of the Islamic month an evil star, which is invisible, lies to the southeast and bring ill fortune to all who travel to the southeast on those days. On the second day the star lies to the south, on the third to the southwest, and so on until on the eighth day it lies to the east. On the ninth day it is underground, and on the tenth day straight overhead and therefore irrelevant to travel. On the eleventh the star again lies to the southeast, and the cycle is repeated through the twentieth day. From the twenty-first to the end of the month the cycle repeats itself again. Also, it is considered inauspicious to travel north on Friday. Once an auspicious day has been selected plans for the wedding can begin.

Most of the celebration surrounding the wedding takes place at the groom's camp. Relatives and neighbors of the groom and bride must govern their behavior on these days in terms of whether they are closer in terms of agnatic ties and residence to the groom or the bride. Those closer to the groom, and those not clearly close to either, gather at the groom's household. Those closer to the bride gather at the bride's household. The celebration begins when those gathered at the groom's camp, excepting members of the groom's household, proceed to the bride's camp to fetch the bride, accompanied by a camel with a specially decorated camel litter (kejebe) intended for the bride to ride back on. At the bride's camp the group is offered a sacrificial meal of rice and mutton (thadagha), provided by the bride's father. Male agnates of the bride show little overt interest in the proceedings and are reserved in conduct. It is considered improper to mention the bride in their presence on the wedding day because of the "shame" they feel in association with a marriage of a close female agnate.

The women close to the bride gather around her in a tent and bar the door. It is then necessary for the women close to the groom to break into this yurt and remove the bride by force. Men not closely related to the bride gather and watch the melee with amusement and, if the fighting becomes too severe, intervene to end it.

Once the bride has been extracted by force she is placed on the special litter prepared for her with two women who stand in the relationship of yenge to her and is taken to the groom's camp. At the groom's camp the bride and her two yenge are placed in a tent set aside for women where the bride sits with her head completely covered. Meanwhile all men partake in a feast and join in entertainment provided by the groom's father. The entertainment consists primarily of wrestling and horse races for which prizes are provided by the groom's father, as well as by the guests who pool small donations of money for this purpose.

In the evening the Islamic ceremony (nekēh) joining the pair as man and wife takes place. This ceremony is not attended, out of "shame," by the bride or groom, or by the father or mother of either. The ceremony is conducted by a religious teacher among three representatives, one for the groom, one for the bride, and one for the bride's father. Both the ceremony creating the marriage and the appointment of representatives must be witnessed by two individuals other than the representatives themselves and the religious teacher, although in practice there are usually several more. After the representatives have been appointed, they gather with the religious teacher and the witnesses in a tent by themselves. Before the nekēh begins, the representative of the bride and of the bride's father have an imaginary dispute with the representative of the groom, claiming as a rule that the representative of the groom owes them some fantastically large sum of money. Eventually the representative of the groom settles the dispute by offering a handful of sweets to satisfy their claim. After this the nekēh begins with the religious teacher asking the representatives whether or not they accept the proposed match. Following the giving of consent by the representatives, the religious teacher recites a portion of the Koran, and then all those gathered for the ceremony join in a sacrificial meal (t͟hadag͟ha) provided by the groom's father.⁵

After this ceremony (nekēh), the heart of one of the animals killed for the sacrificial meals given by the groom's father is divided and a half each is given to the groom and the bride to eat. This is said to assist the development of a bond of affection between the pair. Following the consumption of the heart, the groom is led to his bride by one of the bride's ye̱ṉge. He is taken to her in a tent where he will spend the night alone with her behind a tutī with the bride's two ye̱ṉge sleeping on the opposite side of the tutī. Before being left alone with his bride the ye̱ṉges of the bride preside over a brief ceremony called the eles͟hdermek, "the causing to join together of hands." One of the ye̱ṉge joins the little fingers of bride and groom together and recites a short poem admonishing the groom to treat his bride well.

If the bride and groom are both old enough, as they usually are, the marriage is consummated on the first night after the wedding. Whether the marriage is consummated or not, after the wedding the bride is considered to have undergone a permanent change in status, from that of unmarried girl to that of married woman. This transition is symbolized by a change in her headdress. On the morning after the wedding, women of the groom's family, younger than the bride, pull her tresses backwards where they will henceforth be worn in the manner of a married woman rather than in front of her shoulders in the manner of an unmarried girl. At this time she is also given a gift of coins with which to decorate her hair. A married woman's headdress differs in other details as well, which a bride arranges after returning to her father's household. After making the transition symbolized by this change of headdress, a woman can never again assume the status of an unmarried girl, a qīt͟h. If her husband dies, or if she is divorced (which is improbable), she will assume a different status, that of dul, and if she is subsequently remarried her bridewealth will be that of a widow.

After a wedding the bride and her two ye̱ṉges remain with the groom for two or three nights. They then return to her father's household, and the period of complete spouse avoidance begins.⁶ During this period, although the bride and groom avoid one another as well as all those close to, and senior to, their spouse, the other members of the two households exchange visits frequently. Also, during this period each of the two households begins a practice of sending the breast of each animal they slaughter for food along with a few loaves of sweet bread to the other household. This practice, called

---

⁵ The appointment of witnesses and the crucial part of the marriage ceremony, the inquiry by the religious teacher of the three representatives as to whether they accept the proposed match, are conducted in Turkmen. Only the recitation from the Koran is in Arabic, which the majority of Turkmen do not understand.

⁶ Displaying blood stains, or other proof of virginity, plays no role in the ritual surrounding Turkmen marriage.

straightforwardly "do*sh* ībermek," (the sending of the breast), is carried out between all households related in this way. Most households are tied to several other households by marriage and cannot honor all of them each time they slaughter an animal. They tend, however, to emphasize this practice in relation to the household with which the most recent affinal tie exists.

As mentioned above, spouse avoidance is considered a means of showing respect to the bride's seniors. It is not, however, expected that either of the spouses themselves have any strong scruples about visiting one another if they can do so secretly. It is the business of those senior to each spouse to see to it that clandestine visits do not occur. This is not especially difficult since both parties, and especially the bride, lead confined lives. Occasionally a resourceful groom does manage a secret visit with his bride at night. Plans for such a visit can be arranged through an old woman not related closely to either spouse. Such a woman can speak freely and alone with either spouse without arousing social disapproval and at the same time she feels no compunction about such a clandestine visit. Such meetings are usually arranged near the bride's home at night and entail among other things a liberal supply of bread with which to satisfy the inevitable pack of vicious dogs that stand sentry around every Turkmen camp.

If caught during such a secret visit the groom is beaten by his affines on the spot. Also, in such cases the bride is sent to her husband's household the next day and the members of the bride's household ostracize completely all members of the groom's household. It is then incumbent on the groom's elders, if they wish to make peace, as they usually do, to send go-betweens to plead on their behalf. Most commonly they offer to extend the period of wife avoidance in compensation for the offense and, as a rule, some agreement is worked out, friendly relations are restored, and the bride is again returned to her father's household.

The period of spouse avoidance is marked by two ceremonial visits closely paralleling the du*th* dadi*sh*maq. Each entails visits by a party of women socially close to the groom to the household of the bride where women close to the bride assemble to receive them, and each entails the giving of ekmek. The first such visit occurs sometime during the month which marks the first anniversary of the wedding. This visit is called the innemek, a word meaning in general "an inquiry after something." During the month marking the second anniversary of the wedding, the same sort of visit is made and this time is accompanied by a request that the bride be returned. The name of the second visit, *ch*ag*h*armaq, a word meaning "a request for something," reflects this aspect of the affair. The most common response is that the bride will be returned to her husband in one more year. However, if the bride is unusually young, a request is usually made that the period of spouse avoidance be extended one or two years. The most usual period of spouse avoidance, three years, thus represents the shortest acceptable period.

The parents of both the bride and the groom work out the final date for the return of the bride. Normally this occurs in the month marking the third anniversary of the wedding, the exact day being determined by the considerations mentioned above concerning auspicious days for important journeys. Formalities surrounding the return of the bride, the qaytïrmaq ("the causing to return"), are similar in some ways to those surrounding a wedding. A celebration (toy) is arranged by the groom's father that amounts to an attenuated version of a wedding celebration. The bride is brought back on the same sort of gaily decorated camel litter (kejebe) which is associated with a wedding. However, there are important differences as well. This time the bride's parents prepare the litter and bring the bride to the groom themselves. No party goes out from the groom's camp seeking the bride, and there is no female melee over the bride. In fact, the careful distinctions concerning those socially closer to the bride and those socially closer to the groom are not made in any way during the qaytïrmaq. The nekēh, the giving of a divided heart to the spouses, and the eleshdermek are all lacking.

The one year period following the qaytïrmaq, during which the bride alternates between her natal and affinal households, is not accompanied by further formalities of a festive nature, although the formality of "the sending of the breast" continues on occasions between the two households as well as frequent informal visits between those related as qoda.

This lengthy process by which a wife is acquired is on rare occasions cut short by pregnancy. A marriage is consummated during the two or three nights which the bride and groom spend together after the wedding if both bride and groom are old enough. If pregnancy results, the bride must return to her husband's house to have her child and the period of wife avoidance is terminated. It is also possible that the year during which the bride alternates between her father's and her father-in-law's yurt can be cut short by pregnancy. A third possibility is pregnancy owing to clandestine contact between bride and groom. These are exceptions, however, and normally a groom must wait four years for a full-time wife.

From the above description it can be seen that marriage is surrounded by a large amount of ritual which extends over a period of several years and marks the various stages by which a marriage develops. There are not only a large number of formal rules governing the transaction of a marriage, but also numerous formal prescriptions governing behavior toward affines.

## WIDOWS, WIDOWERS, REMARRIAGE, AND POLYGYNY

The elaborate and gradual process by which a marriage is established is not repeated in marriages of widows, widowers, or married men. Precisely what ceremonial sequence is followed depends, as does the bridewealth, on the marital history of the partners. When a widower takes a previously unmarried girl as a second wife, all of the ritual described above is followed except that the period of spouse avoidance is reduced to a few months. A chagharmaq occurs as described above a month or so after the nekēh and is soon followed by a qaytirmaq. After the qaytirmaq there is no period during which the bride alternates between her natal and affinal households, although like all wives she visits her natal home once or twice a year for a period of a few weeks.

When a widow remarries, the ritual of marriage is drastically different. The festivities on the wedding day are considerably reduced and the dalish, the removing of the bride by force, is omitted. The nekēh is conducted between the bride and groom themselves rather than between representatives, and the period of spouse avoidance is reduced to a period of one week to one month. In such cases, there is no chagharmaq. In cases of leviratic marriage, which are discussed in greater detail below, the period of spouse avoidance is completely eliminated.

When a married man takes a virgin bride as his second wife, the ritual sequence followed is that appropriate for widowers. When a man forms a polygynous union by taking a widow as a second wife, the rituals followed are those appropriate to a widow's marriage. The situation is the same in those rare instances in which a man takes a third or fourth wife. It should also be noted that the Turkmen do respect the Islamic proscription against having more than four wives at once.

## DIVORCE

Turkmen claim that they do not allow divorce. Some are sufficiently aware of the tenets of their religion to be aware that this is a matter of Turkic custom rather than religion. Of 194 marriages recorded in Ajī Quī, 81 have been terminated by the death of one of the partners and one was terminated by divorce. The single instance of divorce involved the only marriage in Ajī Quī of a Turkmen to a Welayet woman (see Table 9). The woman was a widow in her late twenties who was taken as a wife by a widower of 69 for a bridal payment of 700 tumans (less than one-tenth of what would have been required for a Turkmen widow of comparable age). The woman spoke a Turkic dialect as her mother tongue but was completely unfamiliar with Turkmen customs. She was continually and severely criticized for not following Turkmen custom, and, as a result, went out of her mind, sitting still for hours on end appearing to understand nothing that was said to her. Over a period of several months, she alternated between this state and a somewhat more rational one. Finally her husband divorced her in disgust and sent her back to her brothers with a request for the return of his 700 tumans. The money was not returned, however. These events occurred during my stay in Ajī Quī and after the divorce, one informant observed that such wives are indeed inexpensive, but they are worth only what one pays for them.[7] Informants also observed that the disapproval of divorce did not extend to marriages with Welayet.

Rare instances of divorce involving Turkmen wives can be found despite the proscription against divorce. One such case occurred among the Qara Makhtum mentioned above, and the event precipitated a serious squabble. The divorce was desired by the wife who persuaded her father to press demands for a divorce on her behalf. The husband and wife had a common ancestor in the seventh ascending generation. All of those more closely related to the groom than the bride, a lineage of 25 households, vigorously supported the groom's claim that divorce was contrary to custom and therefore could not be tolerated. The bride's father had serious difficulty in mustering support among his agnates, and many refused to support him at all and advocated to him privately that he drop his demand that his son-in-law divorce his daughter and that he send his daughter back to her husband. The remainder of the Qara Makhtum also advocated privately to the father that he desist from his demand, but publicly maintained a neutral position advocating only that the matter be settled without violence. Men of stature, especially religious teachers, from other descent groups also took it upon themselves to intervene advocating a peaceful solution. The efforts of neutral parties narrowly avoided an out-break of violence on a few occasions when tempers got out of hand. Eventually it became clear that the only peaceful solution possible was to grant the bride's father's demand. After this the neutral parties concentrated their efforts on persuading the husband and his lineage-mates that a divorce should be granted, and after some difficulty finally succeeded. It was also agreed that the bridewealth should be returned. Seven years after the event, in 1967, all of the groom's lineage were still completely ostracizing members of the bride's household, pretending that they did not see them when chance encounters occurred.

The conclusion can be drawn that the proscription against divorce is in general taken seriously among the Yomut.

## THE DEMOGRAPHIC CONTEXT

A number of aspects of Yomut marriage can be understood best in their

---

[7] There is no word in Turkmen that means distinctly "to buy," the verb used for buying and taking (almaq) being the same. Presumably, the sentence "shüjüre ayal arthan alıp bolar," could be transalated as: "Such women can be taken cheaply," but the implication of sale is not lost in such a translation. Giving of women is most commonly referred to with the verb thatmak which means "to sell," not "to give." When speaking Persian the verbs kharīdan and furūkhtan, "to buy" and "to sell," are used most commonly by Turkmen to refer to marriage. Anthropological literature is replete with statements to the effect that one should not infer wife purchase from the practice of giving bridewealth. The Yomut, however, have not been much influenced by this literature.

demographic context. Unfortunately data on the demography of the Yomut are limited; this section presents what is available.

The evidence indicates that there is a shortage of women available for marriage as a result of a number of factors: an overall shortage of women in the population, a tendency for widowers to remarry combined with a tendency for widows not to remarry, and polygyny. Each of these factors requires some examination.

A breakdown of the population of Ajī Quī by age and sex indicates that there are fewer women than men in the population, particularly among those over the age of 20 (see Table 8). Since it is relevant to the demographic factors influencing marriage, Yomut and non-Yomut women are distinguished in this table.

There is evidence from other sources to corroborate the overall shortage of women among the Turkmen. Data reported by Lawrence Krader in *Peoples of Central Asia* indicate a preponderance of males over females among the Turkmen population of the Russian empire shortly after the Russian conquests of Central Asia (1963a:175-176). Krader suggests that the figures reported may be in part a result of underreporting of women, although he concludes some preponderance of males is nevertheless to be inferred. As mentioned above, Turkmen do consider it improper to discuss daughters and sisters with strangers and one might suspect underreporting of females in a census as a result. My own experience included some initial difficulty in collecting information about sisters and daughters. However, once sufficient rapport had been established with a few informants it was possible to obtain information concerning the number and ages of their sisters and daughters without much difficulty. It was also relatively easy to get informants to discuss women other than their own close agnates. In contrast to their feelings toward sisters and daughters, the Turkmen have no compunction about

TABLE 8
AGE AND SEX COMPOSITION:
AJĪ QUĪ, AUGUST 1967

| Age | Yomut Male | Yomut Female | Non-Yomut Female |
|---|---|---|---|
| 60+ | 14 | 8 | |
| 45-59 | 21 | 14 | |
| 30-44 | 31 | 27 | 1 |
| 15-29 | 69 | 57 | 2 |
| 0-14 | 84 | 91 | |
| Totals | 219 | 197 | 3 |

discussing their wives with strangers. (When a man marries a close agnate, this is still the situation: the relationship of husband-wife supersedes that of agnate in this regard as well as in others.) Thus, danger of underreporting lies in the early age categories, those below the usual age of marriage. Since the average age at marriage is 15 and the shortage of women lies in the age categories above 15, there seems little cause to worry about underreporting of females in a household-by-household census as an explanation of the small number of females in the population.

The most reasonable explanation of the shortage of women is a shorter female life expectancy. A number of factors appear to contribute to generally poorer health among women. Women have less protein in their diet since the largest share of all meat is consumed by men. They dress less warmly in the winter and, when ill, they receive less care. In addition, the difficulties of childbirth probably account in some measure for a higher mortality rate among women.

Other data support this interpretation as well. For a portion of the terminated marriages recorded, the cause of termination was reported. Of 82 marriages for which these data are available 56 were terminated by the wife's death, 25 by the husband's death, and one by divorce (see Table 9). This information is even more striking since most wives are younger than their husbands. The average age for females at marriage is 15, while that for males is 20 (see Fig. 21).

As mentioned above, the shortage of women available for marriage is aggravated by common practices regarding remarriage of widows and widowers. Reasons for widowers wishing to remarry are obvious from the preceding discussion. Most widowers do eventually remarry if they are younger than about 50, and many older widowers remarry as well. Frequently, however, a widower spends several years raising the bridewealth before he is able to remarry.

Remarriage for a widow poses a problem only if she has children. It is by no means unusual for a young bride to be widowed during the period of complete spouse avoidance, or in the early part of her residence with her husband before any children have been conceived. Such widows are invariably remarried to widowers. If a widow has children, however, residence rules pose a serious hardship for both her and her children if she remarries. If remarried, she would have to reside with her husband, while her children, once they were physically able to be separated from her, would as a rule be required to reside with their agnates. Turkmen do not respect the Islamic dictum that children cannot be separated from their mother before age seven. When residence rules require separate residence, children can be separated from their mother as soon as they have been weaned. Turkmen children are ordinarily weaned at about age two unless a younger sibling arrives before this age is reached. Such separation is difficult for both mother and child and attempts to avoid such

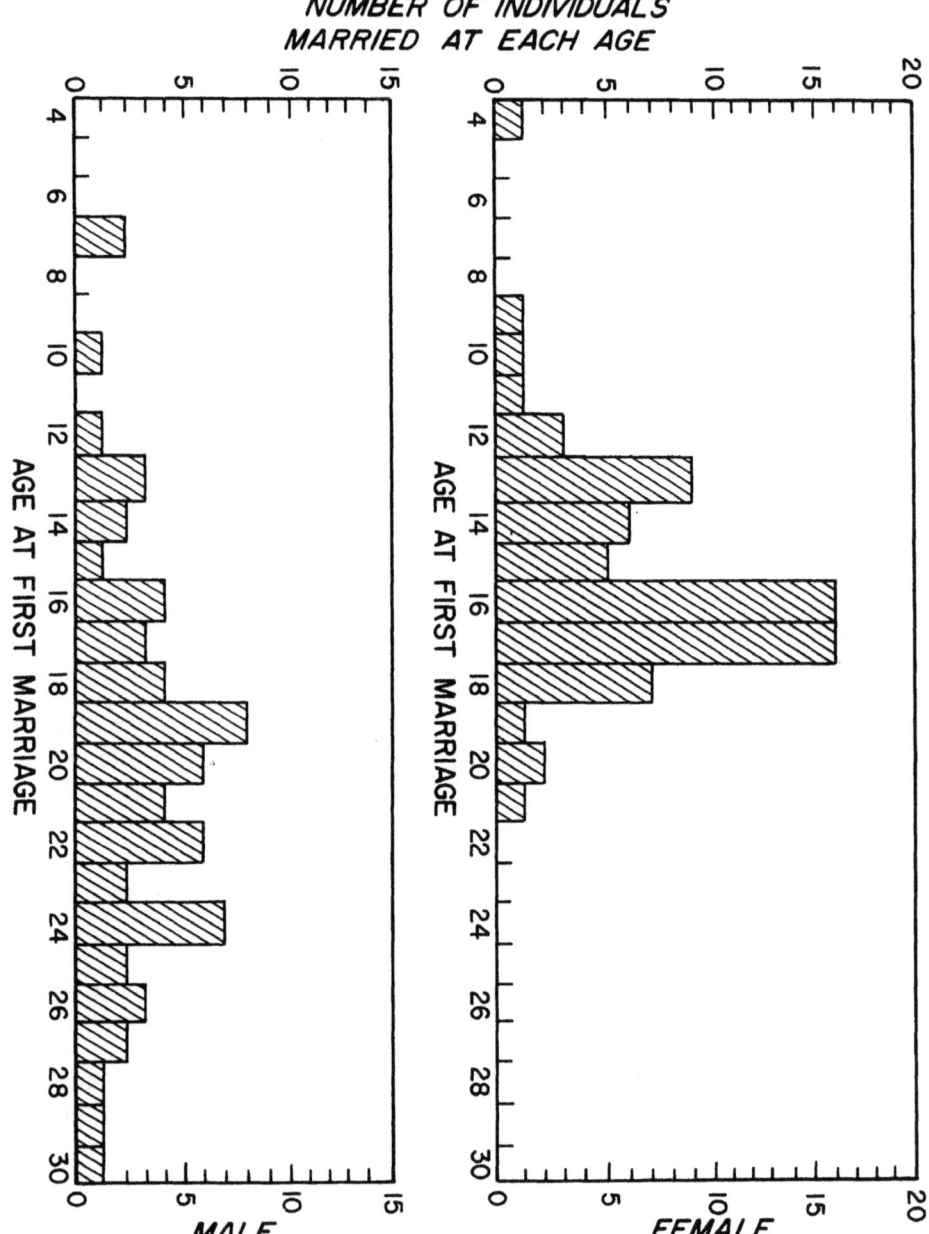

Fig. 21. Ages at first marriage for 133 individuals in Ajī Quī.

separation underlie the somewhat complicated subject of the disposition of widows.

After a woman's husband dies, her agnates have a right to reclaim her and to give her in marriage to another man and collect another bridewealth. At the same time, her husband's agnates have a right to claim her children. A number of means are available which usually avert the necessity of separating mother and child. The most common solution is for the widow's agnates to abrogate their right to reclaim her. Concern for the welfare of one's sister and sister's children is one factor motivating this sort of solution. Another important factor is the age of the widow herself. The bridewealth a widow can fetch on remarriage depends on her age, and, as a woman's potential for bringing in bridewealth declines, there is less concern about reclaiming her. Most widows over 30 simply stay with their children without any compensation to their agnates.

In the case of a young widow, however, the lure of a higher bridewealth can overcome concern for the feelings of a sister and her children. As a rule the bridewealth given for a young widow is higher than that which was given for her as a virgin bride. The usual bridewealth for young widows falls in the range of 14 to 17 mal. This may strike observers of the Turkmen as paradoxical, but a fuller view of Turkmen marriage regulations indicates otherwise. Except in leviratic marriages, only virgin brides are taken for previously unmarried boys; widows are available only for marriage to widowers. If a widower takes a virgin bride, as most widowers prefer to do, he must pay in most instances 20 mal in bridewealth. A widower's situation is also complicated by the preference for giving daughters and sisters to previously unmarried boys. After several years of extra work and frugal spending in order to build up a surplus of 20 mal for a bridewealth, he may have a long search for a man willing to give him his virgin daughter as a bride. Faced with these circumstances, a widower may choose to seek a widow as his second wife in return for a smaller bridewealth. Although he may give a larger bridewealth for such a widow than her first husband gave for her, it is nevertheless a sound proposition from his point of view. Marriage regulations and preferences have placed him in a completely different situation than that faced by previously unmarried boys. For him women are much scarcer and whether he takes a widow or a virgin bride he must offer a higher bridewealth.

If the agnates of a widow announce that they intend to reclaim her, the agnates of her children may intervene on behalf of the children. Under these circumstances they can prevent the children from losing their mother by arranging a leviratic marriage, or by paying a compensation equal to the bridewealth the widow would probably fetch if remarried. This compensation is called otırtma mal, "the causing to stay livestock."

Leviratic marriage is the more common solution since Turkmen religious teachers maintain otırtma mal is forbidden by Islam. Leviratic marriage, however, is frequently little different from the solution posed by the payment of otɨrtma mal. Often although the widow is married to some close agnate of her deceased husband, she does not become a part of his household or in any way assume the role of his wife. In these cases the widow is in effect the head of an independent household until one of her sons is old enough to assume the position. This sort of arrangement occurs when the widow is married to a man who already has one wife. The bridewealth for polygynous leviratic marriages is not higher than that for other forms of leviratic marriage. It is usually assumed that marriages of this sort will not be consummated. However, occasionally they are clandestinely consummated and at times such marriages bear children. In such cases the children are usually raised in the household of their mother separate from their father.

An alternate form of leviratic marriage consists of giving a widow in marriage to a previously unmarried agnate of her first husband. In cases of this sort, the widow assumes an active role as the wife of her leviratic husband who ordinarily does not later seek a second wife. When he establishes an independent household his wife's children by her first marriage become a part of his household.

If the agnates of a widow wish to claim her, and her children's agnates are unable to raise the otɨrtma mal or the bridewealth for a leviratic marriage, the widow may actually be married off elsewhere and separated from her children.

Thus, there are five possible dispositions of a widow with children: (1) abrogation of her agnate's right to reclaim her, (2) payment of otɨrtma mal, (3) a polygynous leviratic marriage which is, in effect, very similar to payment of otɨrtma mal, (4) a monogamous leviratic marriage, or (5) remarriage of the widow to a man not an agnate of her first husband. The last solution usually entails separating a widow from her children, although the children's agnates can also abrogate their right to the widow's children. This is done only when for some reason close agnates of the children are unable to care for the children themselves.[8] The first two solutions have the effect of reducing the number of women available for marriage by placing a fertile woman in a celibate state. The third solution usually has the same de facto effect.

An examination of specific data concerning recently dissolved marriages in Ajï Quï point up the combined effect of the factors discussed above. Table

[8] Thirty-nine of the terminated marriages recorded in Table 9 below had children under 12 at the time of termination. In only four of these cases were the immature children placed with their mother's kin. Three of these were cases in which a widower was left with a child under five, and was forced for economic reasons to take up employment as a shepherd away from his own kin. In such cases, a man cannot care for the child himself, and often prefers to place the child with its uterine grandparents or a mother's brother rather than with collateral agnates. In either case the father loses control of the child, and it is often felt that uterine grandparents or an actual mother's brother will provide better care for a child than would collateral agnates more distant than first cousins.

9 summarizes the causes of termination of marriage and the subsequent marital history of the surviving spouse. Among widows, instances of polygynous levirate marriage involving separate residence are listed separately since this type of marriage is, from a demographic perspective, more like the solution posed by payment of otïrtma mal than like remarriage.

These figures, although they represent a small sample, demonstrate a strong trend. Combined with the figures in Table 8 the following demographic model is suggested. The number of females approaching the average age of first marriage may equal approximately the number of males approaching the average age of first marriage. However, in the later age categories more marriages are dissolved by the wife's death than by the husband's death. This means there are more widowers needing new spouses than there are widows available for second marriage, and the situation is further aggravated by the fact that most of the widows still in their fertile years do not remarry. Although not especially frequent, polygyny to some extent further aggravates the shortage of marriageable women. In effect, boys seeking their first brides, widowers seeking second wives, and married men seeking polygynous marriages must all compete for the same limited number of girls approaching puberty.

The combined effect of these factors leading to a shortage of marriageable women can be seen in a breakdown of the population of Ajï Quï in terms of marital history and current marital status. These data are presented in Table 10. An examination of these data reveals that there are 42 males above the age of 15 who are not married and 15 who are married but not yet living with their spouses. The comparable figures for women are 17 unmarried and 12 married but not yet coresident with their spouses. Two interesting facts emerge from these figures. The first is the large disparity between the number of marriageable men and women. The second is the fact that, despite the shortage of marriageable women, a fairly high proportion of the fecund

TABLE 9
DISSOLUTION OF FIRST MARRIAGE
AND REMARRIAGE

|  | Cause of Termination of First Marriage | | |
|---|---|---|---|
|  | Death of Wife | Death of Husband | Divorce |
| Number Terminated | 56 | 25 | 1 |
| Number of Spouses Remarried | 45 | Polygynous Levirate  5 | Other Remarriage  7 | Husband not Remarried Wife no Information |

women in the population are currently not living with a spouse. The implications of these facts are worth exploring.

If we assume the widowers (and the one divorced person) above the age of 55 are not interested in remarriage, and that the one disabled individual in the 30 to 44 age category is unmarriageable, we are left with 36 males who would like to have spouses but have none. In the female segment of the population there are only six marriageable females, since the badly crippled woman, the feeble-minded woman, and the widows over 30 are all in effect unmarriageable. However, despite the high number of potential suitors for each young woman implied by these figures, these six women will probably not all marry for several years. This can be expected because of the high bridewealth required before a suitor can marry one of these women. The situation is clearly one in which the social conventions exaggerate the demographic fact of a shortage of women. The situation is interesting in light of the Wynne-Edwards hypothesis (1962; 1964:68-74; 1965:1543-1548).

## POPULATION REGULATION THROUGH SOCIAL CONVENTIONS: AN HYPOTHESIS

Wynne-Edwards' hypothesis maintains that animal populations, and some human populations, regulate their size in such a way as to avoid overtaxing their resources and that they do this by means of social conventions which regulate reproduction in a density dependent way. A population that is well adapted in terms of the balance of its size against resources is one which utilizes most of its reproductive potential when density in relation to resources is low, but progressively limits reproduction as density increases. At a certain density, which is well below the point at which the population begins to degrade its resource base, fertility is limited to the replacement level and population size becomes stable.

If through some unusual event it goes above this density—as for example through the shrinkage of a population's territory—fertility would drop below the replacement level until the density declined to the stability level.

Wynne-Edwards believes that most post-Neolithic human populations were not regulated in this way, and the general fact of world-wide human population growth would seem to cast doubt on the existence of such population regulation among most modern human populations. However, the evidence is not all in one direction. Many populations that have been studied by anthropologists have been found to have a density well below the maximum possible one given their resources and mode of economic production (Bender, 1971:32-45). The Yomut, until the early 1950s, clearly had a density considerably below the maximum possible level given their resources and technology. This is evidenced by the fact that until then, arable land existed in great excess of demand and no local group felt that any of its resources were limited enough to make it desirable to exclude new members from joining their group.

In view of this situation it seems a reasonable hypothesis that through a complex of social factors the Yomut did regulate their population in the manner suggested by the Wynne-Edwards hypothesis.

The following model is proposed concerning the social regulation of population size among the Yomut. The fixed high bridewealth of the Yomut and their practice of delaying the coresidence of spouses for several years after marriage inhibit fertility, and this fertility inhibiting effect increases as per capita wealth diminishes. The reason for believing that this effect is density dependent revolves primarily around the fixed nature of the bridewealth. As mentioned above, there is a limit to which the bridewealth can be reduced. Therefore, as a family's wealth is diminished, it can ease its situation with regard to bridal payments only to a limited degree through negotiating lower payments. Beyond that point such a family can only respond to diminishing wealth by delaying the marriages of its sons in order to have a longer time over which to accumulate the bridewealth. This fact is reflected in the great variation in age at first marriage among men (see Fig. 21). A breakdown of this data according to the wealth of the man (or family of the man) entering marriage indicates that wealth differences, more than other factors, explain the variance in age at marriage among men.

The effect of diminishing per capita wealth on ages of females at marriage is more complex. In general, the age at which women marry does not depend on their family's wealth and does not vary as greatly as the age of men at marriage (see Fig. 21). The usual practice for poorer families is to marry off their daughters as soon as acceptable suitors appear, but not to use the bridewealth to immediately marry off sons (if there are any ready for marriage). Rather the usual practice is to delay the marriage of sons and use the bridewealth as income to ease their economic circumstances. Thus, a girl's age at marriage is not affected by her family's wealth, and a poor boy's age at marriage is not affected by the fact that he has sisters who themselves bring in bridal payments.

Despite the above consideration there is reason to believe that a decrease in average per capita wealth of an entire breeding population (large sub-regions of Yomut territory occupied by distinct and largely endogamous descent groups demarcate approximately isolated breeding populations) would increase the overall average age at marriage for females even though it would affect women of the different wealth strata equally. The reasons for this lie in processes involving entire breeding populations. The composition of these populations in terms of age, sex, and marital status may, for the purpose of explaining this model, be assumed to be very similar to that of Ajī Quī as presented in Table 10. If this is so there will be a fairly large number of fecund women in each population who are not married, and, therefore, given

TABLE 10
YOMUT POPULATION OF AJI QUI:
AGE, SEX, AND MARITAL STATUS

| Sex | Age | Marital Status | | | | |
|---|---|---|---|---|---|---|
| | | Never Married | Married: Period of Spouse Avoidance Current | Living With First Spouse | Living With Second or Third Spouse | Widowers, Widows or Divorced Persons | Polygynously Married |
| Male | 60+ | | | 5 | 4 | 3 | 2 |
| | 45-59 | | | 13 | 6 | 2 | |
| | 30-44 | 1[1] | 5 | 23 | 6 | 1 | |
| | 25-29 | | 9 | 9 | | | |
| | 20-24 | 10 | 9 | 8 | | | |
| | 15-19 | 25 | 1 | 2 | | | |
| | 10-14 | 26 | | | | | |
| Female | 60+ | | | 1 | 1 | 3 | 3 |
| | 45-59 | | | 8 | 1 | 4 | |
| | 30-44 | 1[2] | 1[4] | 22 | 2 | 2 | 1 |
| | 25-29 | | | 18 | 2 | | |
| | 20-24 | 2[3] | 3 | 18 | | | |
| | 15-19 | 5 | 8 | 3 | | | |
| | 10-14 | 22 | 1 | | | | |

[1] Crippled and feeble-minded.
[2] Badly crippled.
[3] One of these individuals is feeble-minded.
[4] This woman's family fled the U.S.S.R. to evade difficulties with governmental authorities after she was married but before she had taken up residence with her husband; she therefore, cannot join her husband.

the social context, not exposed to pregnancy. The frequency with which these women marry will obviously correspond to the frequency with which men marry. Thus, a decrease in per capita wealth which diminishes the number of marriages per year will diminish the frequency with which unmarried fecund women enter marriage and begin to bear children. At the same time, the number of women leaving the category of fecund married women through their own death, the death of their husbands, or menopause would not diminish in response to a decrease in per capita wealth. Rather it could be expected to increase in response to diminishing per capita wealth. The end result of all these processes would be that a large permanent decrease in per capita wealth would lead to a large decrease in the number of fecund women who are married and therefore a decrease in fertility.

This, in turn, would be reflected in a later average age at marriage for women. Logically no shift in the average age at marriage but rather the relegation of a portion of the female population to permanent spinsterhood (a result which would also dampen fertility) is possible. However, the requirement that women marry according to their birth order would tend to encourage the former pattern.

It should be observed that a population regulating mechanism of the sort hypothesized here would be successful only if it kept population size at a level well below the maximum level supportable by the existing wealth. In other words what the situation calls for is a healthy margin of safety rather than a fine adjustment ot the overall wealth existing at any one point in time. This is so because wealth is subject to continuous short-term fluctuations and a human population could continually readjust its size to such short-term fluctuations only at great cost. The only adaptation that would make sense would be to keep the population low enough so that during the worst years wealth resources would still be adequate.

The system of regulation suggested above would not be one that could make fine year by year adjustments, but is one that could maintain a long-term balance based on a margin of safety. Readjustments to new conditions would only occur slowly. Thus, a single bad year, although it might cause a few marriages to be delayed a short time, would not affect current population size and probably would not have a noticeable long-term effect. On the other hand if the overall wealth available to a group were to change significantly, either by decreasing or increasing, and remain changed for a decade or more, a long-term readjustment of population size would occur. In the case of a downward adjustment, the fact that population was well below the maximum size supportable before the change would compensate for the fact that such an adjustment could only be accomplished slowly.

It is also worth emphasizing that a significant long-term increase in wealth would lead to an increase in population. Thus, under certain conditions rapid growth, as is currently occurring, should be expected on the basis of this hypothesis. The actual situation among the Yomut since the early 1950s has been one of rapid increase in wealth and rapid increase in population. The test of the above hypothesis under current conditions would have to hinge, therefore, on demonstrating that various subgroups of the Yomut which differ in overall wealth increase their population at significantly different rates, the poorer subgroups growing more slowly than the wealthier ones.

In addition, a population regulating device of this sort, if it operates as hypothesized here, would do so in conjunction with other forces. Thus, a social mechanism of this sort may have worked well in conjunction with the high mortality rates that existed before the 1950s, but may no longer work under the improved health conditions that have recently been experienced by the Yomut. This question will have to await future investigations.

The data currently available on the Yomut are inadequate to test this hypothesis and, therefore, firm conclusions will have to await further study. The hypothesis does, however, offer both an explanation of certain unusual social practices of the Yomut, and a partial explanation of the fact that the Yomut population was much less dense than its resource base would allow until the recent occurrence of a large immigration of non-Yomut into Yomut country. The explanation would be partial because the above model could explain how population and wealth were kept in balance, but would not explain how the production of wealth was kept within limits that would not degrade natural resources (arable land and pasture). Since at least until recently the exploitation of natural resources was kept within such limits, there must have been some factor limiting population growth in terms of existing wealth as well as some factor restricting the exploitation of natural resources for the production of wealth. Again only further investigation can suggest what might be responsible for limiting both population growth and the exploitation of natural resources.

# VII

# DOMESTIC ORGANIZATION AND ECONOMICS

THIS chapter analyzes the effect of household organization on the distribution of wealth among households. The relationship between the number of adults in a household and its economic viability is crucial to this analysis. The analysis is carried out by examining institutions which have conflicting implications. The first part of the analysis is concerned with factors which tend to create an unequal distribution of wealth: the division of society into economically autonomous households each of which has a separate economic fate, and the fact that inequalities in the labor resources of domestic units lead to differences in productivity and wealth. The second part is concerned with institutions which, to a limited extent, counteract the tendency toward economic inequality: bridal payments, ultimogeniture, adoption, and various forms of economic assistance among related households. For convenience these institutions are referred to as leveling institutions. The third section examines the relationship between the kinship system as an economic system and the corporate structure of Yomut society which is primarily political in function. This section attempts to show that the leveling institutions, by maintaining at least minimal viability for most domestic units, preserve the numerical and, hence, political strength of agnatic descent groups.

## DIFFERENTIAL PRODUCTIVITY AND THE DISTRIBUTION OF WEALTH

Central to an understanding of the extensive economy of the Yomut[1] is the fact that a large labor pool, that is, a large number of able-bodied adult members, is a greater source of economic security for a household than is a

---

[1] Material published by Robert Netting suggests that some of the characteristics of the pastoral economy of the Yomut which are discussed below are in fact characteristic of many extensive economies, not just of pastoral ones. In particular, the relatively great importance of labor resources and the limited importance of capital seem to be generally characteristic of extensive economies (see Netting, 1965:422-429; 1968:130-143).

large herd. Livestock are subject to frequent losses due to natural hazards. Large bridal payments also cut deeply into a household's property in livestock. As a result, it is not unusual for a once wealthy family to find itself without sufficient capital for its own support. However, employment as hired shepherds is relatively easy to find and compensation in cash and livestock is generous by local standards. A household with several able-bodied men but no livestock can, through this form of employment, build up a herd sufficient to support itself in a period of four to five years. Thus, a large family does not view even the complete loss of its livestock as more than a temporary setback.

In contrast, a household with few able-bodied males but a large herd is in a more difficult position. It may through careful management, good luck, and the employment of hired shepherds maintain its herd. If, however, through misfortune or mismanagement, it should lose most of its livestock, regaining its former position would prove very difficult. Its good fortune is more precarious than that of a family which enjoys not only wealth but also numbers. A more thorough explanation of why labor is more important than capital requires a more detailed examination of certain aspects of the economy of the Yomut charwa.

## Livestock as a Form of Capital

The natural increase of a herd varies considerably from year to year depending on conditions of weather and pasture. Informants estimate that the portion of fertile females in a herd that reproduce each year varies from 60 percent to 90 percent. The high death rate among lambs and kids usually reduces the number of yearlings to between 30 percent and 60 percent of the number of fertile females in the herd.

The sex ratio at birth is approximately 50 percent males and 50 percent females. The usual practice is to keep all of the female lambs and kids in order to build up the reproductive potential of the herd. Only the three wealthiest households in Ajī Quī could afford to be more liberal in the sale or consumption of their stock. This practice allows an annual increase in the female portion of the herd ranging between 15 percent and 30 percent. Female animals reach maturity in two years, and are kept for between seven and nine years before being fattened for sale. During the period between maturity and sale, ewes and female goats constitute the most productive portion of the herd, providing offspring, milk, and wool. The majority of male animals are castrated in the fall of their first year. Only a small portion of the males born, about one for every 20 mature females, is set aside for stud. Wealtheir families maintain a higher portion of uncastrated males. The castrated males are sold for meat and hides, or are consumed by their owners, soon after reaching maturity.

The striking feature, given these methods of herd management, is the large potential that a herd has for increase. This large potential is, however, offset by a number of factors. Drought, disease, and severe cold can often cause sudden and dramatic losses, while wolves and thieves claim a few animals each year. Occasionally unusually high expenses can cause a family to cut into its productive stock. As mentioned above, still another factor which greatly diminishes a household's livestock at times is the occasional need to make a bridal payment. The usual bridal payment of 100 sheep and goats represents a large enough herd to support a household. Accumulating livestock for such bridal payments requires several years for most families, and often after making such a payment a household is left temporarily impoverished. The high risks to which capital in livestock is subject and the heavy demands represented by bridal payments would make life very precarious for Turkmen pastoralists if alternate forms of income were not available to families with insufficient livestock for their livelihood. The practice followed by owners of large herds of using hired shepherds and the customary generous compensation, therefore, has great social significance.

## Shepherding Contracts

There are two varieties of shepherding contracts. The most common arrangement is one by which a person hires himself to a large herd owner who is himself a nomad migrating with his own livestock. Under this arrangement the hired shepherd migrates with his employer and a part of his compensation consists of being fed and clothed by his employer. Frequently young unmarried men enter into this sort of contract, and in such cases they are also housed in their employer's yurt during those parts of the year in which the livestock and camp are kept close together. In addition to food and clothing, the shepherd is paid in livestock for his labor during the winter and spring. The compensation consists of one yearling for every 15 animals cared for, collected before the spring shearing. Compensation for the remainder of the year, summer and fall, was at the time of my research set at 600 tumans ($80), food, shelter in the form appropriate for shepherds, and necessary clothing. If the employer of a shepherd is especially pleased with the service he has received, he may add an additional suit of clothes to the customary compensation.

An alternate arrangement consists of farming a herd out to a family in another community. This is most frequently done by wealthy sedentary Turkmen who wish to put a part of their wealth in livestock. A herd so placed is called an emanet. The holder of the emanet is responsible for the care of livestock and usually herds them with his own animals. In compensation he receives all of the dairy products of the herd, one-tenth of the wool produced by the herd, and one lamb each summer for each 15 lambs in the herd. He also consumes any animals which must be slaughtered because they are about to die. Animals that die without being properly slaughtered by having their throats placed in the direction of Mecca and slit are forbidden as food. When an animal is sick and in danger of death, it is often a problem to decide whether to slaughter the animal or to gamble on its recovery while risking the possibility that it will die before it is possible to slaughter it. Holders of emanets can naturally be expected to settle more frequently on immediate slaughter as the preferable course. This practice, combined with the possibilities of pilfering, no doubt explains the lower rate of compensation under this arrangement.

The social importance of these two shepherding arrangements lies in the opportunity they provide for translating labor into capital. Because of these arrangements it is possible for a family to subsist without any livestock of its own and at the same time to gradually build its own body of capital in anticipation of eventual economic independence. Employment as shepherds also provides a means by which families with many sons and moderate supplies of livestock can build up the surpluses necessary to acquire brides.

## Agriculture

Agriculture is a significant secondary pursuit among the pastoral Turkmen. The amount of land that can be cultivated in the region inhabited by the pastoral Turkmen is small and the yields are limited and highly variable. What is produced on this land, with rare exception, is consumed completely by the producer.

However, there is another form of agricultural income of greater importance to the pastoral Turkmen. In order to encourage sedentarization the government has been willing to grant land reform deeds to pastoral Turkmen. A portion of the Turkmen in Ajī Quī have taken advantage of this opportunity (see Table 12, Appendix I) and have received relatively productive plots of land in the area immediately north of the Gurgan River and east of Gunbadi Kāvūs. These are 10 hectare plots suitable for dry cultivation of wheat and barley. The Turkmen of Ajī Quī claim that the income derivable from such a plot, if cultivated by the owner, is equivalent roughly to that which can be derived from a herd of 80 sheep and goats. Information gathered from sedentary families relying on such plots of land as their primary source of income confirms this estimate. If rented, the same plot yields a smaller income. Because of the higher productive potential of this sort of land, the acquisition of land reform deeds has changed the economic situation of families holding them. Pastoral families who own such land manage it in a variety of ways. Some sharecrop their land, turning over all of the management of the land to another party in return for half of the yield. Others rent their land for 1,000 to 1,200 tumans per 10 hectare plot. Some manage the land themselves. Since cultivation is mechanized—machinery being held by a few wealthy individuals and contracted out to an entire village at a time—this can be done with a minimum of travel between their camps and their land.

Income from land of this sort, like income from livestock, varies widely, averaging about 2,400 tumans a year for a family that manages its land itself; half this if their land is sharecropped.

In addition, three households in Ajī Quī have claims on irrigated land on the Atrak River. This land is jointly owned by all the households of a particular lineage, three of which live in Ajī Quī. These devote themselves to pastoral pursuits while renting their shares of this land.

Land of such a productive variety provides a substantial income and as a form of capital is subject to less risk than herding. It can be lost only if sold out of economic need. Productive agricultural land can be, and occasionally is, purchased by wealthy pastoral families. Thus, wealth built up in livestock can on occasion be converted into a more secure form.

## Carpet Weaving

The use of wool and goat hair to produce various handicraft items is an important source of income for all pastoral families. The items manufactured include pile carpets, flat woven rugs, felts for the walls and floors of yurts and for use as horse blankets and shepherds' cloaks, and ropes of goat hair. At the time of observation, all items except pile carpets were manufactured primarily for use by the producer's family. Pile carpets, of the variety called Bukharan by Oriental rug dealers, are produced primarily for sale and represent the only source of cash income derived from female labor. The return on female labor invested in carpet weaving is quite high by local standards, but both the limited supply of wool and competing demands for female labor limit the production of carpets.[2] Because of these limitations, several closely related households usually pool their resources in wool and female labor for purposes of carpet weaving, splitting the eventual profit in proportions corresponding to each family's contribution.

## Other Secondary Sources of Income

In addition to agriculture and carpet weaving, there are a number of other sources of income of minor importance. Hunting of partridge and

[2] Wool yields runs about 1.7 pounds per sheep in the spring, and somewhat less in the fall. About two-thirds of the spring wool is suitable for carpet weaving. As a rule, none of the fall wool is suitable for this purpose. Wool not suited for carpet weaving is used to manufacture felts. If the market value of the raw materials for a carpet—wool and dye—are subtracted from the market value of the carpet, and if this figure is then divided by the days of female labor required to produce the carpet, an estimate of the return on female labor invested in weaving can be made. The resulting estimate is about five tumans income (66 cents) for a 12 hour day of weaving. This represents a high return in terms of the local economy.

antelope and gathering of greens and pomegranates provide additional minor sources of subsistence income for all pastoral families.

A few individuals have been trained in religion, and are occasionally given small donations in return for performing various religious services. A handful of households among the pastoral population maintain stores in their yurts where they sell tea, sugar, matches, cloth, and rice. A few act as middlemen on a larger scale by bringing grain and flour in large quantities into the community for local sale. A few individuals are also blacksmiths. Of these secondary sources of income, trading is the only one that can provide a substantial income.

## Wealth Profile of a Particular Community

A more concrete picture of the relationship between economics and kinship among the pastoral Turkmen can be gained by examining the economic situation in a particular community. Table 11 summarizes property holding in Ajī Quī. In order to simplify comparison, the various forms of productive capital have been converted into their equivalent value in sheep. The Turkmen themselves frequently compare different forms of productive capital by converting them into an equivalent value in sheep, and they have standard rates of conversion for this process.[3] A more detailed list of property holdings is given in Appendix I.

A few observations should be made about the data in Table 11 and in Appendix I. First, only productive capital is summarized in this table. Beasts of burden, yurts, and household equipment, although necessary for each family, are not sources of income, and, therefore, have not been included.

TABLE 11
WEALTH PROFILE OF AJĪ QUĪ

| Value of Capital in Livestock and Land (converted to equivalent value in sheep) | Number of Households | Average Number of Able-Bodied Adults in Households of Each Wealth Category |
|---|---|---|
| 400 or more | 5 | 7.8 |
| 200-399 | 5 | 7.0 |
| 100-199 | 14 | 5.1 |
| 35-99 | 15 | 3.7 |
| 34 or less | 20 | 3.0 |

[3] The equivalent values used by the Turkmen are as follows: one she-camel equals 10 sheep; one cow equals five sheep; one mare equals five sheep; three goats equal two sheep; one hectare of marginal agricultural land equals one sheep; one hectare of productive dry land equals eight sheep; one hectare of irrigated land equals 40 sheep.

Second, capital in livestock and land are not the only sources of income for the Turkmen. Shepherding and trade are also significant sources of income. However, any family which gains a substantial income from shepherding or trade will eventually use a part of this income to acquire livestock or land. Thus, capital in these forms reflects fairly accurately a family's economic situation no matter what sources of income other than land or livestock it might exploit. Details of other sources of income, including charity, are included in Appendix I.

An examination of the data in Appendix I reveals that all but one of the families with capital of less than 35 sheep (in equivalent value) have some supplementary source of income. Thus, 35 sheep or an equivalent in other forms of wealth can be taken as a rough estimate of the minimum amount of capital with which a single household can subsist without some additional source of income.[4]

Seven households in 1967 were subsisting almost exclusively on charity. In addition, three households had absorbed closely related domestic groups that were totally impoverished. It is not unusual for such impoverished families eventually to regain a position of economic independence and even substantial wealth. Nine of the households in Ajī Quī that had capital equivalent in value to more than 100 sheep in 1967 had in the past 20 years been in a position of not having sufficient capital for their own support. One of these nine household heads had started with a moderate patrimony and then grown extremely wealthy, and had been able to take four wives, a sign of great affluence. He later lost virtually all of his wealth, but during the last 10 years has regained a position of wealth and ranked fifth in capital among the families of Ajī Quī. Thus, over a period of 30 years he had experienced the extremes of wealth and poverty. The frequency with which this sort of reversal of fortune occurs impresses upon both wealthy and poor the desirability of mutual assistance among close kinsmen.

## Relationship Between Family Size and Wealth

Because of the ease with which labor can be transformed into capital, there is a tendency for families with large labor pools to be wealthier than smaller families (see Barth, 1961:107,117). Figure 22 indicates the extent of the association between wealth and labor resources. The Spearman rank correlation coefficient for these two variables in Ajī Quī indicates that the

---

[4] See Appendix I, Table 13. Also see Barth, 1961:16. Barth cites 60 animals as the minimum herd on which a Basseri family could subsist in 1958. There are, of course, numerous differences between the economies of the Basseri and Yomut which could account for this difference. It is interesting in light of this difference to observe that individuals with 40 or more sheep and goats are obligated to give alms, a fact suggesting that in early Islamic times, a family could subsist with 40 animals.

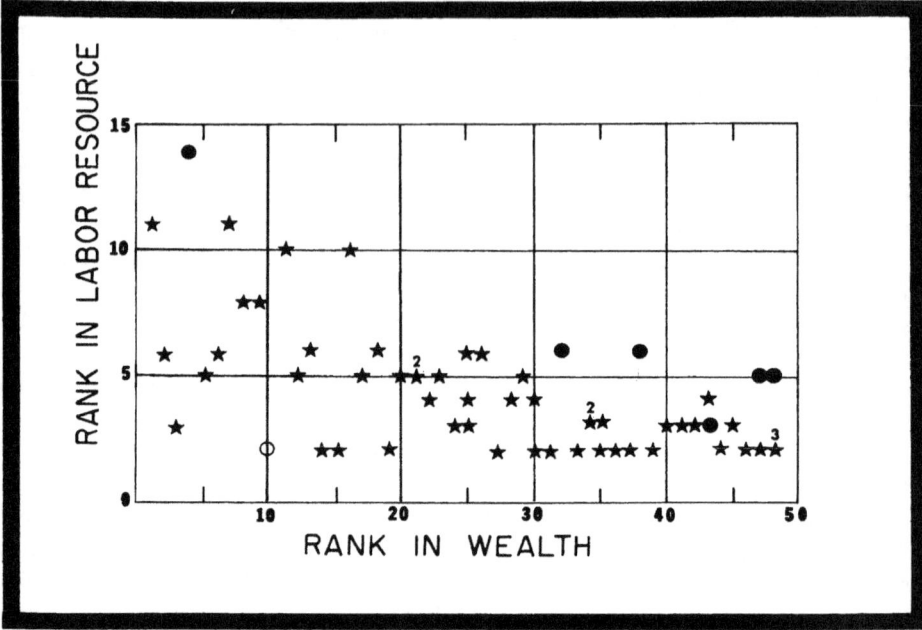

Fig. 22. Labor resources and wealth for the households of Ajī Quī; labor resources are measured by number of able-bodied adults in household.
- ● represents a household which has paid bridewealth in the last two years
- o represents a household which has received bridewealth in the last two years
- * indicates the number of households which fall in exactly the same point, being equal in both wealth and labor resources; because of these overlaps, the 59 domestic units form 48 rankings on the scale of wealth

association between wealth and labor resources is +.66.[5] The qualitative description of the relationship between wealth and labor resources leads to an expectation that there would be a high degree of association between these variables. However, there are a number of factors that would lead one to predict an association substantially less than +1.0. Herds are, as pointed out above, continually fluctuating so that the correlation at one point in time does not reflect perfectly the productivity of each family. Also, there are marked differences in the efficiency of each individual as an economic producer, and, since all households contain only a small number of producers, these individual differences do not average out. Thus, the statistical correlation

[5] The data correlated are those presented in Figure 22, and in Table 13 of Appendix I. Households which have—as indicated in both Figure 22 and Table 13—paid out, or received, bridewealth in the last two years were excluded from the correlation. The correlation would be significant at the .01 level for a random sample (Siegel, 1956:202-213, 284). The sample, of course, is not random, but rather a 100 percent sample of Ajī Quī in August 1967. See also Epstein, 1967:35.

agrees with expectations derived from the qualitative description of the relationship between labor and capital. It should also be borne in mind that while it is easy for a large family to acquire capital, it is sometimes possible for a small household that begins its independent existence with a large patrimony to maintain its position through diligent and judicious management of its capital. For this reason, small wealthy families are more common exceptions to the general association between labor resources and accumulated capital than are large poor families (see Fig. 22).[6]

It should be noted briefly at this juncture that the relationship between wealth and labor resources was probably very similar among the Yomut chomur before the recent development of mechanized commercial agriculture in their region. Arable land existed, as noted earlier, in surplus of demand and the amount of land cultivated by a family depended on the labor resources they possessed. Under these conditions one would expect to find the same sort of correlation between wealth and family size that existed among the charwa of Ajī Quī in 1966-67.

## LEVELING INSTITUTIONS

The basic argument presented about bridewealth in this section is that it can be interpreted as a compensation to the bride's family both for loss of labor and loss of future growth potential, and conversely payment by the groom's family for both labor and growth potential. The economic significance of the other institutions discussed is relatively obvious.

### Bridewealth

Virilocal residence after marriage has clear implications in terms of the advantages conferred by a large labor pool. A bride brings both her own labor and promise of future growth to her father-in-law's household. It is equally clear that one family's gain in this regard is another family's loss. Because of virilocal residence, families can grow only by producing sons, and the birth of a daughter instead of a son is a misfortune in the sense that opportunities for future growth have been missed. The importance attached to the birth of sons is indicated by special ceremonies and celebrations after the birth of a son, ceremonies and festivities that are absent after the birth of a daughter. It is also indicated by extensive magical practices designed to protect sons, especially from the evil eye, practices not used to protect daughters.[7] The

---

[6] Of course, immediately after making a bridal payment a large family is often temporarily poor. However, because such a family regains a position of at least moderate wealth very quickly, there would never be many such families in a large sample.

[7] Daughters are not protected from the evil eye because it does not pose a threat to them. Only objects of envy are in danger from the evil eye.

advantage of having sons is, of course, many-faceted: prestige and political advantages as well as economic ones accompany the growth of a family. Nevertheless the economic advantage of having sons and the economic disadvantage of daughters are well appreciated by the Turkmen. Viewing the situation from a more analytic point of view, it can be said that the random composition of sibling groups in terms of sex is a large factor contributing to inequalities in the sizes of families and thus to inequalities in wealth.

Bridewealth to some extent compensates for these inequalities. The apparently exorbitant bridal payments favor the economically disadvantaged at the expense of the economically advantaged. Families with many sons and few, or no, daughters must labor for many years to raise the extra livestock they need to obtain brides. Families with many daughters, although they have less potential for growth and economic prosperity, receive a large income in bridewealth each time a daughter is married.

The three-year period of spouse avoidance, whatever other effects it may have, increases the compensation to families with many daughters and increases the burden of obtaining brides which falls on households with many sons. A family, in order to obtain a bride, must not only produce a large surplus of livestock but also must do so, in effect, several years in advance of obtaining a bride. A family giving a daughter in marriage enjoys the income from her bridewealth for several years before actually losing her labor.

It should be emphasized, however, that the bridewealth conventions do not place every household in a position of economic equality. For example, families with few, or no, children of either sex are not assisted by this institution. The effect of high bridal payments and of delayed delivery of the bride is to ease the economic difficulty of some families and to decrease, but not eliminate, the number of households that are in an economically precarious situation.

The effect of bridal payments on household wealth can best be illustrated by examining the economic fate of two households, one with a large number of sons and one with a large number of daughters.

The family of K͟hoday Berdī ("God Gave Him"), a man with five sons and one daughter illustrates the situation of a family that is, by virtue of having a large labor force, in an advantageous position. K͟hoday Berdī was originally a very poor man. He was born a Kurd in the vicinity of Bujnurd and taken as a slave by raiders while still an infant. Following the general pattern described above, he assumed a position similar to that of a second-class son in the family that purchased him. His master had only one actual son, Bayram Geldī ("He Came in the Month of Bayram"), a boy 10 years older than K͟hoday Berdī. His master died after both he and Bayram Geldī had reached adulthood and married. The older son was quite tyrannical toward K͟hoday Berdī and eventually threw him out of his household with no property at all. The elders (yas͟holīs), feeling this action unjustified, gathered and discussed the matter with Bayram Geldī. Eventually they persuaded him that although Khoday Berdī had no right to a patrimony he should, nevertheless be given something. Bayram Geldī than gave him a tent with a few furnishings and a few donkeys. Following this Khoday Berdī migrated to a neighboring oba in order to avoid extensive contact with Bayram Geldī.

During his early years Khoday Berdī lived by performing odd jobs for wages: hauling firewood, blacksmithing, performing circumcisions, anything for which a small fee could be given. Being able to save some of his meager income, he gradually began to build up a small flock of sheep and goats. Meanwhile he had the good fortune of having five sons and a daughter over a period of 16 years. His sons began shepherding his small herd when they reached the appropriate age and eventually he accumulated a herd of 120 animals. About 20 years ago a livestock disease reduced this herd to 25 animals. Following this he began gradually to rebuild his herd. Fifteen years before my arrival in Ajī Quī he took a wife for his oldest son, who was then 18. At this point he had not yet accumulated enough livestock to make a bridal payment, but he was able to arrange a daughter exchange (chalshɨq), giving his own daughter of 14 in return for his son's bride.

Eleven years before my arrival his herd had again reached 120 animals, and he took a bride for his second son, paying 70 animals out of his flock, as well as a horse, a camel, and a sum of money. This left his herd at 50 animals, and his sons began again to rebuild the family herd, but soon they suffered a serious setback: the oldest son's wife died. In addition to the personal tragedy involved, this meant a second wife would have to be taken for the oldest son who was then 27. The oldest son found employment as a shepherd for a wealthy man who, like Khoday Berdī, belonged to the Choperlī[8] descent group. Meanwhile the younger sons cared for the family's own livestock. In a period of four years, Khoday Berdī's herd rose rapidly to 210 animals, and it was possible to take a second bride for the oldest son, paying 185 animals and a sum of cash.

This left a herd of 25 animals, but the oldest son continued shepherding. The income in livestock from shepherding caused a rapid rise in their livestock so that at the point of my arrival in Ajī Quī they had 170 animals, and shortly after my arrival they were able to take a bride for their third son, paying 70 animals and the remainder of the 11 mal payment in cash. The third son of the family a few years prior to my arrival had begun trading, buying small items, such as cigarettes, matches, tea, sugar, and also some cloth in the city of Gunbadi Kāvūs and selling them among the nomads. This not only increased the family's income, but also meant that a fairly large portion of their accumulated wealth at any one time took the form of ready cash. Thus, their willingness to use cash as part of a bridal payment increased.

---

[8] Choperlī is a fictitious name.

After the last bridal payment they had 100 animals left, but the oldest son continued shepherding and the third son continued his trading. Thus, after a bad year in which both drought and a livestock epidemic had caused most herds to decline they had increased their holding to 140 animals. This herd produced a poor lamb crop and many adult animals died owing to drought, but their livestock escaped the disease which decimated many of their neighbors' herds. At the same time they enjoyed a good income from shepherding and trade which took the form of cash for immediate expenses and livestock to build up their herd. At this point they had two more sons to marry off and they were hoping to accomplish this in a short period of about five years. Barring serious setbacks, they should be able to do this. The family now has an adult labor pool of eight individuals and, thus, is very productive. The adult members include the head of the household, his five adult sons and two daughters-in-law; the mother of the family is deceased and the third son's wife has not yet joined her husband.

Thus, over a period of some 40 years a man who started with no capital had managed to build up a herd and then see it depleted seriously by disease on one occasion and bridal payments on three occasions. After each setback he managed to recover, and in more recent years with five adult sons he has been able to recover from depletion of his capital very quickly. This illustrates well the advantages conferred by a large labor pool.

If we compare the fate of Khoday Berdī with that of Anna Mengli ("Friday Speckled"), a man with five daughters and two sons, we see a sharply contrasting situation. Anna Mengli was 60 at the conclusion of my research; Khoday Berdī was at that point 69. Anna Mengli, however, was of less humble origin and married some 10 years earlier than Khoday Berdī. As a result he began producing children at a younger age and his first born is the same age as Khoday Berdī's. However, Anna Mengli's first four children were daughters and he did not have a son until he was 40 years old, despite the fact that he married at about age 22. Anna Mengli received a modest patrimony of about 60 animals when he established an independent household, approximately 20 years before my arrival, and shortly after becoming independent he gave his oldest daughter in marriage to a widower, receiving roughly 200 animals and a small cash payment in return. His herd diminished rapidly over the next three years, and he then gave his second daughter in marriage receiving about 100 animals, thus making up for his losses. Again his herd declined for three years until he gave his third daughter in marriage receiving again about 100 animals. Two years later, however, he took a bride for his 12-year-old son cutting deeply into his large herd, leaving him with about 40 animals. Thus, after 12 years during which he had received a patrimony of 60 animals and about 400 animals in bridewealth, and had given out only 100 animals for bridal payment, he was left with a modest herd. Forty animals is close to the minimum on which a family can subsist without some secondary source of income. Until six years before my arrival Anna Mengli's herd stayed at about 40 animals while he enjoyed a very modest standard of living. Six years before my research began, he gave his fourth daughter in marriage receiving the usual 11 mal compensation, largely in livestock. His sons were by then old enough to begin making a substantial contribution to the family income so that their wealth did not decline rapidly after this bridewealth. They had about 120 animals when I left. His sixth child, a boy of 17, and his youngest child, a girl of 14 were both well within marriageable age at the time of my departure, and he was contemplating a daughter exchange. This would provide his second son with a wife without depleting their herd. The household now has a labor pool of five adults, the head and his wife, two sons, and a daughter-in-law. With such a labor resource, it should be able to maintain a good size herd and a reasonable standard of living in the future.

The above discussion illustrates one of the more salient effects of bridewealth. It should be noted, however, that bridewealth has several far-reaching social implications and the above discussion explores only one. The institution of bridewealth also has an effect on the status of women and the stability of marriage, facets of the institution which are not discussed in this study.

### Other Leveling Institutions

The economic aspects of adoption and ultimogeniture are relatively straightforward. A man who has no sons in his household is obviously in a very disadvantageous position economically. The practice described above by which men who fail to produce sons adopt them from close agnates maintains the viability of households which would otherwise be in a very weak position. It is interesting to note that the institution of adoption among the Yomut is primarily economic: an adopted son (oghilliq) assumes the position of son in relation to his adoptive father only in economic terms. His political position and his position in relation to incest barriers are defined by his original parentage. Ultimogeniture has a similar effect of saving independent males from the fate of maintaining a household without the assistance of a dependent son.

Another set of institutions provides a guarantee against economic difficulty: the forms of charitable assistance between closely related households. One conspicuous institution of this sort is thakat, the annual giving of alms for charitable or religious purposes. Although thakat is an Islamic institution, not one of kinship, Yomut inevitably give the required alms to the closest kinsmen qualified to receive them, which, in effect, makes the practice a form of economic assistance to close kin. Among the Yomut, assistance beyond that required by the obligation to give thakat annually is limited to close kin: in the case of consanguines, first cousins or closer; and, in the case of relatives by marriage, those related as qoda (see Fig. 20) in a non-classificatory sense, or closer affines. Economic assistance between such close kin in extreme cases can take the form of merging an impoverished household with a wealthier one so that they become a viable joint household. Three of the households listed in the Ajī Quī census were joint households formed in this way. Assistance can also take the form of gifts of money or livestock that go beyond what a person is required to give as thakat, as well as donations of labor. In addition to helping kin meet their daily economic needs. Yomut frequently help close kin to raise bridal payments. Assistance in bridal transactions can take the form of a gift of livestock, or of offering a bride to close kin for a reduced payment.

Thakat, in contrast, represents a more limited form of assistance, but one that is often given to more distant kin: relatives that are only putative agnates often receive thakat if no closer kin can be found. Thakat, in effect, is very much like a negative income tax, in that it requires that the wealthier portion of the community give a part of its wealth to the poorer portion.

Turkmen reckon thakat as follows: 10 percent of agricultural income, and a fixed portion of holdings in livestock other than beasts of burden. The fixed portion of livestock relevant to the nomads of Ajī Quī is determined in this way: for an owner of less than 40 small animals, no thakat is required; those owning 40 to 120 must give one sheep; those owning 121 to 200 must give two sheep; those owning 201 to 399 must give three sheep; for holdings of 400 or more, the required alms is one of every 100 animals. The thakat on camels and cows is defined in similar terms, while that on mares is calculated as one-fortieth of their cash value. The total wealth that changes hands in Ajī Quī through thakat offerings is quite large. In the fall of 1967 thakat reckoned on livestock was equivalent in value to approximately 7,670 tumans (including 1,700 tumans given from herds held as emanet in Ajī Quī and belonging to relatives of local residents.). The üshür, or alms on agricultural income, in the spring of 1967 was equivalent to approximately 2,340 tumans. Comparing these figures to the number of recipients yields some idea of the importance of this institution. Fourteen families (68 persons) received thakat offerings because of poverty and one additional young man received offerings because he was a full-time student of religion. Thus, the alms received averaged about 140 tumans per person. This figure compares favorably with the per capita income of a family of median wealth in a bad year (see Table 14, p. 179), especially if consideration is given to the fact that most of the families receiving thakat have additional, though meager, sources of income.

### The Overall Effect of Economic Leveling Institutions

It has been shown that the institutions organizing economic production tend to create an unequal distribution of wealth, and that certain other institutions to a limited extent counterbalance this tendency. Bridal payments take a greater portion of wealth from the most productive families, and from families with the highest growth potential, that is, from those with the largest number of sons. Much of this wealth is distributed among families that lack growth potential, that is, families with many daughters. Adoption and ultimogeniture prevent the depletion of labor resources within the family. Finally, obligations of mutual assistance among close kin provide a last line of defense against ruin for poorer families.

It should be noted, however, that the various leveling institutions do not create anything approximating an equal distribution of wealth. The strongest tendency is that created by the division of society into productive units of unequal size, and the leveling institutions simply act as a brake on this tendency, which for the most part amounts to requiring the more productive households to share a part of their greater wealth with less fortunate families.

## Household Size and Economic Viability

What is probably more significant is the fact that these various leveling institutions have the effect of minimizing the number of households that fall below the viable limit in terms of their labor resources. The institutions most prominent in doing this are ultimogeniture, adoption, and the late age at majority among Turkmen males. The norms of deference and avoidance discussed in Chapter V also play a crucial role in preventing conflicts that could lead to an earlier break-up of extended families and a larger number of households too small to be viable.

The contrast between the Yomut and the Basseri nomads of southern Persia (Barth, 1961, 1964) is instructive concerning this facet of Yomut domestic organization. The Basseri nomads differ from the Yomut in lacking most of these institution which encourage the occurrence of households with large numbers of adult members. The Basseri have no consistent practice of ultimogeniture, and men without sons less regularly adopt the sons of other men. It is also the usual practice among the Basseri for men to establish economically independent households soon after marriage in contrast to the Yomut who ordinarily establish independent households at a much later point in life.

In his study of the Basseri, Barth did not address himself extensively to the question of household labor resources and economic viability. It seems reasonable, however, to assume that the situation of pastoral Basseri is not that different from that of the pastoral Yomut, and, until recently, that of the agricultural Yomut. In fact there are suggestions in Barth's study that the situation is very similar (1961:117). If we assume that the relationship between labor resources and economic viability is roughly the same for these two groups, then the Basseri should be characterized by both a lower average household size and a higher porportion of economically unviable households.

That this is indeed true is suggested by Barth's report that a large proportion of the Basseri population in each generation is forced through impoverishment to abandon their migratory pastoral way of life and seek employment in sedentary communities. Barth in fact mentions that men with no children or only daughters are especially likely to become impoverished and forced to settle (*ibid*.).

This contrast is interesting in that Barth suggests that the process of continual sedentarization of a large portion of the nomadic pastoral population is important as a mechanism maintaining a healthy balance between economic resources (mainly pasture) and population.

If this is true the contrast between the Yomut and the Basseri is an especially interesting one. According to Barth, in each generation the Basseri produce a larger population than their economic resources can support and then eliminate the surplus through outmigration. Outmigration is encouraged by a developmental cycle of domestic groups which creates a large number of households that are unviable because of limited labor resources. It is suggested in this monograph that the Yomut, in contrast, have social mechanisms that limit population growth to what the tribal resources can support and then organize the existing population into domestic units which are predominantly large enough to be viable (cf. Irons, 1972).

# VIII

# OVERVIEW

IT has been suggested that several features of the kinship system described in this study are adaptations to the physical and social environment in which they evolved. These adaptations are directed toward two general things: maintaining military effectiveness and maintaining general economic well-being. Certain features of the lineage system have facilitated both the use of nomadic mobility and the uniting of large numbers of people for military purposes, apparently as adaptations to a continual challenge of external aggression both from other Turkmen groups and from geographically contiguous states. Several features of domestic organization appear to have the beneficial effect of minimizing the frequency of small households which are economically unviable. Also a number of practices surrounding marriage appear to serve as mechanisms regulating population size.

These propositions are all theoretical ones which can only be accepted on the basis of empirical testing. At points in the study supporting evidence has been offered. At several points, however, it has only been possible to suggest future empirical tests or to refer to research in progress which may eventually provide a better testing of these propositions. It would be useful as a concluding discussion to explore further the ways in which propositions of this sort can be tested and to point out how such empirical research could shed further light on the ethnography of the Turkmen.

Each of these propositions consists of a statement to the effect that a particular social form has an effect on the population which increases its chances of survival. One obvious way in which propositions of this sort can be tested is to devise empirical studies designed to determine whether a particular social form in fact has the beneficial effect hypothesized. Research of this sort, dealing with the hypothesis presented at the end of Chapter VI, is currently in progress.

An alternate and somewhat broader approach is also possible. This approach would consist of an attempt to relate both historic and ethnographic data to a broader theoretical framework. A theory concerning the origin of adaptive social forms is already available to us (Campbell, 1965; Chagnon, 1974:67-80, 127-161; Irons, 1974:655-657; Newcomer, 1972.). Briefly, this theory states that the evolution of forms of human social organization (as well as other aspects of culture) is a result of a process of variation and selection similar in many ways to that underlying biological evolution. The theory first assumes the existence of distinct and in some ways competing groups, such as the various tribal and lineage divisions of the Turkmen. It further assumes that occasionally some of these groups introduce behavioral innovations. For example it would be necessary to assume that occasionally a particular Turkmen tribe or lineage will change some feature of its social organization from that of its ancestors and that of neighboring and competing groups. In addition it is assumed that some of these variations provide the groups with which they are associated with an advantage relative to other groups (parallel lineages or tribes), while others confer a disadvantage. Advantageous variations tend to be retained and to spread through two processes: expansion of advantaged groups at the expense of less favored groups, and imitation of advantageous innovations by groups which did not originally possess them. Disadvantageous variations tend to disappear through the reverse processes: the contraction and disappearance of groups possessing them, and abandonment of such innovations as a result of some level of understanding of their detrimental effects.

Introducing a theory of this sort into the anthropological study of the Turkmen has several advantages. First, it offers a general justification for the presumption that certain social forms are in some measure adaptive in their local context. Second and more important, it immediately suggests possible relationships between historic and ethnographic data which might not otherwise come to light. Further the introduction of such a body of theory suggests additional lines of empirical enquiry.

The above theoretical model suggests that the historically well-documented process of tribal warfare has been the local manifestation of the evolutionary selective process. The written history of the Turkmen which extends back a millenium records a continual process of intensive warfare both between different Turkmen groups and between Turkmen tribes and neighboring sedentary state societies. History further indicates that not all Turkmen tribes survived the competitive pressures of their social environment. Many groups continually lost territory in military encounters with competing groups and were eventually either absorbed as refugees among larger and more successful tribes, or were pushed out of the Turkmen area (Abul-Ghazī, 1958; Barthold, 1962; Marvin, 1881; O' Donovan, 1882; Qūrkhānchī Saulat Nizām, 1903-4, Rabino, 1928; Vambery, 1865; Yate, 1900). Other groups which were more successful expanded at the expense of weaker neighbors, and eventually fissioned into numerous descendant groups.

The oral accounts of older informants and the more recent written accounts indicate that this competitive process continued up to the time of pacification. In the latter part of the nineteenth century, the Yomut were expanding at the expense of the Göklen, an expansion that had continued over a long time. Originally the entire Gurgan Plain had been occupied by the Göklen, and the Yomut, a group of more recent historic origin, were originally intruders from the Balkhan Mountains to the north. Also during the nineteenth century, the Teke, a group of more recent origin than the Yomut, were expanding from the region of the Kopet Mountains at the expense of the Yomut. After the Russian conquest and pacification of the area north of the Atrak River, the expansion of the Teke ceased, but the expansion of the Yomut at the expense of the Göklen continued on Persian territory until the pacification of the Iranian Turkmen in 1925. Even during the brief period of ineffective administration during the 1940s, certain Yomut tribes took advantage of the situation to expand their territory at the expense of neighboring tribes.

Considering the long period of time during which Turkmen groups have been faced with continual intertribal warfare, and the frequency with which particular groups have been eliminated through this selective process, the argument that the end result has been the development of social forms geared to military effectiveness seems quite compelling. The argument may seem less compelling in terms of the evolution of economic or demographic adaptations. However, it is reasonable to assume that the process of intertribal competition in the form of warfare would lead to the evolution of economically and demographically adaptive forms if the broad range of factors possibly affecting the outcome of such warfare are taken into consideration. Both oral and written accounts indicate that the Turkmen were periodically affected by drought and famine. Although it is difficult at present to document, it seems reasonable that different groups would vary in their ability to survive these threats to their existence. Owing to differences in social organization, some groups may have maintained a better balance between population size and resources than did other groups. A year, or sequence of years, of drought or famine would in such cases affect some groups more adversely than others. One territorial group might emerge from such a misfortune vastly weaker than some neighboring territorial group which had maintained a lower population density in relation to resources. At such a point the situation would be ripe for the expansion of one group at the expense of another. Differences in forms of domestic organization which might lead to a higher proportion of economically unviable households in one group than another could have a similar effect on intergroup competition. Thus, intertribal warfare in the Turkmen region is probably best thought of as only one aspect of a broader selective process that favored not only forms of social organization which contributed to military strength, but also ones which contributed to such things as an effective organization of economic activities, the maintenance of a healthy balance between population and resources, or any of a number of other things affecting a particular population's chances of survival.

It should be kept in mind that, at present at least, it is impossible to document this selective process completely and, therefore, it must remain to some extent theoretical. It can be shown that certain Turkmen groups have expanded and fissioned into several descendant groups, while others have declined and in many cases vanished. It can also be shown that at present different Turkmen groups display differences in social organization which it appears could affect their competitive success. However, there is not a sufficiently detailed historical documentation of the social institutions of various Turkmen groups to allow one to demonstrate that the long-term expansions and contractions of particular groups have been the result of difference in social organization. Also the differences in social organizations which presently exist have not yet been studied thoroughly enough to say what their long-term effect is likely to be on survival in the face of intergroup competition. However, the evidence available does support the theory introduced above, and the theory does have the advantages of both being empirically testable through future research, and of suggesting new lines of inquiry. In particular it would suggest that future studies should attempt to investigate variations in social organization among different Turkmen groups, and also to draw on historical sources in order to gain a better picture of long-term historical process in the Turkmen-inhabited region of the world.

# APPENDIX I

# THE WEALTH PROFILE OF AJĪ QUĪ

Table 12 presents a detailed list of each household's holdings of productive wealth in August 1967. Number of sheep is reckoned on the basis of flock size in the fall when herds are smallest. In Table 13 all wealth has been converted to an equivalent value in sheep (see footnote 3, Chapter VII), and information on labor resources and sources of income other than from capital is included. In both tables households are listed in the order of their wealth, starting with the wealthiest. For convenience, these same numbers indicating ranking in terms of wealth are used to designate household heads in Figures 12 and 13.

### TABLE 12
### HOLDINGS OF CAPITAL IN AJĪ-QUĪ

| Household Rank in Wealth Profile | Sheep | Goats | Mares | Camels | Cows | Productive Dry Land* (hectares) | Irrigated Land (hectares) | Marginal Agricultural Land (hectares) |
|---|---|---|---|---|---|---|---|---|
| 1 | 400 | 350 | | | | | | 5 |
| 2 | 200 | 500 | | 5 | | | | 3 |
| 3 | 500 | 100 | | | | | | |
| 4 | | 60 | | | 30 | 30 | | 4 |
| 5 | 80 | 39 | 2 | | 9 | 20 | 2 | 7 |
| 6 | 280 | 40 | | | | 10 | | 5 |
| 7 | 50 | 40 | | | 1 | 27 | | 10 |
| 8 | 150 | 40 | 1 | 4 | | | | 5 |
| 9 | 110 | 30 | 1 | | | 10 | | 10 |
| 10 | 70 | 20 | 1 | | 8 | 10 | | |
| 11 | 40 | 100 | | | | 10 | | 5 |
| 12 | 90 | 20 | | | | 10 | | 7 |
| 13 | 160 | 10 | | | | 10 | | 3 |
| 14 | 50 | 10 | | 1 | | | | 2 |
| 15 | 10 | 60 | | | | 10 | | |
| 16 | 40 | | 1 | | | 10 | | 2 |
| 17 | 100 | 30 | | | | | | 5 |

| Household Rank in Wealth Profile | Sheep | Goats | Mares | Camels | Cows | Productive Dry Land* (hectares) | Irrigated Land (hectares) | Marginal Agricultural Land (hectares) |
|---|---|---|---|---|---|---|---|---|
| 18 | 100 | 30 | | | | | | 3 |
| 19 | 30 | 10 | | | | 10 | | 2 |
| 20 | 20 | 20 | | | | 10 | | 2 |
| 21 | 30 | | | | | 10 | | 5 |
| 22 | 12 | | 1 | | 2 | 10 | 2 | |
| 23 | | 30 | | | | 10 | | 2 |
| 24 | 20 | | | | | 10 | | 1 |
| 25 | 20 | 100 | 1 | | 1 | | | |
| 26 | 70 | 20 | 1 | | | | | 3 |
| 27 | | 6 | 1 | | | 10 | | 3 |
| 28 | | 10 | 1 | | | 10 | | |
| 29 | 20 | 80 | 1 | | | | | 3 |
| 30 | | | | | | | 2 | |
| 31 | 30 | 30 | | | | | | 5 |
| 32 | 40 | | | 1 | | | | 2 |
| 33 | 40 | | 1 | | | | | |
| 34 | 30 | | 1 | 1 | | | | |
| 35 | 30 | | | 1 | | | | 2 |
| 36 | 15 | 30 | | | | | | 6 |
| 37 | 25 | 10 | | | | | | 5 |
| 38 | 30 | | 1 | | | | | |
| 39 | 35 | | | | | | | |
| 40 | 20 | 15 | | | | | | 3 |
| 41 | | 50 | | | | | | |
| 42 | | 40 | | | | | | 2 |
| 43 | 20 | 10 | | | | | | 2 |
| 44 | 20 | | | | | | | 2 |
| 45 | 15 | | | | | | | 3 |
| 46 | 15 | | | | | | | |
| 47 | | 15 | | | | | | 3 |
| 48 | | 7 | 1 | | | | | 2 |
| 49 | 4 | | 1 | | | | | |
| 50 | 2 | 8 | | | | | | 2 |
| 51 | | 12 | | | | | | |
| 52 | | 6 | | | | | | 2 |
| 53 | | 4 | | | | | | |
| 54 | | | | | | | | 2 |
| 55 | | | | | | | | 2 |
| 56 | | | | | | | | |
| 57 | | | | | | | | |
| 58 | | | | | | | | |
| 59 | | | | | | | | |

*Mostly land granted under the land reform program.

# APPENDIX I

## TABLE 13
### CAPITAL, LABOR RESOURCES, AND OTHER SOURCES OF INCOME IN AJĪ QUĪ

| Rank in Terms of Capital in Land and Livestock | Value of Capital in Land and Livestock: Equivalent Value in Sheep | Number of Able-Bodied Adults in Household | Other Sources of Income | | | | Recent Bride-wealth Transactions |
|---|---|---|---|---|---|---|---|
| | | | Emanet | Shepherd | Alms | Trade | |
| 1 | 637 | 11 | | | | | |
| 2 | 586 | 6 | | | | | |
| 3 | 566 | 3 | | | | | Paid |
| 4 | 434 | 14 | X | | | | 11 mal |
| 5 | 408 | 5 | | | | | |
| 6 | 392 | 6 | | | | | |
| 7 | 308 | 11 | X | | | X | |
| 8 | 229 | 8 | | | | | |
| 9 | 225 | 8 | | | | X | Received |
| 10 | 209 | 2 | | | | | 11 mal |
| 11 | 192 | 10 | X | | | | |
| 12 | 191 | 5 | | | | | |
| 13 | 170 | 6 | | | | | |
| 14 | 149 | 2 | | | | | |
| 15 | 130 | 2 | | | | | |
| 16 | 127 | 10 | | X | | X | |
| 17 | 125 | 5 | | | | | |
| 18 | 123 | 6 | | | | | |
| 19 | 119 | 2 | | | | | |
| 20 | 116 | 5 | | X | | | |
| 21 | 115 | 5 | | X | | | |
| 22 | 102 | 5 | X | | X[1] | | |
| 23 | 102 | 4 | | | | | |
| 24 | 101 | 5 | | | | | |
| 25 | 97 | 3 | | | | | |
| 26 | 92 | 3 | | | | | |
| 27 | 92 | 4 | | X | | | |
| 28 | 92 | 6 | X | X | | | |
| 29 | 81 | 6 | X | | | | |
| 30 | 80 | 2 | | | X[1] | | |
| 31 | 55 | 4 | | | | | |
| 32 | 52 | 5 | | | | | |
| 33 | 45 | 2 | | | | | |
| 34 | 45 | 4 | X | | | | |
| 35 | 42 | 2 | | | | | Paid |
| 36 | 41 | 6 | | X | | | 21 mal |
| 37 | 37 | 2 | | | | | |
| 38 | 35 | 3 | | | | | |

[1] Members of these families received alms by virtue of being religious teachers.

| Rank in Terms of Capital in Land and Livestock | Value of Capital in Land and Livestock: Equivalent Value in Sheep | Number of Able-Bodied Adults in Household | Other Sources of Income ||||| Recent Bride-wealth Transactions |
|---|---|---|---|---|---|---|---|
| | | | Emanet | Shepherd | Alms | Trade | |
| 39 | 35 | 3 | | X | | | |
| 40 | 33 | 3 | | | X | | |
| 41 | 33 | 2 | | | | X | |
| 42 | 29 | 2 | | | X | | |
| 43 | 29 | 2 | | | | | Paid 11 mal |
| 44 | 22 | 6 | | X | | | |
| 45 | 18 | 2 | | | X | | |
| 46 | 15 | 3 | X | | | | |
| 47 | 13 | 3 | | X | | | |
| 48 | 12 | 3 | | | X | | |
| 49 | 9 | 4 | | X | X | | Paid 11 mal |
| 50 | 9 | 3 | | | X | | |
| 51 | 8 | 2 | | X | X | | |
| 52 | 6 | 3 | | | X | | |
| 53 | 3 | 2 | | | X | | Paid 6 mal |
| 54 | 2 | 5 | | X | X | | |
| 55 | 2 | 2 | | | X | | Paid 11 mal |
| 56 | 0 | 5 | | X | | | |
| 57 | 0 | 2 | | X | X | | |
| 58 | 0 | 2 | | X | X | | |
| 59 | 0 | 2 | | | X | | |

# APPENDIX II

# INCOME OF A PASTORAL FAMILY OF MODERATE WEALTH

The income that can be derived from a given amount of either land or livestock varies greatly from year to year in response to natural and market conditions. This combined with the fact that each family's productive capital is subject to continuous fluctuation produces a situation of highly variable income. This fact must be borne in mind in any attempt to estimate long-range income.

Some ideas of the general range of income among the families of Ajī Quī can be gained by examining the income that can be derived in both good and bad years from the property holding of a particular family in Ajī Quī. A family with approximately a median holding and a typical balance between the various forms of capital (the various types of livestock and land), will be most suitable for this purpose. The family that ranks 26th among the 59 households of Ajī Quī satisfies these requirements. This family has 70 sheep, 20 goats, one mare, and three hectares of marginal land. The range of income which can be expected from this capital is shown in Table 14.

TABLE 14
ESTIMATED ANNUAL INCOME FOR AN AJĪ QUĪ FAMILY
OF APPROXIMATELY MEDIAN WEALTH

| Source and Type of Income | Amount in a Bad Year (tumans) | Amount in a Good Year (tumans) |
|---|---|---|
| *Cash Income* | | |
| Sale of sheep for meat | 500 T | 1000 T |
| Sale of goats for meat | 70 T | 350 T |
| Wool and/or carpeting | 200 T | 600 T |
| Sale of colt | - | 300 T |
| Total Cash Income | 770 T | 2250 T |

| Source and Type of Income | Amount in a Bad Year (tumans) | Amount in a Good Year (tumans) |
|---|---|---|
| *Subsistence Income* | | |
| Hunting | 30 T | 50 T |
| Collected greens and pomegranates | 10 T | 40 T |
| Melons | – | 30 T |
| Wheat and barley | – | 160 T |
| oat hair | 40 T | 70 T |
| Wool for felts | 100 T | 200 T |
| Meat | 400 T | 800 T |
| Milk | 200 T | 600 T |
| Total Subsistence Income | 780 T | 1950 T |
| Total Income | 1550 T ($207) | 4200 T ($560) |
| Per Capita Income (family of 7) | 221 T ($29) | 600 T ($80) |

# APPENDIX III

# NOTE ON THE TRANSLITERATION OF TURKMEN WORDS

The Turkmen language has been written using both the Arabic alphabet and the Cyrillic alphabet. However, an attempt to transliterate from either orthography presents serious difficulties. The writing of Turkmen with the Arabic alphabet in Iran is not standardized; not only do different literate individuals use different spellings, but often the same person will vary his spelling of a particular word from one occasion to another. Also much of the material that can be found in Iran written in Turkmen, either in published or manuscript form, does not correspond closely to local pronunciation, having been influenced strongly by other dialects.

The system of writing Turkmen with the Cyrillic alphabet is more thoroughly standardized but does not reflect the pronunciation of Turkmen words systematically.[1] Saadet Çağatay has used a system of transliteration of Turkmen based on modern Turkish orthography (1950:300-324; Dulling, 1960:37), but this system is not satisfactory for the Yomut dialect of Turkmen since it obscures a number of phonemic distinctions. A system of writing Turkmen with the Latin alphabet known as the Unified Turkish Latin Alphabet was developed in the early part of this century, but this also is unsatisfactory since the modified letters used cannot be written with an ordinary typewriter (Dulling, 1960:41). As a result of these difficulties I have attempted to develop a system of transcription of Turkmen words based on the phonology of the Yomut dialect as I understand it. No great authority can be claimed for this system since no thorough phonemic analysis of Turkmen was made. In the course of gaining a moderate conversational command of Turkmen, I developed some notion of the phonemic structure of the language and, lacking anything better, I have used this as the basis for a system of writing Turkmen. The reader should also be warned that my command of Turkmen is in many ways deficient and that not only my impressions concerning the general phonology of the language, but also my renderings of particular words, no doubt contain errors.

Chart 1 summarizes the vowel phonemes of Turkmen, giving the symbols used throughout this book to represent each phoneme.

The vowel system is similar to that of standard Turkish except that there is also a distinction of vowel length. In the case of high, back, unrounded vowels, I was unable to detect a long vowel. Because the vowel system is otherwise symmetrical, I suspect such a distinction may exist even though I was unable to discern it. This doubt is indicated by the question mark in the vowel chart. Long and short back vowels are articulated at the

---

[1] For an explanation of the Cyrillic orthography of Turkmen see G. K. Dulling, 1960. For a discussion of the shortcomings of this orthography see Baskakov, 1960.

## CHART 1
## TURKMEN VOWELS

|  | Front | | | | Back | | | |
|---|---|---|---|---|---|---|---|---|
|  | Unrounded | | Rounded | | Unrounded | | Rounded | |
|  | Long | Short | Long | Short | Long | Short | Long | Short |
| High | ī | i | ǖ | ü | (?) | ɨ | ū | u |
| Low | ē | e | ȫ | ö | ā | a | ō | o |

same points and differ only in length. However, long front vowels are articulated at different points, high vowels being more close, and low vowels being more open.

Rough equivalents are listed below:

| | |
|---|---|
| ī | like the vowel in "eat" |
| i | like the vowel in "it" |
| ē | like the vowel in "hat" except that it is longer in duration |
| e | like the vowel in "bet" |
| ǖ | like German "ü" and French "u" but longer and closer |
| ü | like German "ü" and French "u" |
| ȫ | like German "ö" and French "eu" but longer and more open |
| ö | like German "ö" and French "eu" |
| ɨ | like the vowel in "hut" |
| ā | like the vowel in "father" |
| a | like the vowel in "father" but shorter |
| ū | like the vowel in "moon" |
| u | like the vowel in "moon" but shorter |
| ō | like the vowel in "hoe" without the glide |
| o | like the vowel in "hoe" without the glide and shorter. |

## CHART 2
## TURKMEN DIPHTHONGS

| Front | | Back | |
|---|---|---|---|
| Front Glide | Back Glide | Front Glide | Back Glide |
| üy | | uy | |
| öy | | oy | |
| ey | ew | ay | aw |

Each of these diphthongs begins with the short vowel indicated and is followed by a front or back glide. Some of these diphthongs are very similar to certain English vowels:

| | |
|---|---|
| ey | as in English "day" |
| uy | roughly equivalent to the diphthong in "buoy" |
| oy | as in English "toy" |
| ay | as in English "high" |
| aw | as in English "how" |

APPENDIX III 183

The remaining diphthongs have no familiar equivalents.

It should be noted that occasionally non-diphthongal vowels occur in sequence with neither vowel being audibly modified by the adjacent vowel. Thus, the word quī ("well") contains two such vowels, and is distinct from the word quy (second person imperative of quymaq, "to put," or "to place"), which has a single diphthong.

The consonants are given in Chart 3.

CHART 3
TURKMEN CONSONANTS

|  |  | Bilabial | Interdental | Alveolar | Alveo-Palatal | Palatal | Velar | Pharyngeal |
|---|---|---|---|---|---|---|---|---|
| Stops | Voiceless | p |  | t |  | k | q |  |
|  | Voiced | b |  | d |  | g | q̇ |  |
| Affricates | Voiceless |  |  |  | ch |  |  |  |
|  | Voiced |  |  |  | j |  |  |  |
| Fricatives | Voiceless |  | th |  | sh | kh |  |  |
|  | Voiced |  | t̲h̲ |  | zh | gh |  |  |
| Nasals |  | m |  | n |  | ng |  |  |
| Trills |  |  |  | r |  |  |  |  |
| Latterals |  |  |  | l |  |  |  |  |
| Semi-vowels |  | w |  |  |  | y |  | h |

Rough equivalents of these phonemes are:

| p | like English "p" except that in intervocalic position it becomes a bilabial fricative |
| b | like English "b" except that in intervocalic position it becomes a bilabial fricative |
| t | like English "t" |
| d | like English "d" |
| k | like English "k" |
| g | like English "g" |
| q | like Persian "ك" when it is a stop but voiceless |
| q̇ | like Persian "ك" when it is a stop |
| ch | like the first consonant in "church" (the same as "ç" in Turkish) |
| j | like English "j" (the same as "c" in Turkish) |
| th | like the first consonant in "thin" |
| t̲h̲ | like the first consonant in "this" |
| sh | like the first consonant in "shell" |
| zh | like the "s" in "pleasure" |
| kh | like Persian "خ" |
| gh | like Persian "خ" when it is a fricative |
| m | like English "m" |
| n | like English "n" |

| | |
|---|---|
| ng | like the last consonant in "sing" |
| r | trilled like Persian " ﺭ " |
| l | like English "l" when alveolar |
| w | like English "w" |
| y | like English "y" |
| h | like English "h" |

It should be noted that all of the consonants, except the semi-vowels, occur in geminate form in intervocalic position, and the continuants occur in geminate form in post-vocalic position.

Vowel harmony in Turkmen is simpler than in Turkish, there never being more than twofold (front and back) vowel harmony. However, Dulling's statement that Iranian Turkmen has invariable suffixes, having completely lost vowel harmony, is not true of the Yomut dialect (1960:3,12). Most suffixes do have alternate front-vowel and back-vowel forms, but, apparently owing to historic shifts in the vowels without corresponding shifts in the suffixes, the required suffix does not always harmonize with the preceding vowel. For example, the plural of qīth (girl, daughter, or virgin) is qīthlar, not qīthler, as would be necessary if the vowels were to exhibit front-back harmony. Similarly the plural of gun (day) is guller, not gullar. It should also be noted that the phonemic sequence -nl- always becomes -ll- in pronunciation. There is also a degree of variation in the consonants as well as the vowels in suffixes. Thus, the infinitive suffix has two forms: "-mek" and "-maq."

There are a large number of morphophonemic sound changes, like the transformation of the phonemic sequence -nl- to -ll- noted above. These are too numerous to explain here, however. The only one that appears in the Turkmen words in the text is the shift of final "q" as in aghtiq (grandchild) to "gh" when it is no longer in final position, as in aghtighim (my grandchild).

There appear to be some relatively predictable sound shifts between Turkmen and standard Turkish. These are:

Turkmen "q" usually becomes Turkish "k"
Turkmen "q̄" usually becomes Turkish "k"
Turkmen "th" usually becomes Turkish "s"
Turkmen "t̄h̄" usually becomes Turkish "z"
Turkmen "kh" usually becomes Turkish "h"
Turkmen "gh" usually becomes Turkish "g"
Turkmen "w" usually becomes Turkish "v"
Turkmen "ng" usually becomes Turkish "n"

Less frequent sound shifts are these:

Turkmen "p" often becomes Turkish "f"
Turkmen "b" often becomes Turkish "v"
Turkmen "d" often becomes Turkish "t"

The shifts in vowels and diphthongs between the two languages are not especially regular, but there are a few common shifts:

Turkmen "u" often becomes Turkish "ü"
Turkmen "o" often becomes Turkish "ö"
Turkmen "i" often becomes Turkish "ı"

# APPENDIX III

Turkmen "aw" often becomes Turkish "ev" or "av"
Turkmen "öy" often becomes Turkish "ev"
Turkmen "ew" often becomes Turkish "ev"

Also Turkmen long vowels frequently appear as their nearest equivalent in Turkish.

As noted in the preface Turkmen words which appear frequently in Barthold's "A History of the Turkmen People" (1962) have been spelled as they appear in that source. Listed below are the transcriptions reflecting current Yomut pronunciation of the more frequent such words:

| Spelling in Barthold | Transcription |
|---|---|
| Oghuz Khan | Oghuth Han |
| Teke | Teke |
| Yomut | Yomut |
| Salor | Thalor |
| Sarıq | Tharıq |
| Ali-eli | Alili |
| Ersari | Erthari |
| Göklen | Gökleng |
| Choudor | Chawdır |

There are several spellings of Turkmen current in English (Turkoman, Turcoman, Turkman, Turkmen), and I have chosen the one closest to the Turkmen pronunciation which is Türkmen.

# BIBLIOGRAPHY

Aberle, D. F.
    1953 The Kinship of the Kalmuk Mongols. University of New Mexico Publications in Anthropology, No. 8. Albuquerque, University of New Mexico Press.

Abul-Ghāzī
    1958 Shajarehyi Tarākimeh, A. N. Kononov. Russian and Turkmen. Moscow, Akademiya Nauk SSSR.

Arberry, Arthur J.
    n.d. The Koran Interpreted. New York, Macmillan.

Arfa, Hassan
    1964 Under Five Shahs. London, John Murray.

Arne. T. J.
    1945 Excavation at Shah Tepe, Iran. The Sino-Swedish Expedition, Publication 27, Section 7, Vol. 5, Stockholm.

Aswad, Barbara C.
    1971 Property Control and Social Strategies: Settlers on a Middle Eastern Plain. Anthropological Papers of the Museum of Anthropology, No. 44. Ann Arbor, University of Michigan.

Bacon, Elizabeth E.
    1958 Obok: A Study of Social Structure in Eurasia. Viking Fund Publications in Anthropology, No. 25. New York, Wenner-Gren Foundation for Anthropological Research.

Barth, Fredrik
    1959 Segmentary Opposition and the Theory of Games: A Study of Pathan Organization. Journal of the Royal Anthropological Institute, Vol. 89.
    1961 Nomads of South Persia: The Basseri Tribe of the Khamseh Confederacy. New York, Humanities Press.
    1964 Capital, Investment and the Social Structure of a Pastoral Nomad Group in South Persia. *In*: Capital, Savings and Credit in Peasant Societies, Raymond Firth and B. S. Yamey, eds. Chicago, Aldine Publishing Co.

Barthold, V. V.
    1962 A History of the Turkman People. *In*: Four Studies of the History of Central Asia, by V. V. Barthold, trans. by V. and T. Minorsky. Vol. 3. Leiden, E. J. Brill.

Baskakov, N. A.
    1960 The Turkic Peoples of the USSR: The Development of their Language and Writing. Oxford, Central Asian Research Centre in association with St. Antony's College (Oxford) Soviet Affairs Study Group.

Behnam, J.
    1968 Population. *In*: The Land of Iran, W. B. Fisher, ed. Vol. 1: The Cambridge History of Iran. Cambridge, Cambridge University Press.

Bender, Donald R.
    1971 Population and Productivity in Tropical Forest Bush Fallow Agriculture. *In*: Culture and Population, Steven Polger, ed. Cambridge, Schenkman.

Bobek, H.
    1968 Vegetation. *In*: The Land of Iran, W. B. Fisher, ed. Vol. 1: The Cambridge History of Iran, Cambridge, Cambridge University Press.

Bruk, S. I. and V. S. Apenchenko
    1964 Atlas Narodov Mira. Moscow, Akademiya Nauk SSSR.

Bustāmī, Mīrzā Bābā Valadi Mīrzā Safar 'Alī
    1878 Ti'dādi Naufūsi Astarābād. Teheran, National Malik Library, Manuscript 4330 (3 Muharram 1296/1878).

Çağatay, Saadet S.
    1950 Türk Lehçeleri Örnekleri. Ankara Üniversitesi Dil ve Tarih-Coğrafya Fakültesi Yayımları, No. 26. Ankara, Türk Tarih Kurumu Basımevi.

Campbell, Donald T.
    1965 Variation and Selective Retention in Socio-Cultural Evolution. *In*: Social Change in Developing Areas, Herbert R. Barringer, George I. Blacksten and Raymond W. Macks, eds. Cambridge, Mass., Schenkman.

Chagnon, Napoleon A.
    1974 Studying the Yąnomanö. New York, Holt, Rinehart and Winston.

Coon, Carleton S.
    1958 Caravan: The Story of the Middle East. Revised ed. New York, Holt, Rinehart and Winston.

Cunnison, Ian
    1966 Baggara Arabs: Power and the Lineage in a Sudanese Nomad Tribe. Oxford, Clarendon Press.

Curzon, George N.
    1892 Persia and the Persian Question. 2 Vols. London, Longmans, Green.

Dulling, G. K.
    1960 An Introduction to the Turkmen Language. Oxford: Central Asian Research Centre in association with St. Antony's College (Oxford) Soviet Affairs Study Group.

d'Encausse, Hélène Carrère
    1967a Systematic Conquest, 1865 to 1884. *In*: Central Asia: A Century of Russian Rule, Edward Allworth, ed. New York, Columbia University Press.
    1967b Civil War and New Governments. *In* Op.cit.
    1967c The National Republics Lost Their Independence. *In* Op. cit.

English, Paul W.
    1966 City and Village in Iran: Settlement and Economy in the Kirman Basin. Madison, The University of Wisconsin Press.

Epstein, A. L., ed.
    1967 The Craft of Social Anthropology. London, Tavistock Publications.

Evans-Pritchard, E. E.
    1940 The Nuer. Oxford, Oxford University Press.

Fortes, Meyer and E. E. Evans-Pritchard
    1940 African Political Systems. Oxford, Oxford University Press.

Fox, Robin
    1967 Kinship and Marriage: An Anthropological Perspective. Baltimore, Penguin Books.

Garthwaite, G. R.
    1969 Pastoral Nomadism and Tribal Power. Unpublished paper delivered at the Conference on the Structure of Power in Islamic Iran at the University of California, Los Angeles.

Goody, Jack, ed.
    1962 The Developmental Cycle in Domestic Groups. Cambridge Papers in Social Anthropology, No. 1. Cambridge, Cambridge University Press.

Hanessian, John
    1963 Yosouf-abad, an Iranian Village. American Universities Field Staff Reports, Southwest Asia Series, Vol. 12, Nos. 1-6.

Hsu, Francis L. K.
    1965 The Effects of Dominant Kinship Relations on Kin and Non-Kin Behavior: A Hypothesis. American Anthropologist, Vol. 67, No. 3.

Hudson, Alfred E.
    1938 Kazak Social Structure. Yale University Publications in Anthropology, No. 20. New Haven, Yale University Press.

Iran, Government of
1961 National and Province Statistics of the First Census of Iran: November 1956. Vol. 1, Number and Distribution of the Inhabitants of Iran and the Census Provinces. Teheran, Department of Public Statistics, Ministry of Interior, Government of Iran.

Irons, William G.
1965 Livestock Raiding among Pastoralists: An Adaptive Interpretation. Papers of the Michigan Academy of Science, Arts and Letters, Vol. 50.
1968 The Turkmen Nomads. Natural History, Vol. 77, No. 9, pp. 45-51.
1969 The Turkmen of Iran: A Brief Research Report. Iranian Studies, Vol. 2, No. 1, pp. 27-38.
1972 Variation in Economic Organization: A Comparison of the Pastoral Yomut and the Basseri. *In*: Perspectives on Nomadism, William Irons and Neville Dyson-Hudson, eds. Leiden, Brill.
1974 Nomadism as a Political Adaptation: The Case of the Yomut Turkmen. American Ethnologist, Vol. 1, No. 4, pp 635-658.
n.d. The Wynne-Edwards Hypothesis and Human Population Growth: The Implications of Research among the Yomut Turkmen.

Jarring, Gunnar
1939 On the Distribution of Turk Tribes in Afghanistan: An Attempt at Preliminary Classification. Lunds Universitets Arsskrift, N.F. Avd. 1, Bd. 35, No. 4. Lund: Lunds Universitet.

König, Wolfgang
1962 Die Achal-Teke: Zur Wirtschaft und Gesellschaft einer Turkmenen-Gruppe im XIX Jahrhundert. Berlin: Akademie-Verlag.

Köprülü Zāde, Fu'ad
1931 Turkoman Literature. *In*: The Encyclopaedia of Islam: A Dictionary of the Geography, Ethnography, and Biography of the Muhammadan Peoples. M. Th. Houtsma, A. J. Wensinck, H. A. R. Gibb, W. Heffening, and E. Levi Provençal, eds. London, Luzac.

Kovada, V. A.
1961 Land Use Development in the Arid Regions of the Russian Plain, the Caucasus, and Central Asia. *In*: A History of Land Use in Arid Regions, L. Dudley Stamp. ed. Vol. 17: Arid Zone Research. Paris, UNESCO.

Krader, Lawrence
1955 Ecology of Central Asian Pastoralism, Southwestern Journal of Anthropology, Vol. 2, No. 4, pp. 301-326.
1963a Peoples of Central Asia. Indiana University Uralic and Altaic Series, Vol. 26. Bloomington, Indiana University.
1963b Social Organization of the Mongol-Turkic Pastoral Nomads. Indiana University Uralic and Altaic Series, Vol. 20. The Hague, Mouton.
1968 Turkmen. Encyclopaedia Britannica, Vol. 22. Chicago, Encyclopaedia Britannica, Inc.

Lambton, Ann K. S.
   1953 Landlord and Peasant in Persia: A Study of Land Tenure and Land Revenue Administration. London, Oxford University Press.

Lane, E. W.
   1908 Manners and Customs of the Modern Egyptians. 3rd ed. New York, E. P. Dutton.

Lattimore, Owen
   1962 Inner Asian Frontiers of China. Boston, Beacon Press.

Lévi-Strauss, Claude
   1963 Structural Anthropology. Claire Jacobson and Brooke Grundfest Schoepf, trans. New York, Basic Books.
   1969 The Elementary Structure of Kinship. James Harle Belle, John Richard von Sturmer, and Rodney Needham, trans. London, Eyre and Spottiswoode.

Lewis, I. M.
   1961 A Pastoral Democracy: A Study of Pastoralism and Politics among the Northern Somali of the Horn of Africa. London, Oxford University Press.

Marvin, Charles.
   1881 Merv, The Queen of the World: and the Man-Stealing Turcomans with an Exposition of the Khorassan Question. London, W. H. Allen.

McLachlan, K. S.
   1968 Land Reform in Iran. In: The Land of Iran, W. B. Fischer, ed. Vol. I: The Cambridge History of Iran. Cambridge, Cambridge University Press.

Menges, Karl H.
   1967 Peoples, Languages, and Migrations. In: Central Asia: A Century of Russian Rule, Edward Allworth, ed. New York, Columbia University Press.

Middleton, John and David Tait
   1958 Tribes Without Rulers: Studies in African Segmentary Systems. London, Routledge and Kegan Paul.

Murphy, Robert F. and Leonard Kasdan
   1959 The Structure of Parallel Cousin Marriage. American Anthropologist, Vol. 61, No. 1, pp. 17-29.
   1967 Agnation and Endogamy: Some Further Considerations. Southwestern Journal of Anthropology, Vol. 23, No. 1, pp. 1-14.

Mu'īnī, Asad'ullāh
   1966 Jughrāfīyā va Jughrāfīyāyī Tārīkhīyi Gurgān va Dasht. Teheran, Chāpkhānehyi Sharkati Sahāmīyi Tab'i Kitāb, Isfand 1344 Hijrī Shamsī.

Netting, Robert McC.
   1965 Household Organization and Intensive Agriculture: The Kofyar Case. Africa, Vol. 35, No. 4, pp. 422-429.
   1968 Hill Farmers of Nigeria: Cultural Ecology of the Jos Plateau. American Ethnological Society Monograph 46. Seattle, University of Washington Press.

Newcomer, Peter J.
    1972 The Nuer are Dinka: An Essay on Origins and Environmental Determinism. Man, New Series, Vol. 7, No. 1, pp. 5-11.

O'Donovan, Edmond
    1882 The Merv Oasis: Travels and Adventures East of the Caspian During The Years 1879-80-81 Including Five Months Residence Among the Tekkes of Merv. 2 Vols. London, Smith, Elder and Co.

Okazaki, Shoko
    1968 The Development of Large-Scale Farming in Iran: The Case of the Province of Gorgan. I.A.E.A. Occasional Papers Series, No. 3. Tokyo, The Institute of Asian Economic Affairs.

Patai, Raphael
    1965 The Structure of Endogamous Unilineal Descent Groups. Southwestern Journal of Anthropology, Vol. 21, No. 4, pp. 325-350.

Pehrson, Robert N.
    1966 The Social Organization of the Marri Baluch, compiled and analyzed from Pehrson's notes by Fredrik Barth. Viking Fund Publications in Anthropology, No. 43. New York, Wenner-Gren Foundation for Anthropological Research.

Peristiany, J. G., ed.
    1965 Honour and Shame: The Values of Mediterranean Society. London, Weidenfeld and Nicholson.

Peters, E. L.
    1960 The Proliferation of Segments among the Bedouin of Cyrenaica. Journal of the Royal Anthropological Institute, Vol. 90, pp. 29-53.

Petrushevsky, I. P.
    1968 The Socio-Economic Condition of Iran under the Il-Khans. In: The Saljug and Mongol Periods, J. A. Boyle, ed. Vol. 5, The Cambridge History of Iran. Cambridge, Cambridge University Press.

Pūrkarīm, Hūshang
    1966a Turkumanhāyi Īran. Hunar va Mardum 41 and 42:28-42. 1345.
    1966b Turkumanhāyi Īran, II. Hunar va Mardum 50: 22-34. 1345.
    1967 Turkumanhāyi Īran; Bāzrasiyi Zamīnehāyi Ijtimā'ī, III. Hunar va Mardum 61 and 62:48-64. 1346.
    1968a Turkumanhāyi Īran, IV. Hunar va Mardum 63:25-33. 1346.
    1968b Īncheh Burūn. Hunar va Mardum 71: 43-55. 1347.
    1968c Īncheh Burūn, II. Hunar va Mardum 73:25-41. 1347.
    1970 Turkumanhāy: Dihkadehyi Qusheh Tappeh. Hunar va Mardum 91:38-48. 1349.

Qūrkhānchī Saulat Nizām, Muhammad 'Alī
    1903-4 Nukhbehyi Sifīyeh. Teheran, Library of the National Assembly, Manuscript 690, 1321.
    1909-10 Nukhbehyi Kāmrafi. Teheran, National Malik Library, Manuscript 3935, 1327.

Rabino, H. L.
  1928  Māzandarān and Astarābād. London, Luzac.

Sahlins, Marshall D.
  1961  The Segmentary Lineage System: An Organization of Predatory Expansion. American Anthropologist. Vol. 63; pp. 322-345.
  1968  Tribesmen. Foundations of Modern Anthropology Series. Englewood Cliffs, N. J., Prentice-Hall.

Salzman, Philip C.
  1967  Political Organization among Nomadic Peoples. Proceedings of the American Philosophical Society. Vol. 3, No. 2, pp. 115-131.

Siegel, Sidney
  1956  Nonparametric Statistics for the Behavioral Sciences. New York, McGraw-Hill.

Smith, M. G.
  1956  Segmentary Lineage Systems. Journal of the Royal Anthropological Institute. Vol. 86, pp. 39-80.

Spooner, Brian
  1969  Politics, Kinship, and Ecology in Southeast Persia. Ethnology, Vol. 8, No. 2, pp. 139-152.

Stirling, Paul
  1965  Turkish Village. London, Weidenfeld and Nicolson.

Vambery, Arminius
  1865  Travel in Central Asia: Being the Account of a Journey from Teheran across the Turkoman Desert on the Eastern Shore of the Caspian to Khiva, Bokhara and Samarcand. New York, Harper and Brothers.

Vreeland, Herbert H., III.
  1957  Mongol Community and Kinship Structure. New Haven, Human Relations Area Files.

Wynne-Edwards, V. C.
  1962  Animal Dispersion in Relation to Social Behavior. New York, Hafner.
  1965  Self-regulating Systems in Populations of Animals. Science, Vol. 147, pp. 1543-48.

Yate, C. E.
  1900  Khurasan and Sistan. London, William Blackwood and Sons.

Plate 1. A Yomut woman assembling her family's tent after a migration.

Plate 2. A Yomut woman milking a sheep.

Plate 3. A Yomut man hunting in the Gökcha Hills.

Plate 4. Preparing a hide after the slaughter of a goat.

Plate 5. A nomad camp in the Gökcha Hills.

Plate 6. Setting up camp after a short migration.

www.ingramcontent.com/pod-product-compliance
Lightning Source LLC
Jackson TN
JSHW070313120426
100741JS00007B/42